THE *Age* OF *Ignorance*

Dr. Michael Ritivoi Hansen

BOOKSIDE Press

BOOKSIDE Press

BookSide Press
877-741-8091
www.booksidepress.com
orders@booksidepress.com

Contents

Prologue

Human beings tried to answer two basic questions: how did we come into existence and how to build a comfortable living. At the time when they became able to write, the only intelligence humans seemingly used was that of their own. But, our intelligence is not the highest one; it is the one we used for survival. Empowered by their observations and self-confidence, one may assume that his beliefs are accurate. This confidence motivates one to secure his thoughts into an abstract mental box where they are safely preserved. Therein lies his definition of himself, his defenses and tactics. As we grow, we gradually update our thoughts. To improve our thoughts means that our thoughts are largely opinions, not necessarily truth, and need updating. Still, humans have continuously relied on this tactic to their satisfaction. This concept is evident in even foundational creations like the Bible which was never improved or updated. Why? Is it the Word of God, or, of its writers? Their assumption that God wanted them to exterminate certain people to occupy and resettle in their land, indefinitely, is appalling. Yes… nevertheless, this is what resulted from man's confidence in his creation. So, what is the truth? Truth is a transcendent, fundamental reality, a flawless idea, indestructible and as such it cannot be of physical origin. Anything physical deteriorates in time. The problem seems to be that physically satisfying formulas do not satisfy our non-physical, abstract part of our nature. The physical existence comes with a set of opinions that fail the quality of truth. Is it possible that we had been initially intended to be non-physical as God, our father, supposedly was? We are entitled to know who we are. Does physicality blind us? Was the perfection of our creation so hard to handle that we replaced it with the physical kind of living?

As people, we contemplate our spiritual nature. We built different religions to explain this mystery. But, those attempts have a common problem: our spiritual nature is judged by our physical condition and reflects our physical ignorance of the non-physical truth. Our physical opinions appear evident in all we believe and do. Some experts consider that no single religion is qualified to give us the answer to our spiritual questions. Each religion pursues its local perception of truth. Some concluded that for a more accurate understanding of the spiritual world, it is wise to search all religious beliefs and find their common denominator. That seems to be the closest we can come to an answer. But then, all religions combined, are still a collection of human opinions, all physical. This horizontal approach to the vertical knowledge of life, proves instead our dependence of physical limits. Understanding spirituality requires a spiritual perspective; a quest for meanings is obviously different from a quest for things. This perspective is in its turn considered by materialists to be nonsense. For them everything has to be a logical answer to our physical experiences.

In order to know our identity, we have to rise above our self-righteous opinions. We have to get out of our mental boxes to see the light. Our minds must be connected to the mind of our Creator. Start with the assumption that there is no other mind in the universe but God's. He must have invested something of Himself in His creation of us. That is the connection that can guide us to the One Truth, away from our many opinions. "The kingdom of God is within you." (Luke 17: 21) If so, we should check our minds to find the pervasive truth of creation. Our minds have the extraordinary importance of having the truth built in. All we need is the desire to access it, to get up on our feet and, explore the truth. You either open your mind or, you settle for a long "glorious" rest, on the sidelines.

Truth is abstract, obviously… it is from God! I am aware that, at this point, we may fall into heavy debates: is there a God? How can God create the whole universe from nothing else but His mind, the only existing thing "in the beginning"? Our lack of understanding of reality, is not proof that God's creation is impossible. Rather it is an indication of our inability to understand in our physical condition that which abstract minds can do. So, we come up with pleasing opinions and let this question sit indefinitely. "Only the mind can create because spirit has already been created, and the body is a learning device for the mind." (1) The mind is the only creator. Nothing material can create anything spiritual. On the other hand, there are evidences that consciences may instantly connect the whole universe.

This surprising discovery is generally overrun by our convenient opinion that matter was ever existent and, not created. Don't tell this to Einstein! What if God can truly create matter?

On the subject of the beginning of life there are those who believe that God is its creator and those who believe that life is the result of haphazard combinations of those ever-existent chemicals. Well, simple people like to see value in their simple ways. Still, there is nothing greater than creativity. The materialists believe that matter is all that there is. It was never created; it simply ever existed. Nevertheless, the materialists do not explain where the energy that sustains matter's movement, and therefore its existence and progress, comes from. The permanent movement of its particles of all kinds and sizes, from subatomic to planets, requires a permanent supply of energy. All physical parts from the smallest to the biggest are in permanent movement and that gives it life, and fuels its evolution. Also, for the universe to continuously expand it needs a continuous supply of matter. Can this matter appear as needed, or does it preexist in an unlimited supply, somewhere? Can matter's perfect organization take place in the absence of an organizing mind?

Spiritually oriented people go a step further back in time and believe that matter, its inner energy and its ability to organize is set by a powerful Creator. Well, we see what we want to see. In a car collision I had been involved in, several years ago, the driver of the other car crossed a red light and hit the trunk of my car at full speed, from a 90 degrees angle, as I turned left on the green light. She did so because she claimed she didn't see my car and neither the red light in front of her. She didn't see what she didn't want to see. She was absent minded. We don't see what doesn't interest us. We don't know how God creates life; it is too complicated. Miracles can be a normal part of nature's manifestation. Everything that gets out of line is supposed to be brought back to its place. This is called correction; not miracle. Jesus brought back to physical life people that He knew were alive in another way. He didn't revitalize them. He only brought them back to their previous condition. If God's creation is perfect, then perfection must be a stable and normal state. Illusions and mistakes are therefore imperfections meant to self-destruct, while perfection is built to stay.

On any issue, there are always as many opinions as people. That means that people perceive reality in personal ways and believe that those perceptions, even unbelievable, are valid. In any situation, the truth is one. Here are two problems with those opinions. First, if there are many opinions about one issue it's possible none of the opinions is correct. Only one opinion can be truth. Second, if one's opinions are not true, everything that is based on those false opinions is wrong and doomed.

For someone to open his mind is not that easy. It opens the door to a new world. It implies the acceptance of something unexpected, even unbelievable. Einstein said: "dreaming is more important than knowing". Dreams while awake, can be realities already connected with other thoughts, somewhere in the universe. One may value his thoughts more than his already existing values. For people, their thoughts and beliefs have the value of truth. It is hard for people to perceive what they don't see. We can see a tree, but cannot see God. Regardless, truth is indifferent to opinions and opinions are indifferent to truth. If we believe we are right, we have no reason to change; but then, we are indefinitely stuck in our thinking boxes full of opinions. Anyway, the truth from within us cannot die. Everything we built in the denial of truth, bodies included, dies. Practically, the difference between truth and its perception is the difference between knowledge and ignorance, between heaven and hell, between life and death.

If truth exists, we cannot be indifferent to it. If life is created, it means it has a purpose worth knowing and pursuing. If we are created, a true self is assigned to each one of us; a self that is different from the selves we imagine and believe that we are. Soon after my wife and I decided to have a child, she got pregnant and one day she had a dream of a young boy telling her: "I am the beautiful boy you are supposed to have. If I do come, your life will become more difficult that you can believe. Because of that, for your own good, I decided not to come." Next day, she told me about this dream and instantaneously I realized that, in our case, he is right and I accepted his decision. She did also and shortly after, her pregnancy turned badly. An abortion was definitely required.

If life appeared for no reasons, there is no mind guiding it and doesn't have a purpose; it may fall apart any time; evolution and existence may then be accidental. If evolution is a guided process, we are entitled to ask: where does life's will to perpetuate and improve come from? Who has the mind that guides it? Evolution cannot be constantly supported by accidental self-improvements. Life is too intricate and finely coordinated to be an accident. Truly, life must have a purpose. But then, who gives it that purpose? What is that purpose? Since these are tough questions to answer, some conveniently chose to dismiss them altogether and stay limited with what we know. But of course, by avoiding the question we avoid the answer. So, we miss the truth and, miss the best chance to be more than who we are now.

The atheists work hard at finding and pasting together the pieces of evolution. This is a fascinating process but those physical pieces we have found do not reveal the non-physical forces at work.

The most meaningful direct communication with the world beyond our awareness is provided by Jesus. He didn't find it necessary to answer all the questions we may have. He focused instead on the master question that answers all other questions. The clue to life is the Truth. For God, truth is love and wisdom. It is our ignorance of truth that makes us misjudge what we should already have known. What Jesus did we all can do, if we want. What prevents us is our inability to abandon our cozy thinking boxes. We try in vain to fit truth to our acceptance, instead of fitting our acceptance to the Truth.

Our standard source of spiritual knowledge is the Bible. The overwhelming success of this book is due to our desire to know who we are beyond appearance and opinions. However, our opinions are already an obstacle in knowing the truth. Our questions and our answers build a perfect circle. We answer our own questions with our own physical understanding. But this doesn't give us much beyond the realm of opinion. For example, God is just like us except He's in heaven and we're on earth; readers and writers assume He's just like a familiar father that looks just like us and thinks like us. We are taught that "God created man in his own image" (Genesis 1:27) with the understanding that as we are, He is. Therefore, we confidently conclude that He is like us, even if nobody has seen Him. By understanding ourselves, we believe to understand Him. Consequently, based on our opinions, we gladly transfer our sense of guilt and our responsibilities to Him, who has a higher ability, to properly deal with and, relieve ourselves of obligation. This looks like a conscious neglect of our duty. "The Spirit of God is within you." (Luke 17: 20, 21) We are perfectly created and therefore able to deal with our challenges but, we find it more comfortable to live as we feel rather than as we should. We would rather not attempt to grow to His level, which some may consider to be disrespectful but, here we are. Also, the Bible reassures us of God's commitment to correct what we missed. As a matter of fact, it is disrespectful to let God clean what we mess-up. The Bible suggests that God gave us all the time and ability needed to figure things out. But because we didn't and are getting worse, He sent Jesus, His Messager, to help us sort things out. This is the time to ask ourselves: does the Bible accurately represent God, or it represents the opinions of scripture writers? If the Bible tries to mix physical with metaphysical, it becomes only a matter of time before this odd union between truth and fiction would start to crack. It already started. Inquisitive people cannot miss the Bible's flaws and start to move away from the Church. Regardless, it's time to responsibly ask ourselves what is the truth and, how can we access it?

Truth is available to everyone. It is our own mind-set that prevents us from reaching it. As physical creatures, we pursue physical values. But, with only physical values taking charge of our lives, we cannot achieve anything. If we believe that we already know the truth, we close our minds and stop searching for it. There are limitless internal processes that can only be stimulated by one's inner desires to know and be. Jesus advised us to replace our self-centered tendencies with love, which is the path to truth. Therefore, no spiritual growth can be expected from us unless we open-up our minds to it. Physical values tempt us to chronically desire more goods, unwittingly abuse others and feel more successful and therefore special.

Still, we should be true to our creation and rediscover the way we are meant to be. Spirituality is living according to the internal law of love, versus the external laws of commands, judgment, regulations, or control. Physicality with its laws is the consequence of our judgment of good and evil, not of love. Freedom is spiritual, not physical. The Bible's main message is love and love is perfection. But, do we know what love is?

The purpose of this book is to expose you to ideas that can bring you closer to the Truth. I try to answer the questions you may have in this regard. It may seem arrogant of me to claim having the necessary knowledge for such a task. It may seem so but the fact is, we all should know the truth. God doesn't hide it. It is only that we hide behind personal reasons, opinions and desires that endorse our status quo and separate us from spiritual perfection. We are in our mental boxes assuming we are open minded, out in the open. We assume we are free while we are not. We are slaves to useless rules, obligations, and mistaken opinions. Meanwhile, our call is to know the Truth: "know the truth and the truth shall set you free." (John 8: 32) "Be ye perfect as your Father in heaven is perfect." (Matthew 5: 48) Jesus did access the truth and asked us to do the same (1 Peter 2:21). Don't be shy. Truth is our birthright. I approach this task by clarifying Jesus' teachings beyond the point where his startled apostles left them. Religion is the philosophy of life and the discovery of Truth. For this reason, if practiced correctly, religion's importance is paramount. When we accept our divine Love, we can rediscover God's perfect creation. Only when we return to our original quality, we are back in God's world. The task of returning to reality, is ours. Religion is trivialized these days because our physical concerns are our priority. Religion lost its effectiveness because we made it ineffective by confusing our personal opinions with the truth. Many consider religion to be the way we have formulated it. We would be better by getting out of our comfort zone and think. I don't blame those who get disappointed and abandon the church, but also, I cannot watch from the side how this unique and valuable guide called religion is getting degraded instead of being recognized. Religion is the only valid spiritual guide we have. It is the only teacher of peace and love, available. Yes, today, religion has many flaws. Let's identify them and rise above confusion. Let's change to straight-mindedness. Our happiness depends on it.

I love you. I cannot passively see scores of people wasting their lives. Truth does provide us with everything we need. Aware of the church's error, I try here to reestablish its credentials. Inspired by Jesus' teaching, I disclose religion's flaws and, replace them with truth. This book has four parts:

1. The evaluation of the Abrahamic religions; evaluation of the writers of scripture, the scholars who analyze the holy texts and lastly we, the recipients of this knowledge who filter the received information through our unprepared minds. (chapter II)
2. A survey of atheistic alternatives. (chapter III)

3.	How did we adopt this fantasy, accepted a Marxist style reality and, how our thoughts of "reality" condition our lives. Most important, how to get out of this mental trap. (chapter IV)

4.	The conclusion. (chapter V)

This attempt of exposing religion's mistakes and inaccuracies may seem insulting, disappointing or heart breaking to those who grew up trusting the church's teachings. It also may seem like an attempt to dismiss religion, while it is not. One's belief is a strong pillar in his life. For this reason alone, it is paramount to make sure this pillar of ours is the right one. With an open mind, think about what's written in this book and decide for yourself. Let's replace errors with truth and illusions with reality.

Again, do not be offended by my critical look at the Bible. The Bible has good intentions, but it is limited in its effectiveness by the inclusion of human opinions, presented as God's. Purifying our understanding of the divine is to our advantage. Religion must be respected because it is the only service meant to support divine values. Let's look at it through Jesus' eyes, instead of ours.

What are my credentials? My main credence is my life-long desire for knowing what life is about. I had been fed enough lies during my 35 years of living under communism, in Romania. The desire to know more than communism allowed, guided me to become a dissident and leave my birth country and my seemingly successful career. Once immigrated into the United States, I finally got the opportunity to read most of what interested me. First and foremost I got the opportunity for the first time to read the Bible. Its message of love impressed me more that I could expect. Love is the backbone of life whereas the communist's backbone, as I experienced it, is hate and suspicion. In addition, communism has a deep desire to eliminate any way of thinking that is different than the Marxist one. Communists justified their drive for repression, suppression, oppression, incarcerations, executions, Gulag, isolation and so forth, in ways that only misguided and self-righteous people could conceive. But, can brain-washing be the way to progress? Communism means common ignorance and ignorance cannot be the way to success. How this human painful regression happened in my birth country, Romania, is too involved to explain it here but you will find it in my book, "*The Message.*"

My search for truth didn't stop with communism. Carefully reading the Bible I found it inconsistent, mistaken, tribalistic and puzzling at times. It appears that the Bible writers took liberties they are not entitled to. God must make sense or he is not The God. So, again, what is the truth?

Jesus promised to stay with us to the end of time and He does. Because of my genuine desire to know the truth, he guided me through many inspiring books that loosened my mind-set until I started to read the book called "*A Course in Miracles.*" The book was written by Helen Schucman, a psychologist at the Columbia Presbyterian Medical Center in New York City in 1970's. She claims that she wrote this book under the dictation of a person who identified himself as Jesus. Jesus was a voice only she could hear and, at times, dictated at the first person. The first question you will probably ask is: how do I know that this book is Jesus' direct message and not a fabrication? My answer is:

1.   Dr. Schucman is a reputable scholar with no claims on this book. She stated she is only a scribe, sometimes reluctant, nevertheless respectful, and chosen by Jesus. The voice dictating this book identified itself as Jesus.

2.   The style of the book is unusual, rather heavy, something I never met in published books. Obviously, I didn't read all books but, I am sure all professional authors do their best to make their books as easily readable as possible. Jesus didn't provide any revision to his book.

3.   The novelty of the book's ideas is so deep and unconventional, far ahead of anything written on the matter, that it must belong to a highly intelligent and knowledgeable person. If that person would be a fellow human living on Earth, he would not be limited to one book and his name would be well known by now. While the book is flawless, its author is treated as a pariah, close to how he was treated by religious leaders while living among us.

4.   Jesus gave us this book of 1,250 pages with authority and modesty but, he didn't sign it. What human would do that? Jesus is not interested in personal recognition or monetary compensation but, as always, he is interested in the value of

his message. Nevertheless, He openly stated his authorship down the line, in the text, and corrects some of His improperly quoted statements in the New Testament, as well as some of the improperly interpreted events. In many places, the book is written in the first person.

5.   Through his book, Jesus is faithful to his promise to help us throughout time and, this is a particular time when we need to reevaluate our beliefs. Faithfull to his purpose of teaching the truth, he gave us this book, as the best way to fulfill his promise of staying with us. If he would come on earth, he could not possibly lecture us the 1,250 pages and, have us remember them accurately. "Scripta Manent" (the Latin for: "what is written stays".)

The writing of "The Age of Ignorance" was prompted by my disheartening awareness that religion takes a beating these days. Christians are told they are not relevant any longer. Nevertheless, Christianity is valuable when properly understood and practiced. All we need is the correction of our misperceptions. The information I convey here is inspired by *A Course in Miracles* as well as other readings and, personal inspiration.

I.

You Are Who You Choose To Be

The Age of Ignorance belongs to all times known to history. It started when people decided to live independently, as they saw fit. By replacing God's guidance with their own convenience, people's performance started to decline. Their values changed from eternal to personal, from truth to opinions. Looking for opportunities, people started to search for favorable circumstances and, fair or not, to take advantage of them. Physical separation allows people to relieve themselves from the concerns of others to prioritize their own interests. This is the world of singlemindedness and competition. The glare of personal success becomes more attractive than love. This is a good time for egos. Nevertheless, even if physically independent we still need each other to compare, cooperate and, succeed.

Physicality is the opportunity of having the items we like and need. It is prioritizing our singular identity and our self-interests. As a spiritual group we cooperate, exchange opinions, love and enjoy. As physical bodies we built personal opinions and followed our goals in a race that once started, never seems to stop. A consequence of physicality and its limited supply of things makes some people more "affluent" than others. Some have more desirable things than others. We start comparing, which diminishes our unity and facilitates our slide into competition for personal things and self-interests. Meanwhile, in the Kingdom of God we do not judge each other in terms of good and evil and do not compete because all is available to everyone. In our physical world, life is run according to our rules and values that do not match the spiritual realm. Spiritually, we follow our internal rules, written into our nature and never contested because they are perfect and kept reasonable by our Creator. Physicality has our own imperfect ways and personal value systems; which includes our emotional and tempting possibilities that can upset any time our frail written laws. Physically we need things and become preoccupied with satisfying those personal needs; paying less attention to the others and many times abusing them. We also attribute less importance to the non-physical and less obvious unenforced spiritual traits that are available to all. Both physical and non-physical realities are important and require different kinds of attention. Physically, we have to deal with one person primarily: me. Each one of the two kinds of existence has its own requirements, each having a dramatic effect on our lives. Physicality endorses selfishness while spirituality endorses fairness. Spiritually, we value truth and cohesion. Physically, we drift into privacy, suspicion, pride, and selfishness. What we physically believe is fair, spiritually, it's usually not so. The last desperate attempt to build a fair physical way of living, called communism, was a complete disaster. It singularly focused on the others' selfishness and never on personal shortcomings. Are the rich guilty of exploitation or are the poor guilty of lower ambitions, poor education and poor planning? It seems that the contradiction between selfishness and love arises from the contradiction between physical and spiritual ways of living. Physically we have to produce or acquire what we need. Spiritually, everything is freely available. We seemingly tried to connect the two ways. We try to claim to understand the truthfulness of both having and giving, love and suspicion, knowing and assuming. When we try to combine the two sides, we become inconsistent; we don't fully understand either one of those two choices. Consequently, we look for a compromise; which is not fair to either side and therefore is of limited value.

Each kind of life has its own consequences attached. In a way, each one deserves what occurs. Each one of those choices comes with its own set of opinions that defines a specific life style. Being familiar to us they do not raise too much opposition. We keep our set of opinions in a personal mental box. But, no one can live by two contradicting philosophies and few are willing to invest enough energy to rise above the level of his expected well-being. Each one should choose the proper set of thoughts. This quality of thoughts is achieved spiritually only, because only spiritually we share one truth which is a perfectly balanced scale for thoughts and therefore the fair answer to all problems. Physically we rely on opinions: the reason for never-ending discussions! Feeling right seems more comfortable than being right.

For my own curiosity I made a small survey some time ago among people I could afford to be so intrusive and I asked: "What is the purpose of life, in your opinion?" The college students generally stuck to the purpose of their education: to make a better living, to be prepared for a quality life and so forth. Those who claim to be religious came with statements inspired by their ministers or pastors: "to serve and glorify God," to "learn to love our fellow men," to "grow spiritually," to "repent from our own sins," to "increase our capacity to love". None of them mentioned the supreme Christian goal of salvation from the physical mess we share. It seemed this thought never crossed their minds; while it is the way to a permanently happy life. It appeared my respondents wanted to achieve success by living their lives as they knew it, only more comfortable.

A couple of missionaries said that the purpose of life is to "learn to love more like God." More like God is, on one hand, a sign of utmost respect for Him. But, love is only one kind of feeling or it is not love! Doesn't a father want his son to follow in his steps and to communicate with him on an equal basis? I believe that God wants to have a good communication with his children. Do we love as our Father in heaven loves? For those missionaries to achieve their purpose in life is to willingly stay one step behind their rightful place; preventing them from never reaching it. As a matter of fact, this must be disappointing to Our Father. One church leader said, "The purpose in life is to learn to love even those who don't deserve to be loved." Obviously, he meant that we should judge who deserves our love and who doesn't. This is Adam judging good and evil which is not God's desire to "love your brother as you love yourself." But, how can we do so while we see our brothers guilty for different reasons or, as somebody to take advantage of? How can we love them as we love ourselves while our perception of others is not that great? We should see the others as they had been created, and not as they present themselves.

In my short survey about the meaning of life, those who didn't consider religion's correctness expressed more creative answers: "I don't know . . ., to live the best I can, I guess. Better yet, to carry and deliver DNA, what else?" A lady said with a broad smile: "The purpose of life is to find the purpose of life." Someone else answered: "It is to find a balance between work and play." A friend of mine snapped: "Don't ask me such esoterically minded questions…. It is to survive and struggle and learn some things in the process . . . eventually to find a reason to live. Where did you get the idea to ask such a question?"

The last person I asked was one of my patients whom I had just sat in the dental chair. Since we had limited time, I said: "Don't answer me now. Let's do this filling first. This will give you the time to think about a good reply." When the dental work was done, I asked her," Now, what is your answer?"

"I believe, the purpose of life is to find happiness."

"Yes, we all look for happiness. Nevertheless, on earth this is an impossible task."

"No, it is not."

"Well, we can find short periods of happiness, but not a life full of it. Happiness seems to be too abstract to match this life."

Mary paused a little, wide eyed, watching the distance. "Yes, you are right," and she lowered her eyes. I felt sorry for being "right." What can I do; I was interested in an honest opinion.

"Endless happiness is possible only in the spiritual world," I said. "The immaterial does not deteriorate in time, as things do. Well, this is something to think about. Do you want to see how your filling came out?"

I had the feeling that my patients' interests had been limited to the remainder of their physical lives; seemingly no concern for their life beyond that. They chose physicality. The people I interviewed gave me the feeling that for them, life and faith are only remotely related if at all; the consensus seemed to indicate that we have this life now and we have spiritual beliefs as an abstract escape in the future. We are who we are "now". There is nothing that we appreciate more than what we already believe. Physicality is all about our several years of life on earth … .

Jesus came to earth as a physical person and, being physical, he still lived a perfect spiritual life. This means that we can be likewise: physical and spiritually perfect, if we set our minds to it. We cannot be admitted into Heaven by divine mercy. If we would be, that ideal place would lose its ideal quality. It seems reasonable then, to allow people to learn quality at their own pace by meeting challenges and developing a better understanding of life. Obviously it is more comfortable to do nothing and piously wait for God to do our work for us. But this is not fair. First, God provided us with all we need to keep our minds straight. Second, we are free and responsible for our choices; God would not interfere and change what he perfectly created. Our minds are ours to deal with. God knows we have the potential to discover our best interests. He gave us the ability to grow as well as all the time we need to wake up and, benefit from Jesus' instructions. It seems our inability to straighten up comes from our tendency to justify everything that we think and do. In our minds, we don't have to change what we believe to be right.

All that those people sampled wanted was to find external accomplishments to replace their internal dissatisfactions: associate with a better environment, better people, popular ideas, more money, God's acceptance. This is everything ... but the inner motivation that Jesus asked for: "love your neighbor as you love yourself." My investigation revealed convincingly a paraphrase of Jesus: by focusing on the mote that is inside our brother's eyes selves we ignore the plank in ours. But, awareness starts with us and finishes with us. We are the only ones we can influence and the only ones we should. Salvation implies a change of our minds for the better and this change of mind is a strictly personal job. The problem is that we want to receive enlightenment from God rather than discover for ourselves that which was already perfectly given to us. Our attitude is our personal responsibility.

We are so aware of the past and so concerned about the future that we miss the fact that we live in the thin and fleeting present. It is now when we formulate our choices and every choice we make defines who we are now, and stages our future. Our lives are ours to handle. The outside forces influence our decisions only for as much as we allow it. We don't control the events, but we can control our reactions to them. The way things are: the past is the now that was, and the future is the now that will be. All we have is the brief now: a compressed time when we show who we are, when everything happens and when we can learn and change. Eternity seems to be a continuous now. Now is the moment when we define ourselves. Every thought, word and deed foretells our future. No one else is responsible for our thoughts, but us. Faithful to our tendency to avoid responsibilities, we imagine predestination as another convenient belief that we are innocent victims of God: who set predestination. In our common opinions, He is the one who "decides" our predestinations. The only true predestination is, probably, our future return to whom we had been originally built. And, we are created to be equal, unique, and perfect. After a long chain of individual failures we will finally realize there are no failures, only mistakes. We will know the truth and we will correct our deeds accordingly or, we will stagnate for as long as necessary to learn the truth.

All our decisions are definitions of who we are now. Our lives are all about whom we want to be. Let's take a simple example. If you want to choose an outfit, you have to decide for what situation is it intended. Do you want to look dignified, casual, sexy, colorful, sedate or conservative? Who would you want to impress? What is quality for you? Does a tattoo give you a touch of class? Do street drugs improve your mind? How much do you like to blend in or stand out? Every choice you make reflects your opinions and your opinions are you.

If you want to be in Heaven, you must make the conscious effort to improve the quality of your thoughts so you can fit the quality needed. You are whom you choose to be. For that reason, it is important to define your choices before wasting more time and enduring more anguish. Your treasure is not physical. Your treasure is your mental quality.

Among the pool of endless choices, there is only one choice that can set you on the road to eternal joy. That choice is the truth. You must choose what you value: the absolute freedom or the freedom to make your own decisions no matter how mistaken they may be. This brings us to the question: does God exist or would we rather prefer to be our own god? Jesus didn't leave us any written advice during his first coming. He left us to think over his simple and meaningful words and deeds and, left it up to us to put them on paper.

Because of Jesus' mind-storming teaching and live demonstrations, people treasured everything they saw and had been able to understand. For those who deny Jesus' stories based on their claim of a lack of documents there are written sources outside the Bible that certify Jesus' existence. He is even mentioned in the Koran (not as the Son of God, but as a prophet). The existence of Christians is mentioned by contemporary Roman historians Tacitus, Pliny the Younger and Flavius Josephus. The historian Suetonius (65-135 AD), "while dealing in his '*Twelve Caesars*' at the time of Emperor Claudius, writes: 'He banished the Jews from Rome, since they had made a commotion because of Christus.'" (the Latin word for Christ) The events around Jesus' execution are also mentioned in the collection of letters known as "the Letters of Pilate and Herod" and in "The Letter of Tiberius." There are many apocryphal works that include the "Letter of Pilate to the Emperor Claudius" and "the Letter of Lentulus", a Roman official in Judea at the time of Tiberius Caesar, who saw Jesus and "his wonderful works, his preaching, his endless miracles and other amazing things he wrote about, to the Roman senate." There are also the letters written by Jesus to Abgarus IV, King of Edessa, "long regarded as authentic by Syriac Christians." Jesus is also quoted in the apocryphal Gospel of Peter, the book of James and the Infancy Gospel of Thomas.

The Christian movement was strong enough to convince the Emperor Constantine, at the end of a "journey over time and in his own mind," to become a Christian around 311 AD. I believe, if we have to point to a date for legalizing Christianity in the Roman Empire that would be the spring of 312 AD. The event is known as the "Edict of Milan", attributed to Constantine. At that time, the two Roman Co-Emperors, Constantine and Licinius, declared the power of the "Highest God". Their consensus was cemented by Licinius' marriage to Constantia, Constantine's oldest half-sister who was already a Christian. "Before leaving Milan, Constantine ordered the restitution of property confiscated from the Christian Church during the persecution." Licinius issued his own restoration of property through his edict at Nicomedia in June, 313. So, the Roman Empire was set free to practice Christianity. More than that, Emperor Constantine, aware of the strong disagreements among the eastern bishops, particularly in the way of interpreting the Trinity and Jesus' nature as both divine and human, summoned the Council of Nicaea in 325 AD with the purpose "to come to an agreement on every aspect of this very silly question, whatever it actually is." Constantine approached the Nicaea's Council with the backing of western bishops who had been more level headed and not involved in those "silly" and deadly controversies. He endorsed the unification of different Christian dogmas with a powerful act of public display of reconciliation. After consulting his religious advisers the Emperor Constantine came forward with his own version of Christian beliefs which was meant to set the tone for a unified Christian belief across the Empire. It is now known as the Nicene Creed.

From the earlier years of our A.D. era we have no reports of the denial of Jesus. The Christian message struck a chord in people's minds and souls. It brought to light a deep need for love and fairness. This need is a distant reminder of who we truly are and it's assumed to be a common-sense issue. As time passed, isolated voices started to be heard about different interpretations of Jesus' message. In order to bridge those differences and bring the different Christian factions to agree with the form previously accepted, the religious leaders at that time decided to bring the apostles' letters together in one authorized book, known today as the New Testament. For the compilation of this book some compromises had to be made. From the point of view of acceptance, the Scriptures had been a success. Nevertheless, voices of doubt broke into the open when people felt confident enough to express their opinions. From that time forward we keep getting increasingly bold comments going as far as the denial of Jesus' existence and of his miracles. Despite ongoing differences of opinions, Jesus' message makes sense unlike any other belief system before or after him. Still, his meanings are continuously interpreted by all.

If you believe in God, you believe you are created perfect. "Therefore, you are to be perfect as your heavenly Father is perfect." (Matthew 5: 48) A perfect God cannot create anything imperfect. The confusion arises when in having been awarded freedom of choice, we feel free to choose any way of thinking we want. We can choose any interpretation we desire but what our Creator meant is cast in stone and, this meaning is all that matters. While God's creation is indestructible, ours are subjective and adjusted to our acceptance level and are subsequently flawed and perishable. Jesus came to demonstrate that because he and we are all created by God's perfect knowledge and abilities, we are indestructible also. Nevertheless, having freedom of choice we choose a variety of opinions; not all of them valid. Jesus noticed our confusion and said: "I am higher [than you] because without me, the distance between God and man would be too great for you to encompass." (2) Nevertheless, "there is nothing about me that you cannot attain." (3) This is a matter of "rising up" to a higher level of understanding life. While physicality is limited, spirituality allows one to go as far as one wants. In the end you are whom you choose to be: a perfect spiritual mind, a citizen of the physical world or a debased victim of physicality's trap.

Religion teaches us that God has only one son. In regards to us, the humans, the Bible is less specific. "We have received the spirit of adoption." (Romans 8: 15) Some may believe so but, Jesus never mentioned adoption. Only the human writer of that Scripture could do that. We are created fully equipped: "The kingdom of God is within you" (Luke 17: 20, 21) This means that we have what we need to return to the awareness of who we are: the sons and daughters of God. It means that "you always meet yourself, and this encounter is holy because you are holy " (4). Unfortunately, our spiritual quality is contested by the very institution we've created for the purpose of defending it. It, meaning, our spiritual quality. The established church sees us as wimps who depend on a higher mercy. "For by grace are we saved through faith; and not of yourselves: it is a gift from God: not of works" (Ephesians 2: 8). But, aren't we created "in His image"?

As it is, neither the religious writers nor the atheists can offer a convincing answer to who we are. The scripture's writers present God as they think He must be and consequently, we miss the point. Perceptions and opinions are not truth. Atheists, on the other hand, dismiss God straight out, because His existence cannot be proven through the physical means at our disposal. As monotheists cannot irrevocably prove His existence, the atheists cannot irrevocably prove His nonexistence. So, we are left hanging on to our frail faith or lack thereof. People's attempt to prove one version of truth or the other is ineffective because God doesn't share our physical way of thinking and we don't share His non-physical way. We live in different worlds, run by different principles. The healings which we consider to be miracles are for Him the natural return to the perfection He created; therefore not miracles. As a matter of fact, to be a limited physical body with limited abilities is unnatural and an example of our imperfect interpretation of our universal spiritual nature. We cannot experience the power of truth because we don't know the truth. We only assume that our piecemeal achievements are proof of our abilities. Since we separated from God, we drifted so far away from Him that we don't know Him any longer. Too many mistaken thoughts came between us. Still, we are of God. There is nothing else to come from. "There is but one God, the Father, of whom are all things, and we are in Him." (1Corinthians 8: 6) Consequently, we can still return to Him if we use the means He gave us: straight minds, common sense, faith, love, and Jesus' teachings. So, we can return to our perfect creation but do we want to do that? We are where we are because we wanted to. Do we want to continue going on the same familiar path in the future?

A religion based on spiritual truth and values would be more effective, would satisfy more people's intelligence and would diminish significantly the number of both the confused believers and the ardent non-believers. Nevertheless, changing opinions implies open minds and this is a rare commodity. Besides, people did what they do best: dismantled Jesus' teachings into pieces, then analyzed and rearranged those pieces as they saw fit. People have plenty of time to hone their religion's interpretations smooth and shiny and accept them as truth. We even created a powerful institution for the purpose of defending this practice. Once Jesus died, his followers found themselves in a position of keeping his teachings alive and defending them against interpreters. With no supervision, people started to build personal understandings of Jesus' works. Opinions started to abound. People started to analyze his words and draw conclusions never expressed by Jesus but, appealing to them. We arrived at the point where no one can follow Jesus' legacy ("do what I had done") because nobody understood what thoughts made him do what he did. Even what they did understand, his disciples did not believe that they, too, can replicate what Jesu did. Yes, he asked us to love but, again, do we truly understand love? Why did he allow himself to be caught? Did he really want to pay for the sins of humanity with his murder? Could anybody believe what Jesus does believe? Maybe He wanted to send a different message. Is it even possible to pay for sin with redemption? There is a common expression that "everything has a price". But, is it true? One cannot pay with physical means (money or torture) for non-physical achievements (forgiveness). God already forgave us before Jesus' crucifixion,… do we need another forgiveness? "And the Lord said, I have pardoned according to thy word: But as I live, all the earth shall be filled with the glory of the LORD." (Numbers 14: 20, 21) What better compensation (redemption) can there be for the payment of sin other than God's love?

There is more to Jesus' message than what we assume. "I have many things to say unto you but, you cannot bear them now." (John 16: 12) He will, when we are ready. It's obvious we cannot grow if we limit our understanding to the 2,000 year old opinions that brought us where we are now. In order to increase our quality we have to ponder and change with growth. Interpretations formulated at the beginning of the first century and locking them into our mental boxes is inhibiting For people, the truth in general is what they chose to believe it is. Not surprisingly, none can replicate what Jesus did by using a mentality lower than his.

We use the Bible as our spiritual compass but reading the Old Testament, we can find that it presents God in contradictory ways: revengeful and forgiving, aware and changing his mind, giving us freedom of choice and then severely punishing us if we use it in ways that upset our standards. This suggests that our experts must be mistaken. In the end, it is our duty to find the answer. God gave us everything we need to succeed. But His gifts and guidance do not do for us that we should do ourselves. Doing is our duty, the expression of our desire to be the best we can be. Only we can move our feet along the path of enlightenment. Our duty cannot be delegated.

Religious scholars, for their part, consider that love for God can be proven only by strict subjection to the "divine" Commandments. Meanwhile God does not command, nor require subjection (He gave us freedom of choice); He pursues enlightenment, awareness, knowledge of truth. For the early Bible writers in order to make sure those commandments became thoroughly respected and not cleverly interpreted and overruled, came-up with more than 600 additional commandments that support the original Ten. This made the requirements for holiness so tight that many considered it impossible to uphold them all so they became rebellious. How can one live a perfect life on this imperfect physical environment we have: no sexual affairs, no usury, no lies, no profiting from other's confusions…!? What kind of life is that? Well, a good life can be had, depending on what values we choose. But, as is common, how can we abandon selfishness while it is profitable? Jesus, who "was born as a human," did overcome his own physicality. Once understanding higher values, a person chooses truth and he is not a sinner any longer. Jesus said: "I have given you an example that ye should do as I have done for you." (John13: 15) Notice: "you should do", not: you should expect to be done for you.

What worked for Jesus will work for us all. We are how we think. Jesus didn't claim specialness. He claimed the normalcy of love and wisdom. We expect him to come in glory at his second coming, ready "to execute judgement upon all and to convince all that are ungodly among them of all their ungodly deeds which they have committed" (Jude 1: 15). We should remember that he came to us as a Rabbi, a teacher. He didn't want to change anything but to help us understand truth and fairness. He doesn't punish and doesn't kill.

Adam's choice of judging good and evil leads to the conclusion of inequality and division: if judged, some people are found right and others wrong. In this situation, wrong can be only the one who is judged. The one passing the judgment sets himself above the fray. This is at the very origin of our opinion of unequal qualities among those whom God created equal and are therefore in no need to be judged; nor to be the judge. It is obvious that judgment is needed in our physical set-up only whereby we find it practical to defend fairness, to separate a taker from a giver, to evaluate and correct. Spiritually, we don't have any reason to accuse anyone. All mistakes are correctable and of no consequence in the long run.

The collision between Jesus' teachings and the Jewish religious practices at the time was so extreme that they demanded Jesus' execution. There's a sharp difference between the "holiness" of written laws and the holiness of faith. The Old Testament even deemed that some people are disposable while Jesus maintains that all humans are important to God. It seems incomprehensible: why did we choose to live on earth? Why do some love physicality so much? Physicality implies sinfulness, judgement, inequality, separation among people. Is inequality created by unequal creation or is it a result of the human desire to separate from each other? Isn't it produced by personal subjective opinions, desires and ways ?

Some fundamentalists have taken it upon themselves to kill those who, in their opinion, offended God and consider themselves holy for doing that. Again, a mind can justify anything it wants to justify. Some use their time and talents to harass and even harm those that inconvenience them by claiming that God allowed or even advised them to do so. Little do they know that God doesn't ask anyone to do anything for Him. Nor does He inflict pain. It is only that people like to assume the glory of doing a service "for God", a service that was never asked for but serves the interests of the doer. They may even claim to serve a Higher Purpose. On the same subject, it is highly questionable that God asked any human to do anything beyond being aware of truth. He gave us the freedom of choice. He cannot violate His own principle by imposing demands on us. The writers of the Old Testament overstep the truth by bragging about their tribesmen's abuses and claiming them to be divinely ordained.

If we believe that we are bodies and the whole life revolves around physicality, we cannot get Jesus' message correctly. The writers of the Old Testament claim that God created the first humans from the dust of the earth. But can this be true? The Psalm 149 verse 5 says: "Let them praise the name of the Lord: for he commanded, and they[humans] were created." Here we find no mention of the dust of the ground. Also, "worlds were framed by the word of God, so things which are seen were not made of things which do appear." (Hebrews 11: 3) In other words, physicality is a creation of God. Isn't it possible that Adam's option of a physical life was enacted while he still was a spiritual being? Physicality entails selfishness and selfishness is the opposite of love. Materialists see safety in gathering material assets while Jesus saw safety in immaterial love and knowledge of truth. It is obvious that physicality is a lower form of life in a limited environment where life is run by a simplistic and selfish mentality based on personal physical goals. Spirituality instead is the way of the universe. A simple, physical life is easier to control; it is within our ability to manage. This simplicity made physicality, the "rational" foundation of Communism, palatable at its first look. Control, physicality, and submission had constantly been a central preoccupation of the earliest religious writers. Their early religion itself is focused on physicality, possessions, victories, and everything related. Self-aggrandizement, inequality, domination, specialness, physicality, and everything related are also elements of Adam's physical choices.

For Jesus, everything we need comes from a clear mind which is truth and love. This state of mind cannot be borrowed from another; it is a personal enlightenment born from individual search. Enlightenment is a quest for meanings. Today, people are less interested in meanings and more concerned about possessions. They conveniently accuse others for what they missed and they target the others for punishment.

God is fair (5). If we don't accept His perfection, we don't know Him. If we don't know Him we assume He is the way we are; interested in possessions and power. Usually, we gravitate towards believing He is as we are and therefore thinks as we do. This is where we make our biggest mistakes "in his name". This is when we are proud of ourselves and assume that we are borderline holy. This is when we degrade our opinion of Him.

Judging in terms "of good and evil" is the human way, unrelated to God. The idea of judgment comes from our desire to see ourselves as being "better" than …. We prefer to judge and not be judged. Resultingly, we feel special, accomplished, in control of our personal environment, entitled to use and abuse others and never to be found guilt; only the others are. By believing in evil, Adam messed up his own mind. God doesn't know evil. He cannot consider valid what He didn't create and He didn't create or recommend anything that hurts. Evil is a temporary concept humans use to justify some selfish opinions. The fact that our opinions change in time proves that they are inaccurate. If we really want more for ourselves, we should aspire to raise our own quality to a level that would give us access to plenty. This upgrade of quality is the "Atonement, who was established as a means of restoring guiltlessness to minds that have denied it, and thus denied Heaven to themselves." (6) But, of course, there is a big difference between having the "plenty" available and of gaining plenty through personal cunning. So, where do you want to be?

We take control of our lives with our values quietly guiding our thoughts and deeds. Nevertheless, life is set by God; meaning that He is in absolute control of His Creation. He is life itself. Consequently, He has raised a lot of interest throughout history. As we are, we guide our interests with our choices. We cannot accept what is different from what we consider real, regardless of what God has to say. Our opinion that physicality is real, being mistaken, has no value. Our physical choices are what is preventing us from accessing God. We want to believe what we consider agreeable, which basically are our choices. Then, we have to punish those who do not agree with us. We assume they are guilty of ignorance. Again, we are sacrificing innocent others on our behalf. Guilty is always someone else and someone else should pay for it. This is why our physical life is limited.

This is a good time to remember the Great Depression when people started to believe that capitalism, may not be such a great idea after all. People started to idealize a new and cleverly advertised new system, they knew almost nothing about, called communism. That was their way to accuse capitalism for the financial problems we had and to suggest that communism offered equitable moral values instead. It only took a clever, simple, and palatable transfer of funds from the wealthy to the poor to the disgraced capitalism. The Great Depression was the consequence of human greed, therefore a mistake. Then, we had the self-proclaimed progressive thinkers who wholeheartedly supported communism, thus betraying their own best interests and the interests of their countries. The communist sympathizers from the western countries turned spies, sent eastward large amounts of money and technology. Communism is a big supporter of physicality which also fits the acceptance level of the simple minded and an opportunity for the white middle class to lead the movement and become the new upper class in the future new communist political system. For communist leaders, the material values are much more profitable than moral values. Money may offer a power that override any morality. Everything has a price! By the way, communism, that obviously failed, was not the proper answer to capitalism's crisis. It is not the distribution of money that made a political system fair, but the fair choice of competent leaders. Some thought reforming the existing economic system could be a much better solution then Communist Revolution but, those had been overrun by the new and exciting trend.

A repressive society cannot surpass a free and creative one. In communism, people had been forced to stop thinking freely in order to adopt the Marxist "glorious" mentality. All sources of information had been severely monitored. The problem is that besides accepting the built-in Marxist flaws, by preventing people from thinking freely communism forced them to stop growing. Stop growing means in this case, to stop being people and becoming a herd. Their freedom to create had been obstructed by the stifling central control, self-righteousness, lack of personal means and compulsive indoctrination. As a result, many people from communist countries abandoned all they had and ran in droves to the more free and successful capitalism. Communism lasted as long as it did only because of the accumulation of all power into the hands of a few, street smart, self-righteous and abusive leaders who held tight their political reigns.

People who claimed some dignity in that sea of submission had been communism's most tragic victims. Their fair opinions couldn't be accepted because they had been considered a threat to Marxist purity and therefore prohibited. The free thinkers could only talk to themselves. Any independent thought was considered an attack against the glorious

Marxist philosophy. Independent thinkers could never take the risk of expressing their thoughts. They had been isolated and closely monitored. I remember my beginning years as a dentist in Romania. I was excited by all the knowledge I accumulated in Dental School. I started to create new ways of treating my patients. The last patient I had was a young lady unhappy about her facial profile; affected primarily by her teeth. I redesigned her profile, my way. I emigrated soon after and I never saw her again. Several years later a Romanian patient of mine from my city, who knew her also, told me that she finally emigrated to the United States and was happy with her new face and teeth. This patient never trusted any other dentist to touch my work. I invited her to let me see her and to eventually let me do some free dental maintenance but, she never came. It was probably a too expensive trip for a recent immigrant. In the US I didn't have the courage to assume as much professional freedom as I had in Romania. In Romania I didn't have the necessary dental supplies for what I wanted to do. I was appointed chief of dental services in a creatin area but dental supplies got embarrassingly less and less year after year until I had no choice but to cross my arms and emigrate. The country's budget got oriented towards industrial projects according to our communist luminaires; projects that in the end didn't work-out well. If I could have only received a single supportive word, an intelligent, common sense comment, it could have meant so much to me! That would have felt like a breath of fresh air. But, the communists were relentless in their proud, collective march along their failing path. If Marxism is as correct as they thought it will be, their shining victory is supposed to be around the corner. The mantra was always: the more difficult their path, the sweeter the victory. Trust the "most brilliant philosopher of all time," Karl Marx! And, while holding Karl Marx high, communism collapsed on its own, world-wide. What kind of success was that?

The rudimentary popular sympathy for communist ideas, across the world, had been and still is another form of a transfer of responsibility. Nevertheless, the creative capitalist upper class built the most developed and prosperous countries in the land! I myself rose from absolute poverty to a successful dental business in several years in the heart of capitalism, while communism let me down. We are all created equal but we are not using our abilities the same way. Communism had been seen as progress by those who rose from insignificance to political leadership. It is easy to blame others for one's lack of success. Social stratification cannot be prevented. Communism itself is socially stratified. Leaders and workers have been equally needed in a healthy society. They only need to be able and fair. Guilt is not a monopoly of the wealthy and righteousness doesn't belong to those who cry louder.

For one to be fair, love has to be the main motivating factor and surprisingly it is fundamentally denied under communism. The reason for this denial is that love is the backbone of spirituality, which is not a communist concern while hate, born from the desire to control, is the backbone of communism. For communists to love all people, including the rich, is nonsense! Nevertheless, they highly recommended love for our communist leaders.

In the end, the quality of our lives depends on the quality of our thinking. But, how can we achieve the higher mentality that qualifies us for a happy life, if restricted to know the truth. God's laws are instinctively known but also instinctively prohibited by our materialism's limits on higher knowledge. God doesn't ask for obedience to any external laws. Laws imply obligations and obligations contradict our freedom. Again, we are the ones we choose to be. Nobody else is in charge with how we conduct our own life, but us.

Jesus didn't concern himself with social or political issues, but to the truth upon which life is built. This is the path Jesus successfully chose for himself. Nevertheless, hardships are wake-up calls for mental adjustments. In the end, damage to others is damage to self: we all are a unit!

Atheists and idealists have different kinds of perspectives on life and different ways to achieve fairness and fulfillments. An older patient of mine that had been a religious materialist disclosed her idea of fulfillment as: "I need money not friends. If I would have money, I would have all the friends I want. If I don't have money, I don't have friends either." For God, money is inconsequential. Knowledge, truth and love are consequential.

Communism achieved total ownership and control over one third of the world. Nevertheless, it failed. Unable to fulfill its goal, communism went quietly down the drain hugging its atheist flag.

For Jesus, one's physical condition isn't an issue. He never owned anything and didn't miss anything. For him, things didn't matter; the quality of mind does. The quality of his mind creates miracles. "Don't be concerned of those who want to kill the body but cannot affect your mind" (Matthew 10: 28), Jesus said. The healthy mind provides one with everything he needs. We are those we choose to be.

II.

Monotheism

Long ago, people imagined a variety of spiritual helpers and those assumptions diversified to the extent that Jesus decided to descend from the spiritual realm, be born as a human and teach us what the spiritual world is about. The man-to-man communication is the most effective way to convey knowledge. Unfortunately, his basic teachings upset so much the local church leaders, waxed in their opinions and practices, that they decided to kill him. There could only be either He or they and they decided to have him killed. So, Jesus' direct teaching was interrupted. His followers had been left to make sense of the information they received, the best they could. Jesus' spiritual teachings started to blend in with our long practiced religious beliefs and became accepted as we have it today. But Jesus' spiritual and people's physical natures are two different systems that cannot be mended. Nevertheless, where there is a will, there is a way. People combined Jesus' spiritual nature with his physical crucifixion event and came to the conclusion that his killing was, as a matter of fact, an eternal payment for the sins of humanity. Still, the church continued to ask people to pray for their sins, ever since. Jesus' atonement doesn't seem that solid!

We are created spiritual by our Omnipotent, Omnipresent and Omniscient spiritual Father, "in His own image" (Genesis 1: 27), perfectly equipped for being God's companions in the universe. Humans being humans, one of God's early sons, Adam, found God's advice not to eat fruits from a certain tree, uncomfortable. Surprised by that restriction, Adam thought that this is too much to accept and chose to be removed from heaven and allowed to live a physical, independent life. Why? Ask any rebellious child of today why did he disobey his father. So we, Adam's descendants, started to be born on earth. Many people would like a better or more interesting place. I much prefer myself to be in heaven instead but, here I am and this may not be that bad after all: it forces us to wake-up and desire to be in a better, more mentally stimulating place. In addition to the decision to disobey God's advice, Adam made the wrong decision to proudly refuse to be reminded of his disobedience. Therefore he stuck to his physical ways, avoided God's comments and did not retrace his steps. He didn't want to return to the spiritual world. Why? I don't know. I can only guess: he didn't want to be told what to do but to be left alone to experience his life as he pleases. He got his first taste for control. Well, was this the mistake: taking charge of his life before knowing the meaning of his choices?

Well, all choices had been available to him but only one of those choices could bring him back to heaven. Did Adam know that? Spirituality is more complex than the physical way and more exciting. There is so much more available there than making a living. Learning to read and write is not fun for a young child but it opens larger opportunities for the rest of his life. I remember in the first grade I had a hard time writing for the first time a whole page of letter "a". My father gave up trying to convince me. Fortunately, my mother didn't! Different choices offer different possibilities. Adam supposedly wanted to be left alone to live his dreams. We, his descendants, followed this trend and learned the ropes. We don't have the experience of spiritual life and consequently do not know how it is. But being aware of the spiritual life Adam chose and lived his own understanding of life; that became our physical world. Next, Jesus came to help us realize that life is much more than a quest for physical goods.

Physicality has the big advantage of being obvious and offering exciting opportunities. Without having anything to compare it with, our condition became acceptable and the physical life became our second nature. Physicality demands possessions. Possession implies control, hope, ability to enjoy and trade, specialness, dreams, and the ability to manipulate our social laws; problems and inequality seep in. Inequality generates blame, unrest and potential conflicts. The quest for physical goods makes people lose their equal love, the due respect for each other and their awareness of heaven. As a matter of fact, access to Heaven became impossible in our physical condition. Physicality is limited and limits one's awareness and possibilities. Physically, life itself is limited.

Least of all, physicality replaced God's eternity with the human's idea of time. All objects last for a limited time. The sequence of cause and effects can exist in time only. Since time and eternity cannot be simultaneously real, predestination, future punishments for past sins, consequences of our behavior, forgiveness and so forth can only be human concepts. They do not exist in the spiritual, eternal world. Spiritually, we live our perfection with no negative consequences. Time makes sense to the physical understanding of life, while eternity, truth and love can connect to spirituality only. God's decisions are eternal, while humanity's decisions are temporary only because we have temporary lives. God's eternity allows Him to be instantaneously aware of past and future, something that is not possible in "time". "Into eternity, where all is one," (7) time cannot intrude. Time is our attempt to dissect eternity. "Time and eternity cannot be simultaneously real, because they contradict each other." (266) Our physical understanding of life allows us to understand the future as the consequence of what we presently do. Our finite perception of things brings us to the finite perception of life. To no surprise, we live according to our physical values. Physicality gives us a sense of control in the simple and predictable world we live in. In this world we can understand and manipulate our environment as desired. We don't realize that our desire to be in control is a reminder of our holy origin. Even in this limited state, our personal control tries to overrun the divine influence and separate us from God. Here is where our misuse of control begins. Here is where our separation from our spiritual perfection begins and continues down a path of cloudiness. Because God is love, our misunderstanding of His eternal and perfect love prevents us to understand Him: "For the body is a limit on love. The belief in limited love was its origin, and it was made to limit the unlimited." "Limits on love will always seem to shut God out, and keep you apart of Him." "The body is a tiny fence around a little part of a glorious and complete idea" (8) So, humans created an enclosure where their opinions and their safety tactics are considered acceptable; builders of their own version of progress. Adam used his freedom to build this alternative physical way of life, based on the alternative values that we still use today. Our understanding of physical existence replaced life's spiritual meaning. We have our "mental box" of ideas that guide us throughout life. Because those ideas are our creation, we rely on them and resist those spiritual thoughts that lead to the concept of God. Our ways may not be perfect but they are ours and familiar to us. We know how to handle them.

A physical society, requires a physical legal system. As known, our legal system is not perfect. It cannot be compared with the Divine knowledge of past, present and future and the Divine sense of fairness. God doesn't pursue payoffs. He is concerned with the best outcome in any situation; a solution based on an intimate knowledge of life and not guilt. Meanwhile, our physical system aims for blame, restrictions, punishment, and payoffs. We try hard to punish the "guilty" one but our human judgement has limited knowledge of truth. God is the only one who knows it. No institution on earth is more interested in the truth than the Church. But, the church says ,"And the Lord God formed man of the dust of the ground." (Genesis 2: 7) Is this true? So far our religion is a naive attempt to blend truth with opinions and spirituality with physicality. Truth becomes a supreme unknown, while it is simple and natural!

The church we have, doesn't dare to grow beyond its opinion about life formulated 2,000 years ago and prior. We have to trust that "God created man in His own image" (Genesis 1:27) and treat ourselves with all the respect and wisdom we can mount. We are fully equipped to deal with the challenges of life but, so far, we prefer the easier ways: praise God and ask Him to do our job. This approach allows us to do whatever we can justify, modestly claim that this is the best we can do and hope for God's mercy to save us from any misdeed. This is what we want but, not what we should do. We are equipped to resurrect ourselves from illusions. By not doing so and asking Jesus to do it for us is shameful. As a matter of fact, Jesus didn't come to do what we ourselves should do. He came to teach us how to resurrect ourselves from illusions. God gave us already what we need: common sense, intelligence, ability, truth, Jesus' advice. We are responsible to use those means.

We assume most people are transferred to Heaven once they die, but are they? Do they suddenly achieve the enlightenment needed for Heaven simply by their physical death? Physicality is a weird condition. If people's transition to the afterlife comes with sudden enlightenment, why do so many choose to come back from the afterlife and live on earth again? Nobody becomes born unless he or she wants it. For God, "the body is a learning device for the mind." (9) There is nothing as useful as personal experience! Physically, we have a chance to improve by meeting challenges head on and learning all that we can from this experience until we achieve the enlightenment we need. The perfection we had at our creation is long forgotten after years of a physical life. Landed in this challenging physical environment, the only tool we have for progress is our God-given ability to think and find a way out if it. Unfortunately our minds, under physical stress, do not always find the enlightened way out of our tight enclosure. We customarily justify the comfort of the status quo and revert to it. We find explanations, reasons to hope for solutions, expect God to come and save us and, get satisfaction with appeasing opinions. We justify our inadequate thoughts and stop searching for what Heaven truly is. Ignorance is bliss!? Jesus did try to move us to higher grounds and we showed our appreciation for his intention but before fully understanding his message, the Church leaders of that time demanded and had granted his execution. In his absence we struggled to make sense of his words the best way we could. Obviously our best is not good enough but, it is a good start. As known from the Bible, some did make the transition to heaven and more will.

Disappointments, random hardships and disasters happen for reasons not obvious to us. How can God, who is supposed to be in control and to love us, have allowed the suffering we endure? Our uneducated conclusion is that He has His reasons which we don't understand. As is common for humans we transfer our responsibility for our acts to another; and ultimately to God. Well, He gave us freedom of choice for a good reason, obviously. This reason is to learn and achieve a better understanding of life. This is our world. God gave us all we need to be enlightened but He cannot do it for us as long as we don't want to distinguish right from wrong. He gave us this freedom of choice and He doesn't go back on His word. We have to stay here until we see the light. So far, we have been bent on self-righteousness, selfish explanation and guilt transfer which allow us to feel clean without cleaning anything. Since Adam and Eve, we've always held others responsible for our improper choices. We judge good and evil…, our way. It is surprising that we, the only ones who select our choices, are not aware that we are the only ones responsible for our selection of values and the lives we have. We planned this life that now is ours to handle. Since God is the creator of all that is, it is important to know Him, his reasons, and His ways. We also have insightful writers and scripture's analyzers, giving us their perspectives on divinity. In the end, it is our duty to pay attention, discern and decide how to benefit from all that is available to us. It is our duty to straighten our lives we loaded with so many mistakes. Many try to humanize the divine instead of divinizing our humanness. Thinkers have noticed from antiquity that humanity's quality deteriorates in time; until we may reach the point where, waxed in misconceptions, we won't be able to return to normalcy through personal efforts. That is the time the Bible refers to as "the day of the Lord" when the divine creation of us has to be saved from its own chaos. We love to consider our opinions valid and we build our sense of pride on them. But, those human opinions are generally inconsequential because they miss the truth. God produced Heaven while we produced our physical life. God's creation is perfect, eternal, and therefore real, while ours is an illusion with negative implications that finish in death. Truth is love but we don't know love any longer. While the Church is not entirely aware of its limitations, it still is our only guide to perfection. The Church is the only institution that deals with our moral values and is a window to our spiritual reality. Meanwhile the church, being built by humans, re-defines truth, the human way.

All divinity experts try to explain the often-mistaken scriptures, intellectually justify their inconsistencies and present them as true. So, here we are: we managed to mix truth with opinions. We want to see the truth when and where it is convenient to us. Heaven is the perfect environment we had been intended for. We are the prodigal sons, confused for now, but not in eternity. We have what we need to evaluate any opinion; in other words, to detect and incorporate the truth. It is our duty to know the truth for our own good. Jesus' teachings had been too shocking and presented for too short of a period of time to be incorporated. The holy books and letters, unchanged for thousands of years, had been skillfully presented to fit our physical thinking. But God is above and beyond any books. He is in our souls and minds. One should look for Him in his own heart if he wants to have a fulfilling life. Jesus helps those who want to be helped. God wants us to be enlightened. In His opinion, truth is all that matters.

Therefore, we are justified to carefully evaluate all information received. We are meant to know the truth. For personal clarity and understanding, a brief evaluation in the following pages is the spiritual writers' presentation of their understanding of truth.

1.

THE WRITERS OF THE SCRIPTURES

No doubt, all scripture writers share the desire to portray God fairly. He is the Creator of all that is and He is all that is. "There is but one God, the Father, of whom are all things." (1 Corinthians. 8: 6) Therefore "there is no power but God," (Romans 13:1). He is our only hope for everlasting peace and joy, the knower of meanings, holiness, and life. With such credentials, God cannot be but the owner and organizer of the universe. We don't know Him. We lost touch with him long ago and replaced what we don't know with snippets of insight and, "enlightened" opinions. Gospel writers had been tempted to assume they do understand God better than others and upheld their opinions as divine truth. But, how divine are their opinions if they contradict common sense as well as each other? To prove this point, I will let the scripture writers' present their own case.

The start with, God is presented in the Old Testament as mostly involved in earthly issues and in the New Testament as a teacher of spiritual values. It is surprising that after giving us the freedom to choose, bible writers tell us that He will harshly punish those who do certain things: "all things are lawful unto me", (1 Corinthians 6:12), Baasha and his son Elah provoked "the Lord God of Israel to anger with their vanities." (1 Kings: 16, 13). Also, Jehu "said to the guard and to the captains, go in, and slay them; let none come forth. And they smote them with the edge of the sword." (2 Kings 10: 25) Why? Because they were worshipers of Baal. It would be too cumbersome to list them all. Spiritually, our mistakes are meaningless in eternity; having short term negative effects. God gave us freedom because only in freedom one can face his own mistakes and evaluate their consequences. But, some scripture writers do not allow any expression outside of what is written in their books. Their writings are considered the will of God. But isn't mistake a transient thought and not a fact? A good teacher does not ask the pupils to only obey but guides them to observe and learn at their own pace, through their own will. This is our world, full with justifications, interpretations and accusations of all kinds. Some people created stories about God and Heaven and what God's opinions are while having no knowledge of what happened in Heaven prior to their birth.

In the Old Testament, God is always presented as One while in the New Testament He is presented as a Trinity. Trinity was never mentioned by Jesus. For him there is clearly but one God: our Father, the only One who knew the timing of future events (Matthew 24: 36) and the only perfect love there is. In 381 A.D. emperor Theodosius convened the Council of Constantinople where Athanasius initially proposed the doctrine of Trinity; which became the cornerstone doctrine of the Catholic Church. But, is this opinion justified? We know that God is indivisible and unchangeable. He is also the only One who has perfect love, knowledge and abilities. Also, Jesus cannot be God incarnated. God depends of no one. Jesus, the angels and the Holy Spirit are all creations of His own and consequently are not The God. Jesus once said: "Why do you call me good? there is none good but one, that is God." (Luke 18: 19)

Truth does not need to be defended. In the Old Testament we are asked to display holiness through obedience to written (external) laws, customs and rituals while in the New Testament we are taught to show holiness through having holy thoughts; inserted in our nature at our creation. In the Old Testament, God asked us to pay for our sins with sacrifices while in the New Testament He asks us to dismiss sins as perishable consequences of judgmental mistakes. It is enough to "know the truth and the truth shall set you free." (John 8: 32) The writers of the Old Testament recommend forgiveness of sins through the atoning sacrifice of an innocent other (a substitutional atonement), while the New Testament condemns all sacrifices: "I will have mercy not sacrifices; you should not condemn the guiltless." (Matthew12: 7) In the Old Testament, God's kingdom is presented as the physical Garden of Eden while in the New Testament it is a spiritual condition called Heaven; located in one's mind and soul: "the kingdom of God is within you." (Luke 17: 21). These discrepancies motivate some to claim "that the God of the Old Testament is not the ultimate God. He is a lower and imperfect god, said a popular doctrine spread by a variety of Christians in the 2nd and 3rd centuries. This doctrine, shared by many including the Gnostics, Valentinian Christians and followers of a teacher named Maricon." (The Apocryphal Jesus, by professor David Brekke of the Ohio State University, page 374)

In another section of the Bible the writer claims: "God repented of the evil that he had said he would do unto them." (Jonah 3: 10) But the Bible writer James (1:17) disagrees: "Every perfect gift is from above, and cometh down from the Father of lights, with whom is no variableness, neither shadow of turning." Of the two Bible statements only one can be correct. In another passage, God is presented as selfish: "I am the Lord and my glory will I not give to another," (Isaiah 42: 8). But Jesus said: "sharing is why God created you." (10) Also, "you are part of God," (11) part that makes us His Sons.

Another Bible contradiction is in regards to relieving us of our sins. Sometimes this process is called "Redemption", a form of compensation, and other times it's called "Salvation" from the power and effects of evil. Redemption is a pay back, a repurchase or a paying of a ransom; it is a transaction. But, does God make transactions? With what can one pay for his redemption? With the torture of God's Son? It seems unreasonably cruel and unfair but it was palatable to the early peoples of Biblical times. This local custom carried over to Jesus's apostles and disciples, continuing the idea that the killing of Jesus would redeem all from guilt, forever! The Old Testament has many instances of redemption by executing innocent children for their fathers' sins. The divine Salvation, on the other hand, suggests the deliverance from the illusion of sin. Comparing physical redemption with spiritual salvation which one of the two fits God's nature? He would deny his own nature if He would murder His own creation. People, be aware! God is a creator; not a murderer. He cannot be both.

We hold the Bible's writers as authorities in the knowledge of God. While this is inspiring it also creates a puzzling contradiction: if we are endowed with freedom of choice, it means that we cannot sin. Sins are mistakes and learning experiences; therefore not negative intrusions. "All things are lawful unto me," (1 Corinthians 6: 1) implies that no divine punishment is ever justified and, never happens. There is nothing for the church to save us from. Our decisions have their consequences included.

Mistakes are allowed in order to learn from them before they disappear somewhere into the past. The pain created by mistakes is short lived and spiritually meaningless. Besides, if we are already forgiven, what purpose do sacrifices serve? The writers even threaten us with the nonexistent wrath of God. It should be noticed that Jesus didn't criticize and didn't threaten anyone. His purpose was teaching the truth.

Both the Koran and the Old Testament have stern rules, overseen by stern human defenders of the Divine. This is honorable from their viewpoint but God doesn't need or require to be defended. He only wants love and wisdom. As a matter of fact, God didn't give us any written laws. The Ten Commandments are not laws and neither are they commandments. They look more like physical reminders of our unwritten, built-in creation rules. Still, the clergy believes the love of God should be expressed through obedience to "His" Ten Commandments "delivered" to Moses. To assure accurate and complete submission to those "laws", the early Jewish experts formulated 613 additional laws set in the Torah to protect the ten core demands from being circumvented. It is an air-tight system not allowing any room for mistakes (otherwise allowed by our freedom of choice); a system that to many seems so rigid that it's almost impossible to obey. Some abandoned that system of laws and turned atheist. Others devised practices that allow them to believe their transgressions can be erased through certain ceremonies so that they can make themselves pure again and eventually transgress again and be wiped clean again. One such practice is the recitation of Selichotand in the middle of the blessing for forgiveness. This practice was reported in the Orange County Register of September 14, 2017. This particular article described "the Chabad of Irvine's annual Kappa rot ceremonies." This ceremony: "include a chicken swung over someone's head to symbolize that person's sins are transferred into the bird. The chicken is then slaughtered." It is assumed that by killing the chicken, the person's sins are also killed. Obviously, the "sinner" doesn't have to alter his beliefs or change his ways for as long as such practices are available. It seems that purification through external practices do not involve soul searching and do not require a change or improvement of any kind. Spiritual cleansing by proxy was practiced up until modern times. Christians believe that Jesus, too, was sacrificed as an atonement by proxy.

Our laws are written by men who claim they speak for God: ".….. and the strength of sin is the [external] law." (1Corinthians 15: 56) Those laws are often ignored, thus qualifying their perpetuators as sinful. Nevertheless, our religious leaders get on their high horse and assume the duty to emit laws, interpret Jesus' words, create rituals and practices with the purpose of making us aware of our duty and obedience to God. In this case we should remember that God doesn't require obedience because obedience means submission. If subjected, we are controlled and our growth through life's experiences is stunted. Our growth is achieved through learning (developing our inner abilities through awareness), not through submission to external rules.

The New Testament emphasizes God's love as unconditional and shared with all Creation. Love is perfection. Nevertheless we, the people, figured out a way to love that fits our egos and is therefore adjusted to our selfish desires. So, we search for personal interests and devised ways to justify them. Rather than upgrading our thinking to holiness, we adjusted the concept of holiness to our thinking (acceptance). In the early 400's A.D., Saint Augustine, an adult convert from paganism, introduced the concept of election and predestination. According to him we are selected by God for certain tasks; not all of them holy. That means that no one can change His set agenda. Our only choice is to beg for mercy. Predestination is an interesting idea that contradicts the divine principle of free choice and denies the concept of learning through experience. Marxism boldly replaced learning through personal experience with learning through assimilating Karl Marx's concept of communism. According to Marxist laws, communism is the answer to the inequality generated by physical (financial) arrangements. The glory of communism is its claim that its financial arrangements provide the final answer to the ideal society. Theoretically it seems workable but practically it wastes a lot of talents, prevents creativity, restricts freedoms and creates hopelessness. Spirituality has its own answer to inequality and freedom through the power of truth and love. Truth is the spiritual perfection that leads to the best outcome for everybody involved and does so in complete fairness. Spiritual perfection doesn't have favorites.

The writers of the Old Testament try to prevent sin through fear of divine punishment while Jesus eliminates sin through higher mindedness.

"Love eliminates sins as light eliminates darkness." If one fights darkness he can never win. By fighting it, one gives darkness a recognition it doesn't deserves. Darkness is a nonentity: it is a lack of light. Similarly, sin is lack of wisdom. Fight sin and you give it a legitimacy it doesn't have. Jesus recommends sin's straight dismissal through the awareness of truth. "We cannot solve the problems we have by using the same mentality we had when we created them," Einstein did quote. We have to grow and eliminate our mistakes in order to advance. Holiness is not obedience to laws and rules. It is the love in our heart. Apostle Paul stated, "the strength of sin is the law." (1Corinthians 15: 56) If one disobeys the (legal) law, he is theoretically a sinner; if he does obey, he is its slave. For God's sake, replace the written law with the unwritten one which is: love. Jesus rejected both practices: man's outward display of purity and the subjection to external laws. He required instead purity of mind, in total freedom (live by the inner laws God built in us at our creation). He dismisses our mistakes because they are fleeting human misjudgments and consequently of no value. The fact that our mistakes are correctable means that they are not true. If sins are not true, they cannot be punished. They should be dismissed, (eliminated, not enacted).

Jesus' disclosure of the importance of our mentality didn't impress people. They prefer their personal thoughts. Laws are our creations and our fences that define our accepted limits. "The body itself is a fence the Son of God imagines that he has built, to separate parts of his Self from other parts. It is within this fence he thinks he lives, and dies as it decays and crumbles" (12). Our protection is secured by love. Love has no need for a fence and, consequently, is freedom. Love, being fair, doesn't need laws "for he that loves another hath fulfilled the law." (Romans 13: 8)

When the writers of the Bible mention punishments, they entertain the idea of being tortured forever in hell, "cast into the lake of fire and brimstone... and shall be tormented day and night for ever and ever." (Revelation 20:10) "... go into hell, into the fire that never shall be quenched: where their worm dieth not, and the fire is not quenched." (Mark 9: 43, 44) "Who can stand before His indignation and who can abide in the fierceness of his anger? His fury is poured out like fire, and the rocks are thrown down by him." (Nahum 1:6) and so forth. All this being payoffs for a misdeed we had committed in our brief life. This scenario is obviously unfair and cannot belong to God who "saved us before the beginning of time." (2 Timothy 1: 9). More than that, the writers of the Old Testament amplify His displeasure with us to the level of revenge which is, again, foreign to God but common to humans. While God built Heaven, we built this painful place we call "our world". He built holiness, we built guilt. He brings forgiveness, we punish.

It is expected from double standards to generate double messages. One message is, that we are children of God and consequently capable to overcome our temporary confusion. "You are the temple of a living God" (2 Corinthians 6:16) meaning that part of Him abides in us; that part makes us His Sons. We are asked to "be ye therefore perfect, even as your Father which is in heaven is perfect." (Matthew 5:48) This means we are perfectly capable to clean up our minds and achieve salvation from this mess we are in. We are the prodigal sons that can happily return to our birthplace of abundance and love any time we want. This message seems clear enough but, lo and behold, in the same Bible we confidently read the opposite message: we cannot clean up our minds and we are incapable of overcoming our condition and achieve salvation, "For by grace we are saved through faith, and not of ourselves: it is the gift of God; not of works, lest any man should boast." (Ephesians 2: 8,9)

There are only two possible sources of ideas belonging to the only two creative sources available: God, and humans. Sin, having a negative meaning, is a human's production and consequently is subjected to human will. Therefore, we do not depend on the atoning sacrifice of Jesus Christ as scriptures claim. The humans cannot claim that we are "incapable to overcome it." "Therefore, those who look on sin are seeing the denial of the real world" (13). The real world is sin free, created by the sinless God who has no association with anything negative. Should God sacrifice Jesus for the benefit of a bunch of confused fellows who refuse to renounce their sins? Even if He would want to do that, humans cannot be reconciled through physical torture of an innocent saint. It is not only unnecessary but plainly criminal. Does God resort to criminality? From God's perspective, "I will forgive their iniquity, and I will remember their sins no more." (Jeremiah 31: 34) Also see Daniel 9: 9, Numbers 14: 18, Psalm 86: 5&103: 3 and Joel 2: 32. If God forgives us, why do we need the atoning sacrifice of His Son in addition?

Another confusion introduced in the Bible by its writers is their presentation of God as both loving and jealous. To them it seems that love could go hand in hand with jealousy but, as a matter of fact, the two exclude each other. Love is freedom; jealousy is possession. If you love you desire happiness for your partner, not enslavement. Love is selflessness, respect and the desire for the best for our partners while jealousy obviously doesn't. Jealousy is a display of insecurity that doesn't have anything to do with love.

There are "passages in the Old Testament that show God as ignorant, as changing his mind, as being pleased by the odor of burned sacrifice, as testing people, unsure of how they will respond. He sometimes experiences dubious emotions like anger and regret." (The Apocryphal Jesus, by Professor David Brake).

A significant misrepresentation of God is coming from our assumption that He has preferred or has chosen people and not special others. Why? God doesn't take sides. He created us equally perfect and different because only different minds generate lovely and inspiring conversations. "We are gods; and all of you are children of the Highest." (Psalm 82: 6) "His equal love is given equally to all alike" (A Cours In Miracles, Text, Page 12, 3: 2; also, see Colossians 3:11). God "hath made of one blood all nations of men" (Acts 17: 26). This truth, like any truth, doesn't need to be defended. It is unassailable. All God's children have His total love for God is not partial (14). To affirm that God kills those He does not like or that He discriminates among his sons seems pure human-like behavior. This kind of blasphemous thinking had been first introduced in the scriptures by their writers' partiality to their own kin.

It is a common belief that Jesus is special due to his special creation. Jesus was created long before his latest birth in Bethlehem in year 1 A.D., when it is claimed that he was fathered by the Spirit of God. Some scholars believe he was born from physical parents. Jesus himself stood against the assumption of his special creation and claimed that he had been created the same way we had been. Before his baptism he lived a common life marked by higher wisdom. He claimed that God is fair and denied the idea of special godly favors. Again, we are different due to our own different choices but not due to being created special. Those who believe they are better, implicitly believe they are right. The assumption that God prefers some over others is blasphemous. God is above such discriminating practices. His Kingdom is populated by equally valuable people who, as created, have equal access to all there is. All that God wants us to do is to show and teach love.

Continuing with the Bible's contradictions, is it possible that God really asked the Israelites not to intermarry (Deuteronomy 7: 3 and 1Kings 11:2) and then asked them to do the opposite? (Jeremiah 29:6) An interesting story is in Judges 1-25: The tribe of Benjamin was left at the time with no women and risked extinction. "The children of Israel have swooned saying, Cursed be he that gives a wife to Benjamin." It was a real possibility "that there should be today one tribe lacking in Israel." In the face of this crisis, the Israelites prayed to God and "Then, the elders of the congregation said, … We may not give them wives of our daughters," but then, they went around their own "law" by advising the men of Benjamin to take what they could not have been allowed to "get": "if the daughters of Shi'-low come out of the vineyards in dances, catch you every man his wife and go to the land of Benjamin." (Judges 21: 1-25) And, so they did. Could God encourage His "chosen people" to kidnap and rape? Why had they refused to allow them to legally marry?

Another puzzling question is: can God hate and love at the same time? For us on earth, this is nothing new. Nevertheless, hate and love are opposite feelings. We partook from the tree of good and evil and started to discriminate and categorize based on our freshly discovered union of opposites. Good and evil, among other things, had been a human endorsement of love and hate, truth and opinion, duty and desire, right and wrong, accept and reject, trust and doubt, assume and know, yin and yang as well as any other dualities. Adam and Eve's acceptance of good and evil means their acceptance of everything a human can think of. Meanwhile, God doesn't compare. He knows. He simply states the truth. God gave us access to everything that is. One cannot know good if he doesn't know bad. His creation is one for all and meant to help us know the truth so we can choose our ways wisely. He gave us the intelligence we need to properly evaluate and use in order to get what are our best choices. God didn't create evil and neither division or degrees of worthiness. He created unity based on the uniqueness of truth and love. We, in this free world of ours, may feel free to make a bad choice. If we do, we are equally free to experience, evaluate and learn. We also like to analyze. Little do we know that by dissecting and categorizing a unit, we ruin its essence.

A stunning misrepresentation of God is related to sacrifices. In Exodus 20: 26 God asked Moses to "make an altar unto me, and shalt sacrifice thereon thy burnt offerings." If the altar will be "of stone, thou shalt not build it of hewn stone" because, if touched by his tools, "thou hast polluted it." In other words, if Moses touches those stones with his hands they are not polluted but if he uses tools to fashion them, they are. The meaning is that tools are a source of defilement. How is this possible? No object can project a will.

In Genesis 17: 14 we read: "And the uncircumcised man child whose flesh of his foreskin is not circumcised, that soul shall be cut off from his people; he hath broken my covenant." Did God command such a covenant for a new-born child? How could that eight days old child be held responsible for not being circumcised and having his existence denied? The decision of circumcision belongs to the parents and not to their innocent new-born and yet they, the parents, are unaffected by their decision not to circumcise their baby. This practice of differed responsibility is similar to any other substitutionary atonement where the guiltless is punished for the sins of the "guilty". See Jesus' crucifixion.

A more serious abomination was in Exodus 22: 20, "He that sacrifices unto any god, save unto the Lord only, he shall surely be put to death." Again, this is either an attack of jealousy (see Exodus 20: 5) or an attempt to deny someone's "free will". God doesn't kill. God gave His Sons everything they need to succeed and He had granted them a freedom which cannot be taken away. "From what you want, God does not save you." (15) It is inconceivable that killing that poor soul that sacrifices to an illusion, would result in anything good. God creates life. He doesn't kill and doesn't ask anyone to kill for Him. It makes more sense to allow the mistaken person to live, experience his own choices and in time, learn from them. God is the God of life and life's purpose is learning. An additional shortcoming of this statement is that it misrepresents God in ways that would frighten the bystanders instead of showing them His love. God doesn't scare.

Some Muslim fundamentalists do the same: go around killing everyone who doesn't believe as they do under the assumption that they, the fundamentalists, are the only ones who know what God wants. This type of attitude, prompted the Gnostic Christians to conclude that there must be two totally different Gods out there: the revengeful and jealous God of the Old Testament and the loving and forgiving God presented by Jesus. Only one of them can be the true God.

Jesus set straight the issue of sacrifices by saying: "I desire mercy, and not sacrifice." (Matthew 9:13) and "to love Him with all your heart, with all your understanding, and all your soul, and with all your strength, and to love his neighbor as himself, is more than the whole burnt offerings and sacrifices." (Mark, 12: 33) Jesus is also quoted: "to sacrifice the body is to sacrifice nothing." (16) He knows it first-hand. "I am as incapable of receiving sacrifices as God is and every sacrifice you ask of yourself, you ask of me. Learn now that sacrifice of any kind is nothing but a limitation imposed on giving. And, by this limitation you have limited acceptance of the gift I offer you," Jesus said (17). A judgmental mistake requires a judgmental correction. Sacrifice any mistaken idea! The body is an innocent follower of the mind's decision. A body's sacrifice is therefore useless.

Jesus calls for love and not for a formal show of penitence. This means that mutilations and killings performed with the pretense of pleasing God are proof of ignorance. Did the gospel writers ever contemplate the thought that sacrificing doesn't please God? "I will have mercy, and not sacrifice: for I have not come to call the righteous, but the sinners to repentance." (Matthew 9: 13) "God established no sacrifice" (18). Humans did.

As practiced, sacrifice was the opportunity for a feast where the participants are fed and satisfied. One could feel better by this practice but still, a sin can be removed only through definite repudiation of the thought that brought it up. It is obvious that no physical payoff can remove the dreadful thought that produced any sin. Only the awareness of truth can. Sin and mistake are identical errors separated only by their intensity. Both disappear when meet the truth. As for the atoning sacrifice…:

1. Killing cannot pay for sin.
2. The sacrifice of another doesn't make the sinner see enough of the depth of his mistake, to recant.
3. Sacrificing an innocent victim is itself a crime. It is only assumed by the writers of Scriptures that it satisfies God.

4.   People believed that a crime is not a crime any longer if it is done to honor God!?
5.   The practice of substitutional atonement is similar to paying a debt with stolen money.

To make it worse, sometimes unfortunate sons were sacrificed to pay for their father's sins. The priests even set a particularly cruel way of doing it by placing the child on the scorching arms of a heated bronze statue called Moloch. (Jeremiah 32:35, 2 Kings 23:10, Leviticus 20:2-5 and 18: 21, Deuteronomy 18: 10-13, Ezekiel 23: 37) What a scene! And God was supposed to be satisfied?!

It is worth mentioning that those who wrote the rules for performing sacrifices, usually the temple priests, had a personal interest in doing so. They had been the ones officiating the ritual in the prescribed manner on the temple's altar, thus conferring to the process a higher significance. But more importantly, by officiating the ritual the priests, who wrote the rules, could claim status and respect. They were entitled to a portion of the sacrificed animal and probably certain fees and donations. "Every male among the priests shall eat thereof." (Leviticus 7:6) "The priest shall have to himself the skin of the burnt offering." (Leviticus 7:8) "And every meat offering ... shall all the sons of Aaron have." (Leviticus 7:10 also 7:11-38) Besides personal interest, demanding sacrifices to be performed at the temple under authorized supervision, rather than in scattered private places, was a political measure meant to centralize power in Jerusalem. We find in the Old Testament many condemnations of performing sacrifices in "high places," private or communal. Those places had the societal advantage of easy access but, the praised king Hezekiah found them politically incorrect.

A particular attention is given in the Old Testament to Abraham's attempt to sacrifice his son Isaac. The story goes that God had long promised to Abraham a son but as Abraham approached the age of one hundred and his wife Sarah "was past the age" and still childless, she asked Abraham to have a child with her slave, Hagar, before it becomes too late. Abraham did. Then, Abraham and his wife finally had their promised son. They called him Isaac. Sarah then became jealous of Hagar and her son and they were exiled.

One day God said, "take now thy son, thine only son Isaac, whom thou loveth, and get thee into the land of Moriah; and offer him there for a burnt offering upon one of the mountains which I will tell thereof." (Gen. 22: 2) Why had God called Isaac "thine only son?" Why did He mislead? Perhaps He didn't. Possibly those words did not belong to God but to the writer of that scripture. If so, the scripture writer wanted to create the perception that the son of Abraham's wife is special; more valuable than the son of a comely slave. Being a slave was not proof of Sara's lower quality. Aren't all humans equal in the sight of God? Did Abraham love Isaac more than he loved Ishmael, the son conceived with the slave? When all preparations had been done and "Abraham stretched forth his hand and took the knife to slay his son, an angel of the Lord called unto him out of Heaven, and said…lay not thine hand upon the lad … for now I know that you fairest God." (Genesis 22:10-12) The angel of the Lord stunningly discovered that Abraham fears God! As presented, it seems the whole event was set to relieve the angel's curiosity if Abraham fears God or not.

The fact that God promised Sarah and Abraham a child and then let them wait unknowingly until that advanced age, doesn't present God in a favorable light. If the writer wanted to emphasize God's unlimited power, then he is stretching God's fairness. He could provide any son, any time, if He wanted to. If He would have certain timing in mind, it would be considerate to let Abraham know. If God wanted to test Abraham's faith, this wasn't necessary. God knew him as He knows each one of us from before being born: "Before I formed thee in the belly I knew thee; and before thou came forth out of the womb I sanctified thee;" (Jeremiah 1:5). For Him we are not a mystery that needs to be unveiled. Was Abraham instead put in the position to confirm his own faith to himself? I don't know but it doesn't seem necessary. Abraham's mind was set already and God knew that. It seems the writer of the Scripture wanted to impress the reader with both God's unchecked power and Abraham's enduring faith. But then, this starts to look more like fiction than an objective account of what really happened. God is not collecting proofs and evidences and He is not out to impress. This behavior is more human than divine. He knows the truth in a more detailed way than anyone else does. As stated in other places, God doesn't require sacrifices (Isaiah1: 11, 13,14, 17) and

He doesn't say different things at different times in regard to the same matter. In God's mind "is no variableness, neither shadow of turning" His decision around.

If He truly had said to Abraham to perform Isaac's sacrifice and later told him not to, then He doesn't act like God. If He does act erratically, it means either that He is not The God or that the Bible writers cooked the story. Jesus never brought up the issue of sacrifices and obviously never recommended it. Again, as presented, God acts like a human who claims to know God. The whole idea of sacrifice is so murderous that only humans could bring it up. "Sacrificing in any way is a violation of injunction that you should be merciful even as your Father in Heaven is merciful." Also, "Sacrifice is a notion totally unknown to God" (19). Sacrifice is an unreasonable, useless crime.

After their arrival from Egypt the Israelites had been involved in the massacre of Canaan's inhabitants. In order to proudly justify this genocide it was necessary to attribute this crime to God: God asked for it and the Israelites dutifully obeyed! It implies that they, the perpetrators, are not only innocent but faithful subjects (sons) of God. This perspective is also used by the Muslim Jihadists today. Meanwhile as known, God is not abusive nor suspicious, doesn't change His mind, doesn't ask anyone to do anything for Him, doesn't instill fear and doesn't kill. "God holds nothing against anyone." (20) "He is not jealous," "not angry," and "established no sacrifice." "God weeps at the 'sacrifice' of His children who believe they are lost to Him" (21). Someone reading those Old Testament stories, can easily question their validity and, if not disappointed, will be left with doubts. The way they are written, the scriptures offer a clear presentation of the writers' characters and probably the first arguments in favor of atheism.

Before leaving the subject of sacrifices we should take a look at the most venerate sacrifice of all: the sacrifice of Jesus Christ. The Bible writers present it as the sacrifice of all sacrifices, the one that paid for the sins of humanity so that no other sacrifice would be necessary from then on. "For by one offering he hath perfected forever them that are sanctified." (Hebrews 10: 14) "… he laid down his life for us." (1 John 3: 16) The slate is now clean for all those who believe in Jesus. "Now where the remission of these is (sins and iniquities), there is no more offering for sin." (Hebrews 10: 18).

His sacrifice had been not a redemption but the most powerful endorsement of Jesus' teachings. "The Lord is longsuffering and of great mercy, forgiving iniquity and transgression," (Numbers 14: 18) "Saith the Lord: for I will forgive their iniquity, and I will remember their sin no more." (Jeremiah 31: 34) If He forgives us directly, (as shown in Numbers and Jeremiah) why do we need, in addition, an indirect way to forgive through the sacrifice of Jesus? The issue gets more complicated once we hear Jesus' statement: "God does not forgive because He never condemned" (22). People simply used their given freedom of choice, in the way people do, for people's purposes. If people have freedom of choice they cannot be condemned for using it, no matter how mistaken they may be; they don't need Jesus' forgiving sacrifice. "The real world [Heaven] is attained simply by the complete forgiveness of the old," (23) and, living the truth (love) in the present. We are what we are now. For God, what we call sins are judgments gone astray, easy to dismiss by correcting the thoughts that created them. Nevertheless, we didn't correct those thoughts but we justified them with our convenient reasons. Meanwhile, as previously said, Jesus never valued sacrifices, never practiced or recommended one and never claimed to save anyone through a sacrifice. He said, "I want mercy, not sacrifice." (Matthew 12: 7) "Sacrifice brings nothing." (A Course in Miracles, Text, page 453 9: 2) "God does not believe in retribution. His mind does not create that way. He does not hold 'evil' deeds against anyone. Be very sure that you recognize how utterly impossible this assumption is and how entirely it arises from a human projection," Jesus said (24). Overcome with guilt for abandoning him at the cross and for hiding in fear afterwards the apostles wanted to pay Jesus the highest respects possible and with unity of voice they praised Him with: He saved the world from sin! This adulation was supposed to alleviate their sense of guilt. He only claimed that sin is a human fantasy; therefore not real. He taught people how to save themselves: "To this end I was born, and for this cause I came into the world that I should bear witness unto the truth." (John 18: 37) True, but the way the writers present Jesus' experience is different. They relied upon their old tradition of atoning sacrifices. Jesus' crucifixion was the closing statement of his ministry: His dramatic show of love, the power of faith, the permanence of life and the nothingness of physicality. He showed us, to the end, his commitment to live as he taught. "Fear not them which kill the body, but are unable to kill the soul." (Matthew 10: 28) His resurrection that followed demonstrates the triumph of life. "You can overcome the cross." (25) What God creates is forever.

Jesus, being physically born, spent the first part of his physical life (on earth,) clarifying his identity for himself and the second part helping us discover ours. One must make the truth clear to himself before going out to share it with others. He knew that his message of life will collide head on with the conventional message of the local church and he knew that upholding clearly his message was more important than the pain he may suffer during this conflict. For his horrified apostles though, what had just happened had been not only frightening but hard to comprehend. For them it was much easier and much closer to their understanding the traditional Jewish interpretation of sacrifice being a substitutional atonement. Drawing from tradition, the religious thinkers drew a parallel concluding that he paid with his life for the transgressions of others. In that local tradition the sacrificial lamb was supposed to be perfect and Jesus was perfect and innocent (the perfect "lamb"). People didn't see that the final act of Jesus was not an atonement decided by God but Jesus' own decision to endorse his life-long teaching with his personal example. God doesn't kill; Jesus cannot die. God doesn't guide anybody to sacrifice. He always respects one's choice. Jesus chose crucifixion as a live demonstration of the truthfulness of his own teaching: life is eternal, truth is freedom, love is happiness.

After the resurrection Jesus' reputation reached new heights that stimulated his followers to attribute to his decision the highest possible (known from the earliest times) meaning: substitutionary atonement (God demanding the crucifixion of His Son as a ransom for the sins of humanity). This centuries old concept became one of the Bible's core teaching in the New Testament by the early fifth century influential Augustine of Hippo, one of the greatest fathers of the Catholic Church. This was an interpretation of Jesus' words: "Drink from it, [cup of Passover wine] all of you. For it is my blood of the new covenant, which is shed for many for the remission of sins." (Matthew 10:39) This quotation seems to point to his sacrificial atonement but this is not what Jesus meant. In the decades' earliest gospel of Mark 22 : 24 Jesus is quoted: "This is my blood of the new testament, which is shed for many." In Mark there is no mention of Jesus' blood being shed "for the remission of sins." The Passover wine was simply a ritual and a reminder of this historical ceremony and togetherness; not for "the remission of sins", as said in Matthew 10. "The new covenant" is his new doctrine of love. Love is the same as truth and the unifying force of atonement. If one loves, he is on the right track; he cannot sin, which means that his past mistakes are dead history. Be one of those who drinks from the cup of the divine knowledge of love! Once you know the truth, you cannot return to the life of ignorance. Once one returns to love, he regains his holiness and achieves salvation. Jesus is "leaving us an example that we should follow his steps." (1 Peter2: 21 and John 13: 15) Heaven cannot be reached by being witnesses to his execution or by being tortured. Heaven can be reached by abandoning your false beliefs and adopting truth which is love and wisdom. Jesus did remove the sins of the world through his teachings: sins are human illusions that can be eliminated when one chooses the light of truth. He precluded sin by teaching love. "Whosoever is born of God doth not commit sin; for His seed remained in him: and he cannot sin, because he is born of God." (1John 3: 9) "God, the Father of all, who is above all through all, and in you all" (Ephesians 4: 6); He is not a killer. Free of guilt, we can advance along the road to salvation unencumbered. "I am the way and the truth and the life," Jesus said. (John 14: 6,7)

Jesus' focus was on teaching the way to salvation through personal enlightenment. As Jesus himself is Christ by being enlightened, so can we. Salvation is the same as truth, love, and holiness. "I (Jesus) have given them thy [God's] word; and the world hated them because they are not of the world, even as I am not of the [physical] world." (John 17: 6 & 14) Nevertheless, he let the saga unfold to its sad conclusion for the purpose of showing the power of his message and the value of faith. Three days after he died on the cross, he came back completely healed. Was his crucifixion a sacrifice? The dictionary defines sacrifice as "an act of offering to a deity something precious; especially the killing of a victim on an altar." In Jesus' case, his body was not offered to a deity and he was not killed on an altar. He was executed for dogmatic reasons. Sacrifices at the time meant the victim to be burned and consumed, presumably at the Temple, which again, wasn't so in Jesus's case. Since sacrifices are made to God, would anyone in his right mind give back to God his own Son as an atoning sacrifice? Sacrifices were regarded as an act of reverence. In Jesus' case the

Pharisees, who asked for his execution, didn't even consider it an act of reverence. We can conclude that Jesus was executed; not sacrificed. If Jesus' execution had been a sacrifice, Jesus himself would have acknowledged it as such but he didn't. Peter said, "Spiritual sacrifices [are] acceptable to God by Jesus Christ." (1Peter 2:5) But, Jesus did not endorse his own sacrifice which means, again, that his crucifixion was not a sacrifice and not acceptable to God.

God had not been concerned about sins when He gave us freedom of choice. Validation of the fact that sin doesn't exist is given by the Bible writers themselves: "the wages of sin is death;" (Romans 6: 23). But, Jesus didn't die. As death is not, sin cannot be; with no cause, there is no effect. What dies is our physical image with its opinions and misjudgments. Jesus became subjected to crucifixion for contradicting the powerful religious leaders of the day and not for sins. His resurrection proved that death is not the disappearance of us as created by God, but the disappearance of our miscreated physical life.

An important weakness of the Bible is the significant amount of confusion regarding the origin and power of sin. Sin is incompatible with life in Heaven. Consequently, sin's dismissal is essential if we want to return to the perfection of our creation. We assume we can renounce sins through confessions, repentance, penitence, contrition, absolution, or through Jesus' blood. However, confession only confirms the existence of sin! Confession is the open admission of sin. If one wants to renounce sin, he should simply abandon sinful thoughts. We should be aware that "No one can forgive a sin that he believes is real" (26). Jesus said: "What is opposite to God, does not exist" (27). "Sin is strictly an individual perception" (28). It is a perishable thought, consequently not true. For the Apostle John, "whosoever is born of God sinneth not." (1John 5: 18)

A statement made by the writers of the scriptures, which has created a lot of confusion, is Jesus' description as the "Lamb of God who takes away the sins of the world." (John 1: 29) Jesus never made such a claim and neither claimed that one can pay for others' sins or take them away. He simply denied sin's existence: "Whosoever is born of God doth not commit sin." (John 3: 9) "Sin" is a personal choice that can be aborted any time. If not, death is the disappearance of the negativity called sin, ("wages of sin is death"; Romans 6:23) and of its creators. Because our bodies (brains included) are not our real selves, they die under the weight of sins while the spiritual selves (minds included) remain untouched. After his killing on the cross Jesus proved the meaninglessness of his body when he presented himself to his apostles, physically restored. Sin is a personal decision. We, as well as Jesus, are God's perfect creations and consequently sinless. We, unlike Jesus, are temporarily confused. What makes Jesus special is the fact that he keeps his mind clear: free of illusions and confusions.

God cannot be considered merciful if He demands a sacrifice for our sins. God is the creator of life; not a killer. We, on the other hand, do kill because we believe we should do something, even a "justified" killing, in order to save our honor. This way of thinking is at the origin of the idea of sacrificing for sin's forgiveness. We may believe we are as clean as daisies if the killing is done "for the Lord" or, for a "higher cause". We ignore that God does not require killing for any reason nor hurt of any kind.

A surrogate sacrifice (of another, on one's behalf) is a loss for both. Both are deprived of their life's experience and, not one of them has the opportunity to learn from it. Salvation is a personal affair. One either does what it requires, or stays where he is. "For I have given you an example, that ye should do as I have done to you." (John 13:15) Those who believe to be "saved" or "sealed" due to their opinion that they had their sins "washed" by Jesus' blood, do not know what they are saying. Respectful or not, idleness cannot save anybody.

In his letters to the Galatians where he mentions Jesus, the Apostle Paul speaks of God sending His Son, "born of a woman", but neither here nor elsewhere does he suggest anything unusual about Jesus' conception or birth. He uses the words "born of a woman" rather than born of a virgin. Jesus calls himself "Son of Man" and not Son of God. The gospels of Mark, John, Thomas and even the hypothetical gospel of Q, make no reference to Jesus' birth story. "Even in Matthew and Luke, the idea of virgin birth never reappears after the initial chapters." It should be noticed that at the time, claims of pregnancy of young women by a god was so frequent that in Greece a decree was issued subjecting to a very severe penalty any woman who would pretend that her child was of divine parentage. The claim of divine conception around the time of Jesus' birth was applied to almost every eminent man. The following are some examples. Romulus, the founder of Rome, had been assumed to be the son of Mars and the virgin Rhea Sylvia.

Plato was considered to be the son of Apollo and Perictione. Plato's father, Ariston, is claimed to be the descendant from the god Poseidon. Assyrian Queen Semiramis, according to Diodorus Siculus (based on previous texts), is "the fruit of pairing between the Syrian goddess Derceto and a young Syrian man." Achilles, the hero of the Trojan War, was claimed to be the son of the goddess Thetis. King Minos, the assumed creator of the Minoan civilization in the Bronze Age, was claimed to be the son of Zeus and the Phoenician princess Europa. Alexander the Great decreed he was the son of Jupiter Ammon and Olympia. Claims of "Immaculate Conception" had been made by people in Egypt, Babylon, Arabia, Persia, Hindustan and other places. Roman emperors used to be called "the divine". How those respected personalities had been born is of lesser importance than their contribution to human development.

Jesus is not the most important man in history due to his kind of conception but due to his revolutionary awareness of truth and that he decided to share it with men. His teaching had been endorsed by his personal demonstration. Regardless of our human parentage, God is "My father and your father," Jesus said (John 20: 17). He also calls us his "brothers" (Matthew 12: 50 and Hebrew2:17). God created us long before our birth and, as perfect as He is perfect. We, the people, are His children who lost their way. What made Jesus special is that he stood solid with his original, intended Self. Empowered by the power of his love, he took upon himself to teach us how to get back to who we are, "for both he that sanctifieth and they who are sanctified are all of one." (Hebrew 2: 11) No one can come to the Father alone, but in unity with those he sees as holy as himself. "Thou shalt love thy neighbor as thyself" (Mark 12: 31) means that you cannot love yourself if you don't love your brothers and you cannot love your brothers, who are your equals, if you don't love yourself. We are equally loved by Our Father. Your life is yours to handle in total freedom. In few words:

> One cannot be spiritually saved by killing another.
> Sacrifice one for helping another denies the growth for both. Both are denied the benefit of their life's experiences (learning).
> Salvation is based on a personal transformation through awareness, not by proxy killing. Transfer of qualities is impossible.

You are created equal to your brothers and, perfectly equipped for the life God offered you.

Imperfections stem from physical temptations.

Forgiveness is a prerequisite for salvation. Forgiveness, properly understood, is the healing of the perception of separation and inequality between brothers. The Bible's inaccuracies raise a lot of questions. Nevertheless, most people prefer to sail clean over the mistakes made by scribes for the good of the main message. Most of the Bible inconsistencies are usually not even noticed because they are buried in the text, pages apart and apparently not strikingly important. Even unimportant, those inconsistencies and inaccuracies strike the important question of how can anybody claim that scripture is the word of God and not of man? The Bible writers are the first detractors from truth and the first promoters of atheism.

To exemplify, I include here quotations from a 150 year old book of William Henry Burr (2), printed in 1859, more than thirty years before the Scopes trial. Burr was a newspaper reporter who took upon himself to do what no religious scholar would. He made a concise list of more than 150 contradictions he found in the Bible, enough to fill a whole book. Let's check some of them, as numbered by Mr. Burr:

"2. GOD DWELLS IN CHOSEN TEMPLES.
'And the Lord appeared to Solomon by night, and said unto him: I have heard thy prayer, and have chosen this place to myself for a house of sacrifice. . . . For now, have I chosen and sanctified this house, that my name may be there forever; and mine eyes and my heart shall be there perpetually.' (2 Chron. 7: 12, 16)

GOD DWELLS NOT IN TEMPLES.
'Howbeit the Most High dwelleth not in temples made by hands.' (Acts 7: 48)

4. GOD IS SEEN AND HEARD.
'And the Lord spoke to Moses face to face, as a man speaketh to his friend.' (Ex. 33: 11)
'And the Lord called unto Adam, and said unto him, Where art thou? And he said, I heard thy voice in the garden, and I was afraid.' (Gen. 3: 9, 10)

'For I have seen God face to face, and my life is preserved.' (Gen. 32: 30)

'In the year that king Uzziah died, I saw, also, the Lord sitting upon a throne, high and lifted up.' (Is. 6: 1)

'Then went up Moses and Aaron, Nadab and Abihu, and seventy of the elders of Israel. And they saw God of Israel... They saw God, and did eat and drink.' (Ex. 24: 9-11)

GOD IS INVISIBLE AND CANNOT BE HEARD.

'No man hath seen God at any time.' (John 1:18)

'And he said, Thou canst not see my face; for there shall no man see me, and live.' (Ex. 33:20)

'Whom no man hath seen nor can see.' (1 Tim. 6: 16)

GOD IS JUST AND IMPARTIAL.

'Lord is upright, ... and there is no unrighteousness in Him.' (Ps. 92: 15)

'Shall not Judge of all the earth do right?' (Gen. 18: 25)

'A God of truth, and without iniquity, just and right is He.' (Deut. 32: 4)

'Ye say the way of the Lord is not equal. Hear now, O house of Israel; is not my way equal?' (Ezek. 18: 25)

GOD IS UNJUST AND PARTIAL.

'Cursed be Canaan; a servant of servants shall he be unto his brethren.' (Gen. 9: 25)

'For I, the Lord thy God, am a jealous God, visiting the iniquity of the fathers upon the children unto the third and fourth generation.' (Ex. 20: 5)

'For the children being not yet born, neither having done any good or evil, that the purpose of God, according to election, might stand, ... it was said unto her, The elder serve the younger. As it is written, Jacob I loved, and Esau have I hated.' (Rom. 9: 11-13)

13. GOD IS TO BE FOUND BY THOSE WHO SEEK HIM.

'Everyone that asketh receiveth, and he that seeketh findeth.' (Matt. 7: 8)

'Those that seek me early shall find me.' (Prov. 8: 17)

GOD IS NOT TO BE FOUND BY THOSE WHO SEEK HIM.

'Then shall they call upon me but I will not answer; they shall seek me early but not find me.' (Prov. 1: 28)

17. GOD COMMANDS, APPROVES OF AND DELIGHTS IN BURNT OFFERINGS, SACRIFICES, AND HOLY DAYS

'Thou shalt offer every day a bullock for a sin offering for atonement.' (Ex. 29: 36)

'On the tenth day of this seventh month, there shall be a day of atonement; it shall be a holy convocation unto you, and ye shall afflict your souls and offer an offering made by fire unto the Lord.' (Lev. 23: 27)

'And thou shalt burn the whole ram upon the altar; . . . it is a sweet savor; an offering made by fire, unto the Lord.' (Ex. 29: 18)

'And the priest shall burn it all on the altar to be a burnt sacrifice, an offering made by fire, of a sweet savor unto the Lord.' (Lev. 1: 9)

GOD DISAPPROVES OF, AND HAS NO PLEASURE IN BURNT OFFERINGS, SACRIFICES, AND HOLY DAYS.

'For I spoke not unto your fathers, nor commanded them in the day that I brought them out of the land of Egypt, concerning burnt offerings or sacrifices,' (Jer. 7: 22)

'Your burnt offerings are not acceptable, nor your sacrifices sweet unto me.' (Jer. 6: 20)

'Will I eat of flesh of bulls, or drink the blood of goats? Offer unto God thanksgiving, and pay thy vows unto the Most high.' (Ps. 50: 13, 14)

18. GOD ACCEPTS HUMAN SACRIFICES.

'The king [David] took the two sons of Rizpah, . . . and the five sons of Michal; . . . and delivered them into the hands of Gideonites, and they hanged them in the hill before the Lord. . . And after that God was entreated for the land.' (2 Sam. 21: 8, 9, 14)

'And he [God] said, Take now thy son, thine only son Isaac, whom thou lovest, and get thee into the land of Moriah, and offer him there for a burnt offering.' (Gen 22:2)

'And Jepththah vowed a vow unto the Lord, and said, If thou shalt without fail deliver the children of Ammon into my hands, then it shall be, that whosoever cometh forth of the door of my house to meet me when I return in peace from the children of Ammon, shall surely be the Lord's, and I will offer it up for a burnt offering. So Jephthah came to Mizpeh unto his house and behold, his daughter came out to meet him... And he sent her away for two months; and she went with her companions and bewailed her virginity upon mountains. And it came to pass at the end of two months that she returned to her father, who did according to his vow which he made.' (Jug. 11: 30-34, 38, 39.)

GOD FORBIDS HUMAN SACRIFICES.

'They heed to thyself that thou be not snared by following them [the Gentile nations]; . . . for every abomination to the Lord which he hated have they done unto their gods; for even their sons and their daughters have they burnt in the fire to their gods.' (Deut. 12: 30, 31.)

20. GOD CANNOT LIE.

'It is impossible for God to lie.' (Heb. 6: 18)

GOD LIES BY PROXY; HE SENDS FORTH LYING SPIRITS TO DECEIVE.

'For this cause, God shall send them strong delusion, that they should believe a lie.' (2 Thes. 2: 11)

'Now, therefore, behold, the Lord hath put a lying spirit in the mouth of all these thy prophets, and the Lord hath spoken evil concerning thee.' (1 Kings 22: 23)

'And if the prophet be deceived when he hath spoken a thing, I the lord have deceived that prophet.' (Ezek. 14: 9)

27. KILLING COMMANDED.

'Thus saith the Lord God of Israel, Put every man his sword by his side, and go in and out from gate to gate throughout the camp, and slay every man, his brother, and every man his companion, and every man his neighbor.' (Ex. 32: 27)

KILLING FORBIDDEN.

'Thou shalt not kill.' (Ex. 20: 13)

32. ANGER APPROVED.
'Be ye angry and sin not.' (Eph. 4: 26)

ANGER DISAPPROVED.
'Be not hasty in thy spirit to be angry; for anger resteth in the bosom of fools.' (Eccl. 7: 9)
'Make no friendship with an angry man. (Prov. 22: 24)

44. BAPTISM COMMANDED.
'Go therefore and teach all nations, baptizing them in the name of the Father, and of the Son, and of the Holy Ghost.' (Mat. 28: 19)

BAPTISM NOT A COMMAND.
'For Christ sent me not to baptize, but to preach the gospel. . . . I thank God that I baptized none of you but Crispus and Gaius.' (1 Cor. 1: 17, 14)

52. HATRED TO KINDRED ENJOYED.
'If any man come unto me, and hate not his father, and mother, and children, and brother, and sisters, yea, and his own life also, he cannot be my disciple.' (Luke 14: 26)

HATRED TO KINDRED CONDEMNED.
'Honor thy father and mother.' (Eph. 6: 2)
'Husbands love your wives... For no man ever yet hated his own flesh.' (Eph. 5: 25, 29)
'Whosoever hateth his brother is a murderer.' (1 John 3: 15)

58. MAN WAS CREATED AFTR THE OTHER ANIMALS.
'And God made the beast of the earth after his kind, and the cattle after their kind . . . . And God said, Let us make man. . . . So God created man in his own image.' (Gen. 1: 25-27)

MAN WAS CREATED BEFORE THE OTHER ANIMALS.
'And the Lord God said It is not good that man should be alone: I will make a help-mate for him. And out of the ground the Lord God formed

every beast of the field, and every fowl of the air, and brought them unto Adam to see what he would call them.' (Gen. 2: 18, 19)

65. THE FATHER OF JOSEPH, MARY'S HUSBAND, WAS JACOB.
'And Jacob begot Joseph, the husband of Mary, of whom was born Jesus.' (Mat. 1: 16)

THE FATHER OF MARY'S HUSBAND WAS HELI
'And Jesus being the son of Joseph, which was the son of Heli.' (Luke 3: 23)

69. THE INFANT CHRIST WAS TAKEN INTO EGYPT.
'When he arose he took the young child and his mother by night and departed into Egypt, and was there until the death of Herod... But when Herod was dead, ... he took the young child and his mother and came... and dwelt in a city called Nazareth.' (Mat. 2: 13,14, 15, 19, 21, 23.)

THE INFANT CHRIST WAS NOT TAKEN INTO EGYPT.
'And when the days of her purification, according to the law of Moses, were accomplished, they brought him to Jerusalem, to present him to the Lord... And when they had performed all things, according to the law of the Lord they returned... to their own city, Nazareth.' (Luke 2: 21, 22, 39)

70. CHRIST WAS TEMPTED IN THE WILDERNESS.
'And immediately [after Christ's baptism by John the Baptist the spirit driveth him into the wilderness. And he was there in the wilderness forty days tempted of Satan.' (Mark1: 12, 13)

CHRIST WAS NOT TEMPTED IN THE WILDERNESS.
'And the third day [after Christ's baptism] there was a marriage in Cana of Galilee... Both Jesus was called and his disciples to the marriage.' (John 2: 1, 2)

6. CHRIST WAS CRUCIFIED AT THE THIRD HOUR.
'And it was the third hour and they crucified him.' (Mark 15: 25)

CHRIST WAS NOT CRUCIFIED UNTIL THE SIXTH HOUR.
'And it was the preparation of the Passover, and about the sixth hour;
and he saith unto the Jews, Behold your king… Shall I crucify your
king?' (John 19: 14, 15)

86. CHRIST WAS TO BE THREE DAYS AND THREE NIGHTS
IN THE GRAVE.
'So shall the son of man be three days and three nights in the heart of
the earth.' (Matt. 12: 40)

CHRIST WAS BUT TWO DAYS AND TWO NIGHTS IN THE
GRAVE.
'And it was the third hour, and they crucified him… It was the
preparation, that is, the day before the Sabbath… And Pilate… gave
the body to Joseph. And he… laid him in a sepulcher… Now, when
Jesus was risen early the first day of the week, he appeared first to Mary
Magdalene.' (Mark 15: 25, 42, 44-46; & 16: 9)

88. THE DISCIPLES WERE COMMANDED IMMEDIATELY
AFTER THE RESURRECTION TO GO INTO GALILEE.
'Then said Jesus unto them, Be not afraid; go tell my brethren that they
go into Galilee, and there shall they see me.' (Matt. 28: 10)

THE DISCIPLES WERE COMMANDED IMMEDIATELY
AFTER THE RESURRECTIOIN TO TARRY AT JERUSALEM.
'But tarry ye in Jerusalem until ye be endued with power from on high.'
(Luke 24: 49)

90. CHRIST ASCENDED FROM MOUNT OLIVET.
'And when he had spoken these things, while they beheld, he was taken
up, and a cloud received him out of their sight…x Then returned they
unto Jerusalem, from the mount called Olivet.' (Acts 1: 9, 12)

CHRIST ASCENDED FROM BETHANY.

'And he led them out as far as to Bethany; and he lifted up his hands and blessed them, he was parted from them, and carried up into heaven.' (Luke 24: 50, 51)

94. KETURAH WAS ABRAHAM'S WIFE.
'Then again Abraham took a wife, and her name was Keturah.' (Gen. 25: 1)

KETURAH WAS ABRAHAM'S CONCUBINE.
'The sons of Keturah, Abraham's concubine.' (1 Chron. 1: 32)

97. GOD PROMISED THE LAND OF CANAAN TO ABRAHAM AND HIS SEED FOREVER.
'And the Lord said unto Abraham, after Lot was separated from him, Lift up now thine eyes and look from the place where thou art, northward and southward, and eastward and westward; for all the land which thou seest, to thee will I give it and to thy seed forever... For I will give it unto thee... Unto thee and to thy seed after thee.' (Gen. 13: 14-17 & 17: 8)

ABRAHAM AND HIS SEED NEVER RECEIVED THE PROMISED LAND.
'And he gave him [Abraham] none inheritance in it, no, not so much as to set his foot on.' (Acts 7: 5)
'By faith he sojourned in the land of promise as in a strange country, dwelling in tents with Isaac and Jacob, the heirs with him of the same promise... These all died in faith, not having received the promises.' (Heb. 11: 9, 13)

100. MICHAL HAD NO CHILD.
'Therefore Michal, the daughter of Saul, had no child unto the day of her death.' (2 Sam. 6:23)

MICHAL HAD FIVE CHILDREN.
'The five sons of Michal, the daughter of Saul.' (2 Sam. 21: 8)

103. DAVID SINNED IN NUMBERING THE PEOPLE.
'And David's heart smote him after that he had numbered the people. And David said unto Lord, I have sinned greatly in that I have done.' (2 Sam. 24: 10)

DAVID NEVER SINNED EXCEPT IN THE MATTER OF URIAH.
'David did that which was right in the eyes of the Lord, and turned not aside from anything that he commanded him all the days of his life, save only in the matter of Uriah the Hittite.' (1 Kings 15: 5)

104. ONE OF THE PENALTIES FOR DAVID'S SIN WAS SEVEN YEARS OF FAMINE.
'So God came to David and said unto him, Shall seven years of famine come unto thee in thy land?' (2 Sam. 24: 13)

IT WAS NOT SEVEN YEARS, BUT THREE YEARS OF FAMINE.
'So God came to David and said unto him, Thus saith the Lord, choose thee either three years of famine,' (1 Chron. 21: 11, 12)

107. DAVID'S THRONE WAS TO ENDURE FOREVER.
Once have I sworn by my holiness that I will not lie unto David. His seed shall endure forever and his throne as the sun before me. It shall be established forever. (Ps. 89: 35,36,37.)

DAVID'S THRONE WAS CAST DOWN.
Thou hast made his glory to cease and Hast cast his throne down to the ground. (Ps. 89: 44)

115. IT WAS LAWFUL FOR THE JEWS TO PUT CHRIST TO DEATH.
'The Jews answered him, We have a law, and by our law he ought to die.' (John 19: 7)

IT WAS NOT LAWFUL FOR THE JEWS TO PUT HIM TO DEATH.
'The Jews therefore said unto him, It is not lawful for us to put any man to death.' (John 18: 31)

116. CHILDREN ARE PUNISHED FOR THE SINS OF THEIR PARENTS.
'I am a jealous God, visiting the iniquities of the fathers upon the children.' (Exodus. 20: 5)

CHILDREN ARE NOT PUNISHED FOR THE SINS OF THEIR PARENTS.
'The son shall not bear the iniquities of the father.' (Ezek. 18: 20)

117. MAN IS JUSTIFIED BY FAITH ALONE.
'By the deeds of the law there shall no flesh be justified.' (Rom. 3: 20)
'Knowing that a man is not justified by the works of the law, but by faith of Jesus Christ.' (Gal. 2: 16)
'The just shall live by faith. And the law is not of faith.' (Gal. 3: 11, 12)
'For if Abraham were justified by works he hath whereof to glory; but not before God.' (Rom. 4: 2)

MAN IS NOT JUSTIFIED BY FAITH ALONE.
'Was not Abraham our father justified by works? . . . Ye see then how that by works a man is justified, and not by faith only.' (James 2: 21, 24)
'The doers of the law shall be justified.' (Rom. 2: 13)

119. NO MAN IS WITHOUT SIN.
'For there is no man that sinneth not. (1 Kings 8: 46)
'Who can say, I have made my heart clean; I am pure from my sin?' (Prov. 20: 9)
'For there is not a just man upon earth, that doeth good and sinneth not.' (Eccl. 7: 20)
'There is none righteous, no, not one.' (Rom. 3:10)

CHRISTIANS ARE SINLESS.
'Whosoever is born of God doth not commit sin; . . . he cannot sin,
because he is born of God. . . . Whosoever abideth in him sinneth not.
He that committeth sin is of the devil.' (1 John 3: 9, 6, 8)

120. THERE IS TO BE A RESURRECTION OF THE DEAD.
'The trumpet shall sound and the dead shall be raised.' (1 Cor. 15: 52)
'And I saw the dead, small and great, stand before God; . . . and they
were judged, every man according to their works.'　　(Rev. 20: 12, 13)
'Now that the dead are raised even Moses showed at the bush, when
he called the Lord the God of Abraham, and the God of Isaac, and the
God of Jacob.' (Luke 20: 37)
'For if the dead rise not, then is not Christ raised.' (1 Cor. 15: 16)

THERE IS TO BE NO RESURRECTION OF THE DEAD.
'As the cloud is consumed and vanisheth away, so he that goeth down to
the grave shall come up no more.' (Job 7:9)
'The dead know not anything, neither have they any more a reward.'
(Eccl. 9: 5)
'They are dead, they shall not live; they are deceased they shall not rise.'
(Is. 26: 14)

123. THE EARTH IS TO BE DESTROYED.
'The earth also and the works that are therein shall be burned up.' (2 Pet.
3: 10)
'They shall perish, but thou remainest.' (Heb. 1: 11)
'And I saw a great white throne, and him that sat on it, from whose face
the earth and the heaven fled away, and there was no place found for
them.' (Rev. 20: 11)

THE EARTH IS NEVER TO BE DESTROYED.
'Who laid the foundations of the earth that it should not be removed
forever.' (Ps. 104: 5)
'But the earth abideth forever.' (Eccl. 1: 4)

128. THE FRUIT OF GOD'S SPIRIT IS LOVE AND GENTLENESS.

'The fruit of the spirit is love, peace, joy, gentleness, and goodness.' (Gal. 5: 22)

THE FRUIT OF GOD'S SPIRIT IS VENGANCE AND FURY.

'And the spirit of the Lord came upon him and he slew a thousand men.' (Judg. 15: 14)

'And it came to pass on the morrow that the evil spirit from God came upon Saul . . . and there was a javelin in Saul's hand. And Saul cast the javelin; for he said, I will smite David even to the wall with it.' (1 Sam. 18: 10, 11)

130. POVERTY IS A BLESSING.

'Blessed be ye poor. . . .Woe unto you that are rich!' (Luke 6: 20, 24)

'Hath not God chosen the poor of this world, rich in faith, and heirs of the kingdom?' (James 2: 5)

RICHES ARE A BLESSING.

'The rich man's wealth is his strong tower, but the destruction of the poor is their poverty.' (Prov. 10: 15)

'If thou return unto the Almighty then thou shall be built up. . . .Thou shalt then lay up gold as dust.' (Job 22: 23, 24)

'And the Lord blessed the latter end of Job more than the beginning, for he had 14,000 sheep, and 6,000 camels, and a thousand yoke of oxen, and a thousand she asses.' (Job 42: 12), in the house of mirth.' (Ecl. 7: 3, 4)

142. MOSES WAS A VERY MEEK MAN.

'Now, the man Moses, was very meek, above all the men that were upon the face of the earth.' (Num. 12: 3)

MOSES WAS A VERY CRUEL MAN.

'And Moses said unto them, Have ye saved all the women alive? . . . Now, therefore, kill every male among the little ones, and kill every woman that hath known a man.' (Numbers. 31: 15, 17)".

One more inconsistent Bible story from William Henry Burr's book (numbers 81, 82, and 83): the four gospels claim different numbers of women coming to the sepulcher where Jesus was buried. John (20: 1) tells of ONE woman, Mary Magdalene. "The first day of the week cometh Mary Magdalene early, when it was yet dark, unto the sepulcher, and seethe the stone taken away." In Matthew (28: 1) we read of TWO women, "Mary Magdalene and the other Mary." In Mark's story, (16: 1) THREE women came. "And when the Sabbath was past Mary Magdalene, Mary, the mother of James, and Salome had brought sweet spices." In Luke's account (24:10) there were MANY women who came: "It was Mary Magdalene, Joanna, and Mary, the mother of James, and other women that were with them."

Those Bible contradictions are cherry-picked from "Self-contradictions of the Bible" by William Henry Burr, an amateur in the field of biblical scholarship. His book had a modest effect at its time (1859) and went out of print in 1890. Nevertheless, it was a common-sense approach to religions aberrations. It seems that religion was propelled by people having no religious training and no thinking outside of conventional mental boxes, like Moses, Jesus, Martin Luther. Moses was not an ordained priest and neither was Jesus and they are the most important mind changers of all time. Ordained priests, ministers and titled authorities in the realm of religion, instead, seem dedicated to the instructions received at their training. They are groomed to uphold the dogma of their training; they did so and continue doing so. The purpose of the Christian Church is to spread Jesus' teachings "to all nations and baptize them in the name of the Father, and the Son, and of the Holy Ghost." (Mathew 28: 19 & 20,). Martin Luther was the first ordained priest I know of that introduced some common sense into religion's assumptions.

Mr. Burr's book is far from exhausting these issues. During one of the church services I attended, I was surprised by one quotation: "We love Him, because He first loved us." (1John 4: 19) But, isn't love unconditional? We love because we are love, not because we are loved. Love is not a trading back and forth.

After reading the Bible, I felt confused about who are the proverbial twelve tribes of Israel. So I went back to the Bible trying to get a clearer account of them. Since the twelve tribes are named after the eleven sons and one daughter of Jacob - later renamed Israel - I made a list of Jacob's eleven sons and one daughter born from four women as described in Genesis, chapters 29 and 30: Reuben, Simeon, Levi, Judah, Dan, Naph'tali, Gad, Asher, Is'sachar, Zeb'ulun, Dinah, Joseph. Another count is made when the aged Israel gathered his sons for blessings (Gen. 49). This time there are twelve sons. Dinah is omitted and Benjamin is added. The tribes of Israel are listed again in Numbers 1: 1-16: "And the Lord spoke unto Moses in the wilderness of Sinai, . . . saying, "Take ye of all the congregation of the children of Israel, after their families, by the house of their fathers". On this count, there are also twelve tribes, but with a change. Levi, Dinah and Joseph are replaced with Ephraim, Manasseh and Benjamin. In Numbers 1: 26, Moses took "the sum of the people," for another count. This time there are thirteen tribes due to the addition of Pallu. Then, in First Chronicles 2:1 where their number is reestablished to twelve by eliminating Ephraim and Manasseh and listing instead their father, Joseph, adding Levi again and eliminating Pallu.

A good opportunity to check the consistency of the Bible is the comparison of parallel stories. How do the four gospels relate to the same events? How do they record the last words of Jesus on the cross, for example? All four use quotation marks, which is an indication of accuracy. Mathew (27: 46, 50) said, "And about the ninth hour Jesus cried with a loud voice, saying, 'Eli, Eli, lama sabachthani?' which is to say, 'My God, My God, why hast thou forsaken me?'. . . . Jesus, then he had cried again with a loud voice, yielded up his spirit." Mark (15: 34) gives a similar account. Luke said (23: 46): "Then Jesus, crying with a loud voice, said, 'Father, into thy hands I commit my spirit!' And having said this he breathed his last." John's account is different (19: 30), "When Jesus had received the vinegar, he said, 'It is finished'; and he bowed his head and gave up his spirit." From other sources, on the cross Jesus didn't say a word and didn't make a sound during the whole process.

The experts agree that Luke's and John's are the oldest of the gospel letters, when people's memories may falter. Everything Jesus said is important, including his last words, and the accuracy of the reporting is equally important. If the Bible is the word of God, then all four quotations should be the same.

Another parallel quotation of Jesus is given at the time of his arrest. The stories are told in Matthew (26: 50), Mark (14: 48, 49), Luke

(22: 52, 53) and John (18: 5-12). In some of these stories Judah identifies Jesus with a kiss; in others, Judah only guides the official guards to him. In the first three gospels Jesus was simply arrested. In John, the mob and the officers fell to the ground when Jesus identified himself. Then, they pick themselves up and arrested him. In Matthew, Mark and Luke the apostles were stunned during the arrest while in John, Simon Peter took out his sword "and smote the high priest's servant and cut off his right ear. The servant's name was Malchus." To take Peter off the hook, Jesus healed the wound. Meanwhile in Romans 8: 32, Paul simply said that Jesus had been "delivered up."

A flagrant inconsistency I found was between the two genealogies of Jesus given by Mathew (1: 1-16) and Luke (3: 23-38). In Matthew, between Jesus and David there are twenty-eight male descendants while Luke lists forty-two descendants, almost twice as many as Matthew lists. In Matthew, the genealogy goes from David through Solomon followed by Roboam while in Luke it goes from David to Nathan followed by Mafata. None of the descendants' names between David and Joseph match in the two genealogies. But here is another problem. Joseph was not Jesus' natural father. Jesus' mother wasn't impregnated by Joseph but by the Spirit of God. This makes Joseph a stepfather, not a blood relative. In Galatians 4: 4, Paul affirms that Jesus was "made under the law" which means, born as a human from two physical parents. In a letter sent by Clement, the fourth bishop of Rome, to the church of Corinth we read that Jesus came from Jacob "according to the flesh." In Romans 1: 3, 4, Peter says, Jesus was "made of the seed of David according to the flesh; and declared to be son of God" . . . "by the resurrection from the dead."

The writers certainly had a deep reverence for Jesus who was so much more advanced than they had been. The best of their abilities could only explain the differences between He, Jesus, and all others was only through His privileged creation: fathered by the Holy Spirit. It is thus implied that, according to the Bible writers, we can never become like Jesus because we don't have the same high parentage. For Jesus, as mentioned, we can match his performance. If Joseph is Jesus' natural father or his stepfather is of little consequence; Jesus' significance rests in his knowledge of truth. As for his birth, isn't every birth a miracle of God? Aren't we all sons of God? Isn't He "My father and your father"? (John 20: 17) In Proverbs

23:26, God calls us "my son"; also, "all of you are the children of the most High" (Psalms 82: 6). Jesus called us his brothers created by "one God and father of all."(Ephesians 4: 6) He is also quoted as calling us "my brother" in Matthew 10: 32 and 12: 50. After all, "There is but one God, the father, of whom all things are." (1 Cor. 8: 6) Our natural parents are mere custodians; caretakers of us during our formative years. Otherwise, we all belong to the one creation which is not complete until we all are back where we belong.

Of a more important significance are the stories that defeat reason. Some questions are raised by the story of the Magi. The Magi were apparently astrologers who had "read the stars" that informed them of the arrival of the Messiah. The New Testament prefers to call them either Wise Men or Kings. The term *"magoi"*, used in the Greek Bible, means magicians but this translation raised the hair on the back of the Bible writers. So they used instead the politically correct "Kings" or "Wise Men". If God created everything, then everything is good and there's nothing demeaning in calling them Magi, as they had been.

And the story goes, "Now when Jesus was born in Bethlehem of Judea in the days of King Herod, behold, there came Wise Men from the East of Jerusalem, saying, where is he that is born King of the Jews?" The magi came as a group from east of Jerusalem; but, from how far east? It is assumed it was quite a distance and possibly Asia; some experts assume it may be Mesopotamia. This claim is supported by their freely disclosed abilities as being magi, unusual in Canaan, by their lack of knowledge of the topography and local politics as well as by the uncommon gifts they brought for Jesus. If they came from far away, they could not arrive "when Jesus was born," due to the difficulties of traveling at that time. With poor roads, if any, the required time to prepare and organize the group of most probably bodyguards and servants all traveling on foot or camels, it could have taken them a full year to reach Jesus. At that time Jesus was not any longer in the manger and no longer a newly born. This belief is supported by King Herod's decision to kill all children in Bethlehem "from two years old and under, according to the time which he had diligently enquired from the Wise Men." (Matt. 2:16) Then, there's that star "which they saw in the East, that went before them till it came and stood over where the young child was." (Matthew 2: 1-9) That "star" as described, seemed to be a spot of light.

The Flood is another story blown out of proportion. The Bible had been written about 800 B.C.E. It is estimated that the flood took place before 1000 B.C.E in a cataclysmic event described in Plato's **"Critias"** and other writings. "The ancient Greeks recalled not one but four major cataclysms" (Frank Joseph, Survivors of Atlantis) between the years 3100 and 1198 B.C.E. that culminated with the disaster of Atlantis and the worldwide Great Flood. After each such cataclysm, many Atlanteans left their damaged island and established colonies on both shores of the Atlantic. Better recorded are those in Egypt, Mesopotamia, Asia Minor, the Americas and other places. This was the time when the megalithic constructions had been built in those areas. Atlanteans' creativity and efficiency made them successful in all those places. They are mentioned in older texts as promotors of the bronze era and as effective sea fearers or "Sea People". "Around 3000 B.C.E. an ambitious mining enterprise opened with great suddenness along Lake Superior's shores of the Michigan Peninsula and on the Isle Royale in Lake Superior. Here is evidence that over the next twenty-two centuries the mining of a billion pounds of the world 's highest grade copper was excavated from five thousand pit mines;" most of it sold in Europe. (Atlantis in Wisconsin, 1995 by Frank Joseph) Atlanteans are connected to the sudden appearance of advanced civilizations in the bronze age.

The Bronze Age had a "sudden end around 1200 B.C.E., [when] pre-classical civilization everywhere collapsed or went into irreversible decline" (Frank Joseph "Survivors of Atlantis"). 1200 B.C.E. was also the year of the cataclysm that created the world-wide flood and the destruction of Atlantis. The Sumerians that were neither Semitic nor Indo-Europeans identified the survivor of the Flood as Utanashpitim. "The ziggurat at Sippar marked the location where Xiusthros, the Babylonian flood hero, buried a history of the world until his time. His Deluge account generally coincides with the sudden beginnings of both the Mesopotamian and Nile civilizations following the arrival in the eastern Mediterranean of culture bearers from seismically wrecked Atlantis." Due to the memorable importance of the Flood, the Sumerians categorized their ruling dynasties as ante-diluvium and post-diluvium. In addition to the Bible the Flood is also related in the four-thousand-year-old great Gilgamesh Epic where the god Enki betrayed the secret plan of his fellow gods, who were intending to punish the humans for their inequities, and informed the one good man from the village of Shuruppak, in the middle of the Euphrates, about the coming flood.

"The Phrygians, ...with roots in Armenia, knew the Deluge myth whose hero was Nannakos. In all Sumerian accounts of the Great Flood, the ark does not come to rest on an Armenian mountaintop but landed instead at the seashore." It is worth noticing that "in 1604, the Dutch merchant Peter Jansen built a faithful reconstruction of Noah's ark using the same ratios given in Genesis: 300 by 50 by 300 cubits, meaning a 120-by-20-by-120 foot craft that proved to be remarkably stable with its cargo full and able to weather heavy swells, implying that the ark belonged to a "sea people" with "oceangoing tradition."

It is assumed that that catastrophic Flood eliminated all corrupt people and that only the righteous Noah and his family remained to be preserved. But, "Noah began to be a husbandman and he planted a vineyard: and he drank of the wine, and was drunken; and he was uncovered within his tent. And Ham, Noah's son and the father of the people of Canaan saw the nakedness of his father." "And Noah awoke from his wine and he knew what his younger son had done unto him. And he said, Cursed be Canaan." (Genesis 9: 20-25) Well, it looks like the flood didn't eliminate the human inequities. Those inequities continued from within Noah's own family and spread from there. Did the flood stop the human moral problems? Josephus, based on ancient records, quoted the third-century B.C.E. historian Berossus who described the Noachic flood and its hero, called Xisuthrus. "Chaldean historian Abydenus (circa 200 B.C.) who claimed to have had access to primordial texts," stated that Noah is the Chaldean King Sisithrus. A Sumerian text, as mentioned, called him Ziusudra. Regardless, the journalist Charles Berlitz reported that "there are over 600 variations of this legend among ancient nations and tribes and the story had been told through the millennia in all quarters of the globe."

Since a considerable amount of time passed between the event and its description in the Bible, the story had plenty of time to be interpreted: the flood could not be world-wide and Noah could not take on board "every living thing that is, of all flesh, both of fowl, and creepeth upon the earth," (Genesis 8: 17) additional "clean beasts" for sacrifice (Genesis 8: 20) and food to hold them all for about 200 days. Cooking and burning sacrifices could be difficult on that wooden ark. Also, a huge effort would be needed by Noah and his three sons to clean the ship of droppings and leftovers from so many animals.

"The total destruction of the human race is of course not involved [and neither could be observed in faraway places or from sparsely populated areas], nor is the total destruction of the inhabitants of the delta (at least some of the antediluvian cities survived into historic times) but enough damage could be done to make a landmark in history and to define an epoch." "It was the open villages of the most barbarous Semitic-speaking folk that felt the full fury of the waters." (30) The Sumerian Noah is agreed to be Uta-Napishtim, from Shuruppak. The instruction to "multiply and replenish the earth was literally fulfilled by the Sumerians' occupation of the empty land" (31) left by the receding waters.

To do justice to the story, each human race from antiquity has its own flood account that affected its own people, its own Noah and his ark and a local mountain where he landed. All ancient cities were built along major rivers that occasionally could swell beyond their banks, with catastrophic consequences. In all, there are four hundred such myths that are known. Some contend that the non-Bible stories had been copied from the Old Testament account, "but the Hindu, Chaldean, Babylonian and Egyptian accounts antedate the Hebrew version by many centuries."

A significant bias of the Bible emphasizes the Jewish tribes as God's favored, chosen for special privileges due to the faith of their ancestor, Abraham, to the extent of allowing the extermination of Canaan's inhabitants to make room for themselves. "And in thy seed shall all the nations of the earth be blessed," (Genesis 22: 18) remained a wish, more like the communist claim of the ideal classless society lead by an enlightened elite, perpetually. The problem with this claim of specialness is that God doesn't have favorites; He created all humans equal: "there is neither Greek nor Jew, circumcision nor uncircumcision, Barbarian, Scythian, bound nor free: but Christ is all, and in all." (Colossians 3:11) "His equal love is given equally to all alike." (32) Nevertheless, "Thou shalt love thy neighbor as thyself." (Matthew 22: 39). Specialness separates people and prevents one from loving all humans equally. If some are "chosen" and others are not, if one is special and others are not then the unity of creation is broken. In this case, a scale of perceived worthiness is established and conflicts are guaranteed. Is it possible that God wants us to abuse and murder one another? No, of course. God and His creation are not physical; therefore, abuse is not possible. Specialness is a human creation and the byproduct of the physical way of living.

A radical difference is seen between historical narratives and the Old Testament unique and fantastic claims in Exodus. In the Old Testament the Israelites had never been abusive or unfair with their Egyptian hosts. Historically, the data are reversed; the Egyptian hosts had been abused until they could not take it any longer. According to the existing documents the Israelites aggressively installed their own Pharaoh in the most productive section of Egypt, the Nile Delta, and strategized to occupy the rest of Egypt. The Egyptian scholar, Manetho, talks about the Hyksos (ancestors of the Jewish nation) who temporarily ruled in Egypt, "more than a millennium prior" to his writing. The Hyksos settled gradually in the most prosperous part of the country, the Nile Delta, and when they reached a significant number they started to display an overbearing arrogance and occupied the northern part of the country (Nile Delta included). Manetho called those people "heqakhasut" "meaning 'beduin-like Shepherd Kings' rendered simply 'rulers of/from foreign lands', foreign rulers - a term that later evolved into the Greek, Hyksos."

"Thought to originate from an area in modern day Israel, the Hyksos arrived on the scene during Egypt's 13th dynasty. Egyptian rulers were able to hold them off until about 1650 B.C., when the Hyksos, growing more militarily powerful, captured the ancient royal city of Memphis." This event put an end to Egypt's Middle Kingdom in a way described by Manetho: 'Suddenly, from the regions of the East, invaders of an obscure race marched in confidence of victory against our land. They easily seized it without striking a blow; they burned our cities ruthlessly, raised to the ground the temples of gods, and treated all the natives with a cruel hostility.'" (288)

This particularly brutal rule that "treated all the natives with "cruel hostility", massacring some and leading into slavery the wives and children of others," (5) generated the revolt of the kings of the Thebaid and the rest of Egypt which resulted in the defeat of the Shepherds [Hyksos] and their expulsion from Egypt. Memphis, along with the Hyksos strong-hold of

Avaris, in the Nile delta, were recaptured by the ruling pharaoh, Ahmose I, around 1521 B.C., at the end of a campaign started by his mother and others before her. First, Ahmose seized the gold rich territory of Namibia to the south. Hyksos, that ruled the northern part of Egypt, had forged an alliance with Namibia hoping to squeeze and defeat the Egyptians in the middle. But Ahmose, after defeating his enemies from the south, turned to the Hyksos in the north and conquered them too. The story of Hyksos' cruelty is backed-up by their indiscriminate massacres during the occupation of Canaan, as described in Joshua 11: 14, ("And all the spoil of these cities, and the cattle, the children of Israel took for a prey unto themselves; but every man they smote with the edge of the sword, until they had destroyed them, neither left they any to breathe.") Also, in Joshua 10: 40 we read: "So Joshua smote all the country of the hills, and of the south, and of the vale, and of the springs, and all their kings: he left none remaining, but utterly destroyed all that breathed." It seems, according to the scenario described by Hecateus and by Manetho, if the Pharaoh truly sent his troops after Moses and his group, he did so to make sure they don't come back. As for the parting of the sea, it is glorious but doubtful. Was it necessary? A logical choice (for Hyksos who knew the country well) would be to go from the Nile Delta to the east and circle the Red Sea around its north end, rather than going south first and facing the more difficult task of crossing the Red Sea through the middle of it, where the Red Sea was about 100 miles wide. Crossing the Red Sea in that area raised important challenges: the Israelites didn't have boats and didn't know God's intention to part the sea for them. If the sea was miraculously parted, as claimed, was its bottom flat and dry for an easy advance? What matters in the end is that the Hyksos departed and were left by themselves for forty years with no other tribes or nations to use and abuse. Resultingly they became a nation. "Most of the scholars agree with the core of [Manetho's] stories", as mentioned in Peter Schafer's account.

Scholarly research of this subject is done by Scott Alan Roberts and John Richard Ward in their 2014 book *The Exodus Reality*. The book mentions on page 105: "The pharaoh who had elevated Joseph to power as his vizier is the same pharaoh who had also given this land [Goshen, in the eastern Nile Delta, the 'finest land in all of Egypt'] to Joseph's family. But, in fact, he was not an Egyptian pharaoh. More likely he was one of the

'Shepherd Kings,' the *heqakhaseshet* – the Semitic race of Hyksos, people from Syria and Canaan who had migrated and infiltrated Egypt." Hyksos rule had been harsh .... "for all shepherds are detestable to the Egyptians" who had allowed them to come to their fertile country in times of need. The overthrow of the Hyksos king, or pharaoh, through a popular revolt helped by a neighboring Egyptian leader, made them loose the privileged position they once had and brought them into servitude under Ahmose I with the purpose of paying for their previous damages done to the country. After a while, Moses came into play.

It is recorded that Hyksos had been driven out of Egypt by force due to their cruelty and abuses they subjected their Egyptian hosts to. "The legend can be traced back to the early third century B.C.E. and reached its literary climax in the 'grand syntheses of anti-Jewish tradition written by Tacitus."The earliest account of the Exodus in pagan literature is to be found in Hecateus of Abdera's lost *Aegyptica*, which has come down to us as an excerpt from Diodorus Siculus' *Bibliotheca Historica. Aegyptica* had been written during the reign of Ptolemy I, around the year 300 B.C.E. and, it starts as follows:

"When in ancient times a pestilence arose in Egypt, the common people ascribed their troubles to the workings of a divine agency; for indeed with many strangers of all sorts dwelling in their midst and practicing different rites of religion and sacrifice, their own traditional observances in honor of the gods had fallen into disuse. Hence the natives of the land surmised that unless they removed the foreigners, their troubles would never be resolved".... "But the greater were driven into what is now called Judea, which is not far distant from Egypt and it was at that time utterly uninhabited. The colony was headed by a man called Moses, outstanding both for his wisdom and for his courage."

The Ten Plagues described in the book of Exodus (Old Testament) are unlikely since there is no direct nor indirect evidence of them. As for crossing the Red Sea, "the Hebrews did not cross at the wide expanse of it, but rather a place referred to as the *yam suph*, most probably identified with the Lake Timsah region, a few miles north of the Red Sea" (33). That route of retreating eastwards, north of the Red Sea, makes sense since it was next to the center of Hyksos power, the Nile delta. The Red Sea is "a mistranslation in Septuagint."The accurate translation is the Reed Sea or the Sea of Reeds. It was possible that the Sea of Reeds could be crossed on foot. Sometimes "in the spring and summer, strong winds can dry portions of the shallow lake and one could cross on the dried-out bottom of the lake." (33) In order to emphasize the greatness of the crossing, the writers of the Old Testament described the physical impossibility "that 1.2 million fleeing slaves, loaded with animals and possessions plus 300,600 Egyptians soldiers with 600 chariots and 50,000 horses entered the Sea of Reeds in one single night." (Exodus 14)

Legends always have a core of truth wrapped in colorful layers of tribal pride. The Bible mentions that Jewish servants "borrowed from the Egyptians jewels of silver and jewels of gold ... And they spoiled the Egyptians." (Genesis 12:35) Here "borrowed" is a figure of speech since the Hebrews had never returned and pay the Egyptians back. It seems those "borrowed" jewels and precious metals (the Israelites came into Egypt while impoverished) were later used by Israel's descendants to cast the Golden Calf while waiting forty days and forty nights in the desert for Moses to return from the mountain.

The story is more involved. What matters in the end is that God is fair to us all. He is addressing us in a personal, way. He doesn't exalt his appreciation to close-by friends or relatives. "God is All in all in a very literal sense." (34) Jesus never displayed specialness either. Specialness is a form of inequality and segregation which is incompatible with God's desire for unity and love. If God favors some over others, he is not fair and, we are not equal. If not equal, we cannot all be loved by God or by anyone else in the same way and we cannot love our neighbor as we love ourselves so: we cannot reach Heaven. This is a possible explanation why some who consider themselves special foresee their eternal life as a reincarnation in a perfected physical environment where they can continue to have a privileged position. The idea of specialness, which is physically palatable, is also at the origin of conflicts, wars, occupations, sectarianism, division, classification, competition, exploitation, hate, inequality... where the hardness of life begins. Like any mistaken thought, specialness is a major contributor to the human hell.

Heaven is a state of perfect love, wisdom and fairness that we can return to but we can't do so automatically, by simply crossing the threshold of physicality. We do so when we return to the perfection of our creation. "

The Kingdom of God is within you," (1 Corinthians 3:16). "Within you" doesn't mean within your body. "The Holy Spirit's temple is not a body but a relationship. The body is an isolated speck of darkness; a hidden secret room, a tiny spot of senseless mystery, a meaningless enclosure carefully protected, yet hiding nothing. Here, human egos would drag their bodies, holding them in its idolatry. Here it is 'safe' for here love cannot enter." (35) The Kingdom of God is not a place but a condition. We believe we cannot achieve that perfect condition because it cannot fit into our physical understanding of life. We see our aberrations as "inherited tendencies", as "the sin that dwelleth in me", "the law of sin in my members (body)." (Romans 7:17 & 23) We cannot break free from what we, on earth, consider normal and true. Our sights and feelings remind us constantly that physicality is real. Heaven is a quality of the mind that we either activate or not. This process of correcting our thinking is the REAL Atonement. The quality that makes us eligible for Heaven requires a conscious effort to reevaluate our opinions, "free yourself from the past," update our thinking and rediscover love. Our interpretations of Jesus' words still prevents us to follow Him 2.000 years after his departure. So if you want to join heaven, adopt Jesus' ways and doings as true. Not true are what our senses identify all around us, all the time, and we candidly accept as our world .

Also in many places of the Old Testament, people are made aware: "The fear of the Lord is the beginning of knowledge." (Proverbs 1:7, 1: 29, 8:13, 9:10, 31: 30; Psalm 19: 9, etc.) God doesn't frighten anyone so forget about fear; just take it seriously. If the writer of the text means "respect", why does he consistently call it "fear"? Isn't it a reminder of the fearsome punishment for non-believers the Bible's writers consistently mention? Jesus said that God doesn't threaten people. Reading through the Bible, I noticed: "because I have called, and ye refused, [to answer]"... "I also will laugh at your calamity;" (Proverbs 1: 24 and 26). In other words, you do it to me, I'll do it to you. Is this valid?

As you may notice, while I pointed out many of the Bible writers' questionable personal opinions I believe that the writers tried to do a good job. Sometimes they overdid it, sometimes they didn't understand their subject, may have boasted with pride and specialness, played politics ... but many times they said the right thing. We all want certainty but for the time being, certainty, which is truth, belongs to God and not to man. Men settled for perceptions. In regards to my seemingly unfair judgements, I quote only what I have reasons to believe reflects the truth. Statements from respectable sources show clarity, common sense and provide a deep sense of peace. What is from God does not include threats, contradictions, exaggerations, or partiality. What is from God thrives on universal love.

2.

THE BIBLICAL SCHOLARS

Once Jesus had gone, people had been left on their own to make sense of their recent holy experience. From the start, Jesus had the challenge of convincing us of his spiritual nature. Is it possible to be a physical person and have spiritual abilities at the same time? To our knowledge, the two groups, the spiritual and the physical, are not interconnected. The spiritual group is non-physical and the physical group is physical and not spiritual. Then, Jesus arrived on the scene. He came to us as a man, trained as a carpenter and performed spiritual demonstrations. As he grew, his spiritual demonstrations diversified: walked on water, made food appear, healed deformities and he raised people from the death while having a regular human existence. How did he do it? The only way he could was through using his pure mind. God created the whole universe in his mind. This is hard to accept but, the mind is all that God had to work with. Why did Jesus even bother to come? He came to teach us to do the same thing he did: use our abstract, clean minds in a non-compromising way to provide what already spiritually exists. I assume that people, having spiritual abilities, have also access to fulfilling their needs. I don't know how it happens, but it makes sense. Inner consciousness could set the whole universe on a coordinated action. All I know is that Jesus manifested everything he needed. Even more interesting, Jesus said that we likewise can do as he did. We can and should build this ability within ourselves! Let us build pure intentions, no rivalries, no selfishness and no petty opinions. Can our physical bodies attain this perfection that can eventually build a perfect world? Let's take an example seen in our businesses which cannot employ all the unemployed people of society. Can our businesses pay all employees well enough to satisfy equally each one's needs? Not likely. We should create our own perfect world based on truth, wisdom, honesty.... . Give all love and respect and let them be. I don't believe I've said anything new up to this point. Perfection is our duty to know. The two different perspectives, spiritual and physical, are the outcome of two different value systems that contradict each other and cannot be simultaneously accepted. When Jesus did his miracles on earth he was a spiritual leader, not a carpenter. This is all that I can say and hope to still seem valid.

The spiritual content of the scriptures is searched by the Church authorities who then take for granted the validity of the scripture writers' words. However, Jesus' apostles were confused. They trusted Jesus but they could not go beyond their physical experiences. While Bible historians analyze the scriptural writers' narratives, certain church authorities develop motivational speeches that do not bring the message far enough. Truth is eternal but the way we try to blend it with our physical life, we tarnish it. All that matters in this world is the truth. We instead sugarcoat the truth of our activities with good words and, call them "truth".

One of my acquaintances who had learned more details about the works of the Council of Nicaea (325 A.D.) told me with a broad smile: "I became a born again Christian. Now I am an agnostic." I replied: "Well, if the Council of Nicaea accepted many political compromises, it doesn't mean that Jesus does not exist or that he is not right. There are reasonable and believable arguments in his favor. You should research them if you want to develop a more balanced decision."

My acquaintance flushed a winning smile and responded, "Well, I'll wait for your book then."

Once we endow an opinion with all the attributes of truth we then worship it as truth. This leaves unanswered the question: what is the truth? Briefly, "truth" is perfection.

Interestingly, the four universally recognized gospels are not written by Matthew, Mark, Luke and John. The four apostles had been technically illiterate and dead at the time when their Gospels had been written, decades later. For the sake of consistency, when the Bible was put together the church experts accepted limited changes in those books considered authentic. Yet, at the same time these experts also included in the Bible books of suspicious authenticity which offered the advantage of fitting the unified message the church wanted to convey. As already shown, different writers have different perspectives. This is probably why for a very long time the Bible, that was hand written in Latin, had its reading reserved for priests who, in turn, would present it to their parishioners as being the church's monolithic interpretation.

In the search for consistency, in addition to excluding valid books, some writings of questionable origin had been incorporated into the New Testament. They were written in the name of the apostles by someone else. The gospels themselves "were written decades after Jesus' crucifixion by unknown authors who had inherited their accounts about him from the highly malleable oral tradition". Nevertheless, those gospels have value due to their spiritual content. What happened during Jesus' life among us is endorsed by many informed and honest people and proved valid by their letters' core message of love. The fact that they had been assigned to one person or another is less important than the message they convey. Those working to put together the New Testament relied on stories told by those who knew people who knew people who knew an eyewitness too impressed to lie and endorsed by too many to dismiss. Their memories may not be perfect, but they had been honest. After all, Christianity answered our need to believe in love, and love is truth.

"During its [first] two and a half centuries, Christianity comprised a number of competing theologies, better said, a number of competing Christian groups advocating a variety of theologies. There was as yet no established 'Orthodoxy,' that is, a basic theological system acknowledged by the majority of church leaders and laity." (Bart D. Ehrman "The Orthodox Corruption of Scripture", page 4) At no point in its history has religion constituted a monolith. The diverse manifestations of Christianity in the first three hundred years - whether in terms of social structures, religious practices, or ideologies - have never been replicated." (Ibid, page 3) The council of Nicaea (today the city of Iznik in western Turkey) was summoned by the Roman Emperor Constantine with the specific purpose of creating a common ground and unifying religion across the empire. He couldn't allow his empire to be ripped apart by petty opinionated squabbles. He used his political skills, backed by the counterbalance of the more level-headed western bishops, against the contentious North African bishops in order to create an aura of unprecedented universality. In the end, the council created a compromise that everyone could agree with. The council symbolically set Jesus' unknown birthday to be celebrated at the beginning of the new year. I believe the Council made a good choice to celebrate the Christian spiritual renewal, at the time when the whole nature is coming back to life after a cold winter.

Before the Council of Nicaea, in A.D. 325, Eusebius introduced the term "Orthodox [meaning 'right opinion'] Christianity" referring to the kind of belief preached by the apostles and their followers from the beginning, as opposed to the deviations that came afterwards. This approach remained the backbone of the Christian Church as of today. Another important achievement of the Nicaean Council was the adoption of the Nicene Creed as a unifying Christian belief across the Roman Empire, in those turbulent times. That unity has been a success but, also, a stop-motion. It cast Christianity into the frame of mind dominating around the year 300 A.D. It was a major spiritual achievement but prevented further introspection and therefore advancement of our knowledge. Once Jesus had gone, he couldn't provide further direct instructions. From that moment on, we had been left with our memories and their interpretations. Opinions multiplied since. Those opinions had been mostly accommodations of spirituality to our physical thinking and, the beginning of The Christian Church as we know it. Jesus didn't give us more than we could assimilate at the time: "I have many things to say unto you, but you cannot bear them now." (John 16: 12) Then, Jesus' time to further teach us was cut short by his crucifixion. "It takes great effort and great willingness to learn" high concepts. Many are convinced that they already know what they need to know so, they don't have to make "the great effort". And, our understanding stopped at the crucifixion of our divine teacher. The vertical growth he offered had been replaced by a horizontal spread across the field of opinions.

"Early Christianity embodied a number of divergent forms, no one of them representing the clear and powerful majority of believers against all others. Only when one social group had exerted itself sufficiently over the rest of Christendom, did a 'majority' opinion emerge; only then did the 'right belief' represent the view of the Christian church at large." As it happened, this kind of Christianity was found in the Church of Rome, who had a superior administrative power and vast material resources. They also had been better organized.

Regardless, the competition for recognition among different Christian parties hovered around the original faith for quite some time.

A Christian church with broad attendance in the Eastern Roman Empire was the Coptic Church, that claimed to be established by Saint Mark in A.D. 42, in Alexandria, Egypt. The Coptic Church takes its pride from being mentioned in Isaiah 19: 12 and from the narration that Joseph (Jesus' stepfather) had been advised by an angel to stay in Egypt until King Herod of Israel would be dead, thus unable to hunt for the young Jesus, (Matthew 2: 12, 13). The Coptic Church is taking its name from the Egyptian Coptic language spoken at the time in that area (Nile delta). The Coptic Church was a distinct Christian body that during the Council of Chalcedon in A.D. 451 stated its claim, accepted as of today, that Christ is perfect in His divinity and perfect in His humanity as well. During those times, the nature of Christ was fiercely debated among Christian churches. From being the dominant Christian Church throughout the Middle East, the Coptic Christians subsided today to 18 to 22 million members world-wide, most of them in Egypt, due to the Muslim expansion. It has its own Pope and it had the oldest Catechetical school in the world where students were taught by renowned scholars as Athenagoras, Clement, Didymus, Origen (considered the father of theology). The school taught, besides religion, basic sciences. It also used for blind students and scholars an earlier form of Brail; 15 centuries before the Brail of today. After the Muslim invasion (639 A.D.), the Coptic Church had been faced with strong opposition and started to diminish to the numbers they have today. One of the main reasons had been the tax placed on non-Muslim Christians by Umayyad rulers and the competition from the influential Catholic Church. Nevertheless, smaller churches upheld their own understanding of Christianity for as long as they could, making the field varied and combative. We should mention that the Gnostics, besides being an early Christian church, were also a loosely organized religious and philosophical movement. Gnosticism struck a chord among those prone to think: our problem is not sin but the ignorance that creates confusion and sinful thoughts.

A major controversy that shook the church was the nature of God: is He one entity or three parts closely related: God the Father, Jesus Christ and the Holy Spirit? Today the Church agrees (under the pressure from the combative north African Christians) that the Godhead is a Trinity and being as such from the very beginning. But then, if Jesus had been created by the Father, he couldn't have been with Him from the "very beginning" and neither equal to Him. Jesus said, "He who believes in me, the works that I do shall he do also; and greater works than these shall he do; because I go unto my Father." (John 14: 12) Does this mean that Jesus could not do "greater works" at that time? If he couldn't, indicates that he was not equal to God and neither God incarnated. On this subject, it is significant to quote Jesus: when he was called Good Master "He said unto him, Why callest me good? There is none good but one, that is, God." (Matthew 19:17) It is obvious again, that Jesus didn't consider himself equal to God or God Incarnated. As for the Holy Spirit, isn't it the thought of God, "the highest communication medium," ever created? The Holy Spirit is God's messenger and consequently, not equal to its Creator. Jesus and us, we are His sons meaning, not Him. We are His created partners meant to amplify love across the universe by exchanging it among ourselves and between us and Our Father.

It is of no surprise that in the middle of such competition for being right, the original texts, copied by hand, had been adjusted to become a source of significant points that could uphold one church over the others. In the New Testament today there are twenty-seven books. In addition, "from the early Christian period, we have a world of 'apostolic' gospels, acts, epistles, and apocalypses by the dozens, most of them pseudonymous, nearly all of them late from the second century and beyond." This practice was strongly condemned at the time, even within documents that are themselves forged.

In an extensive research, Bart D. Ehrman, professor of Religious Studies at the University of North Carolina and a leading authority on the Bible, found "over a hundred writings from the first four centuries that were claimed by one Christian author or another, to have been forged by fellow Christians." Even more disheartening is that several forgeries already had become included in the Bible. Such are the Second Letter to the Thessalonians, the Book of Revelation, the letters of Jude and 2 Peter. Also 1 and 2 Timothy and the book of Hebrews are "particularly debated".

"One of the striking occurrences is the orthodox Apostolic Constitutions, a book of ecclesiastical instructions, ostensibly written in the name of Jesus' apostles, which warns its readers to avoid books falsely written in the name of Jesus' apostles." (The Orthodox Corruption of Scripture, page 14) "The Apostolic Constitutions is in fact an orthodox production, as is the 3 Corinthians, forged by an Asia Minor presbyter" who, upon his dismissal, claimed "he did it out of love for Paul." 2 Thessalonians, which cautions against letters falsely penned in Paul's name, "many New Testament scholars believe is itself non-Pauline." The jury is still out on the Epistles of Colossians and Ephesians. Also, the authorship of 1 Peter remains an open question. We have also a long list of forged documents that serve theological ends and had never been included in the New Testament.

More important than the forgeries themselves are the questions: what damage did those forgeries do and how did this affect the average believer? The answer is, probably not much. Most of those alterations and forgeries had been done with sincere intentions, some even inspired by the Holy Spirit, and consequently harmless. Nevertheless, the exposure of forgeries did affect the upper-end Christians.

When the New Testament was compiled, around the year 350 A.D., the clergy in charge took all necessary steps to come up with a unified text. On one hand, the selection of books to be included in the New Testament had been made with the purpose of upholding the view of the most influential church over the others and, on the other hand, of pursuing consistency as much as possible. Different letters projected the understandings of the different writers and those differences had to be minimized for the sake of unity. The victor of those doctrinal infightings was, as mentioned, the Church of Rome. Consequently, the absolute ruler of Christianity became the Catholic Church.

With this absolute control, pretty much like under any totalitarian leadership, comes the danger of abuse. With no checks and balances it is easy to lose touch with reality and fall into self-righteousness. One important such "fall" was Pope Urban II's decision to launch the Crusades. The First Crusade tried to stop the Turks who had been advancing in Asia Minor toward Constantinople. This 1095 decision was taken following the plea for help made by the Byzantine emperor Alexius. By the early eighth century the Christians had lost North Africa, Palestine, Syria and most of Spain, Sicily, parts of Andalusia to the Muslims. The Byzantine emperors ruling from Constantinople, which was what remained of the Eastern Roman Empire, went on the offensive in the second half of the tenth century trying to save their diminishing country. The violent attack of the European crusaders, took the Muslim world completely by surprise after having been relaxed after so many victorious wars. They were in a state of political disunity which obstructed the speed and efficiency of their preparation for war. Crusaders' victories inspired the pope and the Christian world to recover Christian properties taken over by Muslims and, restore the independence of Christian people in the areas where Christianity had been born. The Crusades embraced the idea to repel the Muslims' advances, and this seemed logical at the time. People believed that Jesus Christ himself authorized the Crusades. They even organized a children's crusade, that fortunately didn't take place, with the belief that children's innocence would give them divine protection. The Pope overlooked the spiritual "thou shall not kill" and got engaged in killing the nonbelievers. The fight for Jerusalem was a total disrespect for "The kingdom of God is within you" (Luke, 17:21) not outside of you. The fact that, "The Most High dwelleth not in Temples made with hands," (Acts 7:48) didn't raise much concern, and the quest for the "Holy City" of Jerusalem became a constant preoccupation for 700 years from March, 1095 (the First Crusade) to June, 1798 (the fall of Malta). In the process, many Temples that were not "made by hands" had been destroyed.

The Pope found an ally in the warrior class, who had started to lose their glamour of fighting in Europe where education had begun to raise the standards of civilized behavior. The developing economic climate in Europe made some of those warriors with resounding pedigree to need better incomes and they looked eastward for opportunities. The Pope, on the other hand, wanted to bring the "Holy Place" under Christian administration. He became the promoter and financier of this military operation. The Crusades had been a complex and poorly organized movement. Regardless, the crusades cost a lot of money and the church had a hard time to come up with the needed funds. One source of funds was the sale of indulgences and other non-spiritual financial exactions.

As the Church's effort to increase its revenue tilted the balance of fairness one way, the "enlightenment" became more proficient in tilting it the other way. Martin Luther, who was a deeply religious man, felt hurt by what his church was doing and debated his objections by posting them on the door of the church at Wittenberg; a custom bulletin board for the local University. From the Fall of 1508, Luther himself taught theology at the newly founded University of Wittenberg where he also received two bachelor degrees and earned his doctorate in 1512. His simple phrases were posted there on October 31, 1517, known today as the "Ninety-Five Thesis," and stirred the whole Catholic Church. Thus, the Age of Reformation began: Indulgencies could not be spiritually justified, priests had been allowed to marry, science became free of the church's intervention, the Bible had been printed in the spoken language (versus Latin) and made available to those interested. It was a timely coincidence that Johannes Gutenberg invented the printing press in 1439! From then on, the Bibles could be easily copied and made available. The Catholic Church control on teaching the Bible was weakened and, along with it, had been weakened its unified interpretation of the scriptures. Protestant churches started to appear. Each church upheld its doctrine and claimed significance. This attitude created separation among God's one creation united by one love and one knowledge of one truth presented in one book, the Bible.

But then, how can we claim that the Bible is the valid word of God when, as a matter of fact, we don't have any longer His original words? What we finished having are only error-ridden hand-written copies. We cannot interpret the words of the scriptures while we don't know to whom those words belong, God or men? In the third century, Origen, looking through different copies of the Gospels, complained: "The differences among the manuscripts have become great, either through the negligence of some copyists or through the perverse audacity of others; they either neglect to check over what they have transcribed, or, in the process of checking, they make additions or deletions as they please." (36) Different copies of the same letters that survived to our time are different from one to another. An example is the story of the woman caught in the act of adultery and brought to Jesus to be stoned in accordance with the Law of Moses (John 7: 53 to 8: 12). The story doesn't mention the man she was caught with. Both of them were supposed to be stoned by the Law. More important, this "story is not found in our oldest and best manuscripts of the Gospel of John." "What does survive [today] are copies made over the course of centuries, or more accurately, copies of the copies of the copies, some 5,366 of them in the Greek language alone." (37) "Strikingly…, no two of these copies are exactly alike in all their particulars. By far the vast majority [of differences] are purely 'accidental,' readily explained as resulting from scribal ineptitude, carelessness, or fatigue." But, some textual changes are deliberate.

How else can an additional twelve verses at the end of the Gospel of Mark be explained? In the last twelve verses of Mark "that are absent from our two oldest and best manuscripts of Mark's gospel, the writing style varies from what we find elsewhere in Mark." (38) "In many English translations [the last twelve verses of Mark], are marked as inauthentic, and in later Greek manuscripts are indicated as not an original."

One more occurrence: scholars doubt the value of the entire Book of Revelation of Saint John. Even earlier critics said that it was "unintelligible, irrational, and the title false . . . [that] it is not John's, and not a revelation at all." (39) Elaine Pagels, Professor of Religion at Princeton University, adds: "Noting the many differences between the two writings, [gospel of apostle John, son of Zebedee and the brother of James, and John the author of the Revelation]. Dionysius concludes that the author of the Book of Revelation must be a different John. He [Dionysius] points out differences that literary critics have noted ever since; for example, that John of Patmos [the probable writer of the Book of Revelation] often mentions his own name but never claims to be an apostle; that the tone of his writing, the style, and the language he uses is 'not really Greek' but uses, 'barbarous idioms,' that are distinctly different from those of the fourth gospel." (40)

Still, can the Book of Revelation be the book of the end, and a good conclusion for the Bible that starts with "in the beginning"? True or not, this Book seems to make a good closure. For Elaine Pagels, "What John did in the Book of Revelation, among other things, was to create anti-Roman propaganda that drew its imagery from Israel's prophetic traditions, above all, the writings of Isaiah, Jeremiah, Ezekiel, and Daniel." "John was invoking prophetic images to interpret the conflicts of his own time, just as the prophets Isaiah and Jeremiah had interpreted the Babylonian War around six hundred years earlier." The Roman occupation was a big issue for the Jews and talking about it could take place only in figurative ways that wouldn't raise Roman awareness, but be clear to the Jews.

The writers of the New Testament left for us a lot of information, both accurate and perceived accurate. To abbreviate, we may say that while the Old Testament is marred by tribal specialness, internecine squabbles and self-righteous postures, the New Testament is limited by its writers' inability to fully comprehend Jesus' message. Both Testaments tried to explain our relationship with God and both lack the ability to reach their too distant target. If so many things are inaccurately presented in the scriptures, then what are the right ones?

Once Jesus had gone, no human mind could comprehend the full meaning of what he said and did. In the end, we finished with interpretations that make sense to us and detract from Jesus'. To rise above confusion means to atone, to harmonize with the mind of our Creator. Our minds come from His, after all. Atonement, being a state of mind that cannot be offered to us, means that it cannot include torture either. If we do not do anything to upgrade our thinking, we cannot atone. What others are doing, is the others' experience and their conclusions. The divinity teachers looked into the holy books written by fellow humans and never asked themselves if those fellow humans are not too human to understand divinity. They still morn Solomon's temple in Jerusalem, rather than search the alive temples where the living God abides. Atonement is a personal act of reconciliation. It is done through understanding and believing, not by passing its news around. It cannot be given to us, not even by Jesus. Enlightened people can only inspire us to think and be. The divinity scholars assumed the scriptures are true: Jesus atoned for us. He made for us remarkable demonstrations but, as a matter of fact, he didn't atone for us. He only showed to us that extraordinary things are possible. Once accepted, these demonstrations became our understanding of "truth" which can motivate us to follow his example. Divine miracles are very convenient but we cannot be saved from this physical life for as long as we don't harmonize our thoughts with the Spirit of God. We need to have divine purity in order to join the divine Kingdom. That purity cannot be given. Jesus' sacrifice is misunderstood and therefore ineffective as presented. His sacrifice does not purify us. We are called to purify ourselves. Due to the fact that we continue to sin, we are not sinless and neither able to get into the holy world. We have the potential but we don't have the quality yet. Well, we are not even willing to attempt to understand holiness for as long as we believe that He will do it for us. As we customarily project our sins to another, we can also assume that we can project our guilt to another too and be considered innocent. But, the projection of any thought is an opinion and not a fact; it is a thought. Jesus is fully aware of our mental activity and our mental activity cannot be upgraded from outside of ourselves. The religious experts, nevertheless, claim that He paid for our sins! Well, in this atonement process, don't we have a part to play? The Scriptures don't say anything about the sinner's role in his own atonement. The sinners are the ones who need to atone! Atonement cannot be bought or given. "No force except your own will be strong enough or worthy enough to guide you. In this you are as free as God, and must remain so forever." (41) Atonement is your return to a sane mind, by your own will. If one doesn't return, he wastes a lot of time. Aware of this fact, Jesus tries to guide us today as he did in the past. "I am with you always, even to the end of the world." (Matthew 28: 20) As in the past, he doesn't attempt to do for us what we have to do for ourselves. He is only guiding, advising and demonstrating. We need to desire to walk the walk and the only way to prove this desire is by walking. Nobody else can do it for us. One's desire to raise his/her awareness is personal. Only he/she is in charge with his/her self. The desire to succeed cannot be borrowed and success cannot be given. It has to be individually achieved. No one can improve his quality without his direct, personal participation. Heaven cannot be handed to you as you are now. We voluntarily chose to live a lower quality life and to adopt a lower mentality which neither one can match the quality we yearn for. We are here because we chose to be here. If you want to reach Heaven, you have to choose to be there and mean it. We have to free ourselves from the trap of our own thinking boxes. Heaven is a quality we are born with, but since we didn't use it for a long time, we forgot it. Fully aware that we have the ability to set our minds on the highest goal and achieve it, God allows us to freely do it. One can see the truth if he wants to. "God has given you everything." (42) We have both the potential and the needed help. Do not expect Him to infringe upon our given freedom and do for us that we should do ourselves. We cannot delegate this kind of work. Unfortunately, people want physical miracles handed to them and not to learn how to perform miracles themselves. We seem to be too self-righteous to re-evaluate our thoughts and too comfortable with our judgments, to change them. We are hesitant to go for a future we don't know any longer. People want ready-made knowledge, computer style, and divine miracles given to them upon request, so that they do not have to personally pursue perfection. People want money, not jobs. People want what the truth brings, not the truth itself. We want to be declared right about our own beliefs so we don't have to advance to where being right is.

3.

THE PEOPLE

G od, Jesus, biblical scholars, priests, all try to help us discern meaning
from appearance, knowledge from opinions, truth from illusions.
Nevertheless, at every step humans interpret reality according to what
they can or want to accept. Our ancestors chose physical life probably
because it is more obvious, has a more tangible feel and has a practical
use. This is why we had and still have so many problems. We did what we
thought we needed to do and, what we want to have. Of course, one can
believe whatever he wants to and he wants what he has found desirable.
In this physical world we consider it true everything we see and touch.
Nevertheless, it seems that the lucky ones are those who accept that reality
exists well beyond what they see and touch. There is a whole new world
out there. Not to mention, the real world is the one meant by its Creator
and, the only perfect one.

I remember a short story from the Refugee Camp where I had
stayed for a while after I left Communist Romania. It was there I met a
small and hearty group of Romanian Pentecostals who had been allowed
to emigrate because this cohesive group could not be infiltrated by the
government. They didn't have a leader who could be bought; a communist
common way to infiltrate any organization. Those Pentecostals attended
a small Romanian church next to the refugee camp. That congregation
gave me my first Bible in Romanian; the only fluent language I knew. No
western language was of any use for common people in our communist
realm. Since Pentecostals from that church had been friendly, I tried to
encourage an older man, a former anti-communist guerilla fighter, to
attend that church also. It could be an interesting way to spend an hour
every week, with no strings attached, instead of waiting in frustration for
a country to accept your application for emigration.

"Oh no" he said. I don't deny they may be ok but I feel more comfortable with our traditional Orthodoxy. All those visions and prophesies are too much for me. You know, I once had one of their kind of spiritual experiences. I was walking between crops on a small country road. I avoided bigger roads at the time, an old fear of exposure. As I was walking, I saw two peasants talking while sitting on the grass by the side of the road. At the same time, I saw two other men walking while involved in a conversation. When they passed by the siting peasants, one of these men casually and softly raised his right hand, like in a blessing, without interrupting their walk. The sitting ones acquired suddenly a white aura each. These peasants stopped talking; stunned. One, confused, softly ran his hand over his head and sheepishly looked at the other. This is the only miracle I ever saw. But still, this cannot motivate me to get more involved with these Pentecostals."

"I don't want to make you a Pentecostal. I am not a Pentecostal myself. Going there is only an interesting way of spending time. I don't know much about Pentecostals," I murmured. We believe only what we want to believe. Those auras where not physical phenomena; it seems they were intended as a blessing. The two walking men kept on going and talking, undisturbed.

We chose, long ago, a different kind of life than the one God had prepared for us. The problem is that while God's world is spiritual, Adam and Eve preferred to live a physical life. "God did not create bodies," Jesus said. (43) Adam and Eve can only be the ones who wanted their lives to be physical rather than spiritual. Nevertheless, the scripture writers expressed their opinion only in writing that the first human was created from the dust of the ground: "God formed man of the dust of the ground, and breathed into his nostrils the breath of life, and man became a living soul." (Genesis 2: 27) Well, how did the writers know? They, themselves, were not created yet. Any-way, Genesis 1: 27 gives a spiritual narration of our creation: "Let us (…god) make man in our image, after our likeness." This sounds much more authentic.

Physically, every choice comes with its own built-in consequences. The spiritual world doesn't even mention consequences; loss never happens. As Jesus demonstrated, spiritually everything is spontaneously provided. Therefore, for us humans the main spiritual concern is to protect the quality of our divine minds which is the creator of all we need. In the physical world, we depend on having physical items, using other people for help, evaluating them, comparing, justifying our individual demands and so forth. The physical way of creation requires a different way of thinking than God's. In spirituality we are instead exchanging love, mutual support and interesting ideas. On earth we are concerned with winning competitions. Spiritually we enjoy fair exchanges. Physically we enjoy material results, the satisfaction of our desires and taking advantage of others. The main advantage of physicality over spirituality is that it provides us with the feeling of achievement and of justifying the specialness that God doesn't offer. God created us all equally gifted and equally able to provide for ourselves. Holiness cannot include specialness because this would negatively affect our connections and our equal love. If God would create unequal sons, He would contradict His own perfection and His own definition of love: "love your neighbor as you love yourself". Since God created us from Himself, having sons of different qualities would mean that He may have multiple personalities which is impossible! God created a perfect world, as we can see in every aspect of his creation. Shouldn't we prefer to belong to his spiritual world?

But, what about the physical life we have chosen for ourselves since Adam? Well, he being the first in line, it is possible that Adam made a wrong decision! He wanted to be special but he didn't know what specialness implies. He probably thought that specialness means total independence; in full control of his life. All right but, this choice brought him into a mess. After a length of time on earth, it became too late for Adam to change course and we subsequently followed. He got accustomed to having his kind of personal control and obviously, Adam didn't want to go back. What for? To learn a new normal? He and we discovered that life is complicated and hard to control: this is the consequence realm. Our growth had been hindered from day one. Ignorance is bliss!

What makes us appear different is our different interests that bring us to different outcomes. Anyway, our different interests do not mean different qualities. Quality wise, we are built the same. Spiritually, no one is interested in leading others; everyone wants to be aware, loving and fair. If I remember correctly, this is how Romania was before the arrival of communism. We should notice that tight leadership is a specific consequence of the physical world. Leadership is a position of utmost physical authority; leading to domination, control, covered-over "independent" local potential and, therefore, counterproductive (see communist leaders): a powerful destruction of the unique and finest human abilities. Spiritually, leadership is an unknown. Spiritually, the only authority is God; the one who created all that is. Spiritual authority is perfection: freedom, fairness, independence, love, creative abilities, free access to everything we need. I felt His righteousness so deeply that I treated all my dental patients equally well. I saw perfection in every one of them no matter how confused he/she became at the time. I respected their given perfection and I felt their respect in return. One patient told me that his wife is an actual dog that he sleeps with. Well, what could I say? Regardless of who is the one he was sleeping with, he still received the quality dental work equally given to all my patients. I felt I was trusted well enough for him to openly tell me his privacy and I respected him for that.

"Mistake", as previously mentioned, is the physical face of a misjudgment. No misjudgment means no mistake; and, no mistake means no sin. Mistakes should not be fought with restrictive laws, but willingly dismissed.

We are concerned about sins but we don't agree about what sin is. Is it a physical act or is it the thought that created it? If sin is evil then that evil has a name; some call it Satan. So, is Satan an entity lurking around looking for opportunities to intrude or is Satan a thought available to anyone who is too selfish to be spiritual?

Wisdom is paramount for success. The way we understand wisdom here, on earth, does not come even close to the wisdom shared in the kingdom of Heaven. Wisdom is not just simply being technically smart. It is also being holy; avoiding doing any harm to anybody. Let's take an example: our "wisdom" tells us that it doesn't make sense to turn the other cheek after the first one had been already stricken. Meanwhile, Jesus advices us to do exactly that: do not get angry and do not retaliate. This is precisely what He did when judged and crucified. Why did He give us this advice to respond to an aggression with love and forgiveness? He gave this advice because this thought of hitting back is proof that the attacker is a sinner and, as such, deserves to be rebuked. But, this means to perpetuate the sin while it is supposed to be denied. If we deny the sin we uphold the holiness of both the attacker and the one who had been attacked. If we deny the sin we obviously don't have to strike back.

Why do we prefer to believe in sin's existence? Probably because sin is the fall-out from physicality; our choice of living. Physically we depend on others. Spiritually we grow in others' positive company. Nevertheless, we feel more comfortable with our simple physicality. It is what we have experienced for so long that it seems normal. This is how our life is: a mild inconvenience justified by inequalities. If unequal, one may feel privileged and may prefer to see his afterlife as being preferred forever. We call this version of eternity redemption (returned as physically privileged) and we consider ourselves able to enjoy forever our inequality and dominance over others as God supposedly promised to Abraham: "I will establish my covenant between me and thee and thy seed after thee in their generations for an everlasting covenant, to be a God unto thee, and to thy seed after thee." (Genesis 17: 7) "And I will give unto thee and to thy seed after thee the land where you are a stranger, all the land of Canaan for an everlasting possession; and I will be their God." (Gen. 17: 8) Why? Because they are redeemed by God. Spiritually we are resurrected, returned to our original wholeness as spiritual entities. Again, redemption is preferred by those who see themselves privileged. As mentioned in the Bible, "they that are in the flesh cannot please God." (Romans 8:8) Therefore they have to be resurrected to a higher quality in order to be resurrected as bodies. Physical thinking cannot fit spiritual quality and neither can it fit Heaven.

In the end, we physically die because we are not meant to be physical. All imperfections die along with our selfish thoughts. At one time, we decided to put our egos in charge of our minds because we thought that our ego would defend our favorable self-image, attribute our mistakes to others and never complain about our errors; ego is "the part of our psyche that serves as the organized mediator between the person and reality." (Merriam-Webster Dictionary) Another definition is: "the part of the mind that believes your existence is defined by separation" (337) from other people and from our environment. To harmonize the two definitions, ego is the belief that we are separated and independent; that our physical nature is real and consequently true. Ego guides us through this thicket of independent bodies, each running subjective, independent thoughts unaware that we are meant to be part of the unit called the Divine

Kingdom. Ego believes that we live together because we need the benefit of each other's abilities. Spiritually meanwhile, we live together because of our joy of communicating love.

The spiritual and the physical understandings are two different ways of thinking that bring us to two very different outcomes. We are physically living a dichotomy and the proof of its illusion. One way provides access to infinite; the other is bound to physical limits. Nevertheless, physicality offers the bonus of living whatever we like to imagine and, we imagine what we are able to know. Ego is perceived as victory over God for awarding to ourselves the desired specialness. To God, we are all perfectly built and equally gifted; none is special.

Since God is love and communication, ego, which is distorted love and self-promoted speech, cannot be created by God. What else but our judgment can be the creator of our private ego that is meant to serve our private interests in disregard of others? We stubbornly believe in ego because it makes us feel special, soothes our failures, projects our guilt to others and promotes self-righteousness. All ego does is to make us feel protected, special, "justifiably" angry with those to whom we assign our own guilt. "You never hate your brother for his sins, but only for your own. Learn this, and learn it well." Jesus said. (44) If ego helps us be content with where we are, why change? For ego, Heaven is just a dream; a soothing illusion; a claim of specialness. Luckily, we are created in Heaven, by His standards. Heaven is part of our spiritual reality. Meanwhile, since we set our physical opinions we feel that we should rather stay put, on our firm ground, and, allow God to save us whenever He decides.

Ego is a private way of thinking which provides favorable opinions of self and the perception of specialness. This comfortable set-up of ours, generates our resistance to Jesus' teaching. Throughout our existence we are guided by our firm reliance on ego. We cannot easily detach from our cozy set-up we've created. We are what we chose to be! We even devised a Church which endorses our opinions and gives them a divine credence. It can be rightfully called the Church of Ego. We explain why we cannot replicate what Jesus did because we believe that God created us inferior to Him. He has a higher parentage! The Bible is not specific about our inferiority but it is specific about having earth;y parents, while He doesn't. At one point it even states that we are formed "of the dust of the ground."

Consequently, God is the one responsible for our lower performance so, we expect Him to come and save us from it.

Meanwhile, Jesus made it clear that we are built the same as he; having the strength that can enable us to rise to his level and even higher. But we find it prudent to believe that we should wait for God to carry us. It is safer and more comfortable; even if it is a dereliction of duty on our part.

Opinions generally endorse the comfort of not growing. If we want to have the physical condition recognized, we must rely on our opinions and consider them valid. Knowing less gives us less to think about so why should we get stressed out to understand what we do not? Because our way of thinking is ours, we trust it. From this trust comes our resistance to change and the hope that God will do it for us. Since people cannot easily accept their ignorance, they cannot accept truth either. Truth is vastly different from what people can admit. We prefer the plasticity of opinions that finds explanations for everything we want. God, instead, uses the truth as the foundation for life and the justification for eternity. His realities are slowly and constantly pushed aside by our thoughts to make room for what we are more willing to accept instead: our opinions and often our desires. If we are right, then we may perceive the Divine as more human-like and consider our religion as we have set it, as valid truth.

When make-believe religious practices got a hopeless hold on people, Jesus came to break this mold and set things straight. It is not the ceremonies, sacrifices, houses of prayer, symbols and gifts that protect us, but an honest, intimate desire to do things right, make faire evaluations, have open mindedness, love for each other and faith in the only living God. "To this end I was born, and for this I came into the world, that I should bear witness unto the truth." (John 18: 37) Notice that Jesus came to show us the truth; not to be sacrificed.

Some Gnostic Christians claimed that one cannot see the Kingdom of Heaven unless he knows the "secret teachings of Jesus". This doesn't mean that Jesus kept secrets from us but that he supposedly taught more advanced concepts to those able to grasp them. Gnostics didn't have the clout of the main church and neither its unity of views. Nevertheless, they hit an important point: "the fundamental problem in human life is not sin, but ignorance." It is ignorance that makes one "sin". Later, plenty of educated men stimulated by the gospel's esoteric connection tried to look beyond the surface and unlock at least part of its mystery. But, "Let no man deceive himself. If any man among you seems to be wise in this world, let him become a fool, that he may be wise." (1 Corinthians 3:18) Wisdom and truth are God's way and, this is how He created us: wise, not "smart".

Once Jesus had gone, dogmas never mentioned by Jesus but interpreted as being his intentions started to emerge. Thus, we are taught that Jesus is the only son of God, "begotten not made" which explains why he is so much more advanced than we. All right but, the Old Testament mentions others who had been begotten and didn't come even close to Jesus' quality, as far as we know. Keep in mind that Jesus was created long before his birth from Mary. Knowing the person who was his physical father, is of lesser significance. Significant is what he did for us. Jesus is what he always was. Nevertheless, Jesus' highly developed mind makes us feel unable to be at his level. The Bible say that while Jesus is God incarnated, we, the humans, had been created "in His own image" from "the dust of the ground, and breathed into his nostrils the breath of life." (Genesis 1: 7) Well, both Jesus and Adam had been created in God's image, the only image God has, but they chose different values to live by. "Things that are seen had been made from things that are not visible." (Hebrews 11: 3) All are a matter of choice. The clergy sails clean over the fact that Jesus' and Adam's lives are created by the same God from the same source: Himself. Humans could not be created as inferior to their Father. No parent wants his sons to be inferior to him. No fair exchange can take place unless among equally enlightened parties. Not to mention, a perfect God cannot create anything that is not perfect. Imperfect is one's choice of misalignment with the perfection of his father. Imperfect is our self-serving or self-pleasing physical choice.

Perfection excludes specialness or inequality. Jesus saw us as his "brothers" who, "the works that I do shall he do also; and greater works than these he [the one who believes] shall do." (John 14: 12) There is only "One God and Father of all, and through all, and in you all." (Ephesians 4: 6) The Lord's prayer, as given by Jesus, starts with "our Father." He is "my Father and your Father," Jesus said. (John 20: 17) We are all Jesus' brothers! If one doubts, "ye shall know that I am in my Father, and ye in me, and I in you." (John 14: 20) "Because I live, ye shall live also."(John 14:21) Humans, and their church, like to categorize people as "good and evil" and thus separate those who are meant to be one. For this reason, our separation seems familiar to us but is nonexistent to God. He knows that physicality means separation and, therefore, failure.

Jesus didn't accuse anyone of committing sin. Sin is the consequence of a misjudgment, not a fact. It is an abstract opinion and therefore dismissible back into the pit of choices. This means that we don't have to fight the thoughts called sin; we just have to avoid them. We are in charge of our choices and decisions. Our thinking is our responsibility; improve it! Sin is a concept created by humans who cannot admit their own mistakes. We prefer to see sin as real in somebody else or somewhere else. "You do not really recognize what arouses anger in you, and nothing that you believe in this connection means anything. You will probably be tempted to dwell more on some situations or persons" and attribute sin to them. (45) The idea of sin being a human thought, doesn't qualify for truth. Consequently, sin doesn't require a sacrifice in order to get dismissed. It only requires awareness. Again, awareness is a quality that when subjected to personal interpretations loses its value. As a brief reminder, our emotions tell us that we must be crazy to turn the other cheek once the first one was struck. Meanwhile wisdom tells us to do just that: do not get angry and do not retaliate.

How can God justify the lack of retaliation to an attack? How could He advise us to respond to aggression with love and forgiveness? He can. God didn't create any sinner. If one sees the attack on him as a slip of emotions not worthy of consideration, then he denies that the perpetrator is a sinner. By denying the effect (your retaliation), you deny its cause (his evil intention, or sin) and this is forgiveness (affirmation of holiness). Jesus never condemned those who crucified him. Jesus could not see neither his accusers nor himself as sinners but holy sons of God caught in an emotional upheaval. Because "the wage of sin is death," (Romans 6: 23) you should avoid it. But, how can one do that while subjected to pride and anger? Notice that Jesus acknowledged everyone's divine identity and dismissed any mis-interpretation of events. We can too, if we rise above the belief that we are only our temporary bodies subjected to all kinds of thoughts and emotions. When he came among us, Jesus did rise from his assumed physicality to the awareness of his spiritual self. He wanted to connect with us and share his knowledge from one man to another. He did not blame anyone no matter what they did. Some believe that we, who had been spiritually created long ago, ("Before I formed thee in the belly I knew thee; and before thou came forth out of the womb I sanctified thee"- Jeremiah 1:5) chose to live physically in order to acquire a unique life experience. "Body is a learning device for the mind." (46) Live through the challenges of the world, learn their nature and the best way to deal with them. God created us spiritual beings and part of His spiritual world. Our physical death is not a disappearance. We are eternal.

Again, sin is the consequence of an improper opinion and therefore is not the truth. The denial of sin is the way to uphold the holiness of both the attacker and the attacked. This is what Jesus did on the cross. He forgave His attackers, did not retaliate, did not complain, did not accuse and, by doing that, he upheld the holiness of God's creation. If angry, we believe we are much less than who we really are. Anger is nothing else than an attempt to make someone feel guilty. Guilt is not godly. We don't realize that if angry, we share destructive emotions rather than denying them. If we accuse anyone, we accuse God of miscreation. If we accuse it means that we believe in guilt; a thought which separates us from each other and from God. If we choose to consider that we are separated persons having different qualities, rather than having the same qualities and different interests, we make our return to Heaven's unity impossible. Heaven is the acceptance of our perfect creation as truth. In conclusion, the concept of "turn the other cheek" is extremely important. It defines a whole philosophy. Forgiving the attacker is a spiritual decision that stands against everything we physically learned and against our standard physical behavior. If we believe that we are bodies, the attack on our bodies is considered an attack on us. In its turn, this kind of belief prevents us to access a higher mentality. The apostles themselves didn't quite understand the deepness of Jesus' words. Simon Peter himself cut off the ear of the high priest's servant, who came to arrest Jesus (John 18: 10).

Can you believe that what you perceive in others, you are strengthening in yourself? If you see sin in the others, you live in a world of sin and you think in terms of sin. By physical standards, one accuses another to project his own guilt to the other and away from himself. Little does one know that as you forgive, you are forgiven; as you love, you are loved; as you condemn, you are condemned. The world can give you only what you give to it.

A pure mind knows the truth and this is its strength. In the end, it is you who has to find the truth about yourself, for your own good.

The way you understand life, is a reflection of you. You have the responsibility to answer any challenge you meet. It doesn't matter what other people may believe. It matters what you think. The quality of your thinking qualifies you for your kind of life. The mind is a very powerful tool. Upgrading it is a great achievement that requires a significant effort most people don't understand and don't want to take. The inconvenience of upgrading your understanding motivates people to settle for effortless horizontal interests and justify what ego makes you believe. Ego makes one feel good without any effort, reinforces no need to grow and allows feeling innocent by not admitting to making any mistakes. The price of convenience is the avoidance of truth and the acceptance of falseness. Meanwhile, for God, truth is singular, clear and complete. Since the first humans, we have the proneness of judging good and evil and by doing that we feel righteous while missing the truth. Truth can be known only by a clear mind.

III.
An Open Question

The question is, does life have a purpose or it just happened? If it has a purpose, it is important to know what that purpose is. If we know, we have the opportunity to be more effective in living our lives. If not, we just linger around.

If life has a purpose, avoiding it would be an embarrassing mistake. Still, this is what we do: we choose the easy way, guided by our trusted egos. Obviously, if we settle for a physical understanding of life, we value everything physical, including the comfort of doing nothing beyond looking for food and safety. In this scenario, progress must depend on something else: that something else must be creativity. For once, mind's creative activity doesn't require any physical cooperation. On the other hand, in our physical condition we are stuck to the needs of our bodies. Otherwise, "Only the mind can create." (47) If so, why don't we give our minds the important attention it deserves? Why don't we promote higher thinking rather than horizontal opinions about what we observed one time or another. All conflicts in the world consume huge amounts of personal energy and resources all due to our lack of understanding the purpose of our life. Are we hopelessly selfish; or hopelessly ignorant? I don't know but we have to avoid whatever makes us losers.

Life is best served by truth and truth is knowledge and wisdom. We created social laws to safeguard a fair life but those laws have a lot of loopholes we learned to use to our advantage. We also have internal laws written in our minds at birth but those laws are not enforceable so we feel free to ignore them. Well, we are free only to a point: as a matter of fact we are already in prison for braking the laws of our creation. Our prison is called earth. After a life-long experience we got so much used to it that we don't feel "locked in". We would rather continue going forth with our external rules. They have the advantage of being our own creations that do not frighten us any longer. True, but shouldn't we aim for something more effective? Jesus was more explicit: "he that believes in me, the works that I do shall he also do." (John14: 12) The choice is: heaven? or, earth?. This information is exciting; but, does anybody care? We feel rather comfortable where we are. Who is God beyond what we already believe He is? More than that what do we believe His world truly is? "Only the mind can create." "Only the mind is real because only the mind can be shared." (48) Everything is accomplished through life, and life is of the mind and, in the mind. (49) "Body is a learning device for the mind." (50) Jesus said. If we want to fix physical issues, we have to deal with the cause of that issue not with its consequences. This is a whole life makeover.

Who and what can keep the whole universe in order, other than the Mind who created it? "Things which are seen were not made from things which appear". Who, other than God, holds things coordinated, big and small, in a certain relation to each other? The chemical reactions, the movement of the planets, life itself, everything takes place in a predictable way, as organized by His Mind. It is interesting to notice that light, that propagates as waves, the moment it is observed in the lab, changes its propagation to particles (photons). Can the mind change light's mode of transmission by observing it? It is identified as waves outside of space and time (the domain of potentiality) and as particles, in the physical domain of space and time. "From a quantum perspective, the universe is an extremely interactive place. A physicist's observation determines whether an elementary particle, say, is behaving like a fluid wave or as a hard, tiny particle; eventually, decides which path it follows in traveling from one place to another…. "According to the rules of quantum mechanics, our observations [thoughts] influence the universe at the most fundamental levels. The boundary between an objective 'world out there' and our own subjective consciousness of it, a boundary that seem so clearly defined in classical physics, blurs in quantum mechanics." Everything happening in the universe must be coordinated by a mind of which we are a part, a mind greater than ours that keeps everything in harmony. Everything we know is built with the same subatomic particles. If we are built with the same elements, we belong together. This sameness endorses spirituality's claim that we come from the same source we call: God. Also, God's realm is perfection. In the whole universe no deviation from His well thought decision exists. What makes humans different is our abilities to choose different thoughts. Our choices allow room for change, while God's rules are well planned, infinitely eternal and firm. Our different manifestations are created by the way our identical elementary particles function under the control of our minds. Our minds supersede physicality. The creator cannot be subjected to its creation.

Scientists are looking for an elementary particle that is the constituent of all subatomic particles in existence. They call it the "God particle", the basic building block of everything that is. Not much is known about it. Is it a jolt of energy or the smallest object that can be imagined? If the "God particles" are jolts of energy, then the whole material world is nothing but a form of energy. If this is the case, matter is immaterial; and, abstract. A thought provoking question is: how is it possible to build different particles with different properties by using the same, identical, building blocks? It is assumed that even more importantly than the particles themselves, is their particular way of vibrating. But then, who decides how those building elements move? Who provides all that energy that keeps matter in a state of permanent interaction? Who personalizes that interaction that makes the same particles develop different expressions, different shapes and different characteristics, in different instances? The way those particles interact makes the whole difference; it defines both objects and living beings. In order for those interactions to make sense, a Mind that is beyond the space-time frame must control it all. The only such Mind in existence is God. This source of all creation must be outside of matter because He is its creator, living outside of his creation. Matter is a consumer of energy; not its creator. When the energy is withdrawn, the material particles collapse together and create a black hole where those particles disintegrate into what they had been before. Matter and its works are, after all, the creation of a Mind and dependent of that Mind. Of course, scientists take care not to pass judgment on any connection between those particles and God because they don't have any scientific proof of this connection. Nevertheless, this connection makes sense. The universe is recycling itself. We have both the expanding universe and the collapsing black holes. We have our own bodies that, in the end, collapse into their own black holes we call graves. So much about physicality! Who created it? It must be God because He is eternal and his creation, we included, is eternal. What makes His creation eternal and indestructible is its perfection. As a parenthesis, is the assumed divine predetermination, possible?

How can we prove that God exists? Isn't our persistent belief in His existence, which remains steady despite all the attacks on it, proof enough? Should we dismiss our personal experiences of His presence? Are the many recorded near death experiences of no value to knowledge? Who are we? What is the reason for our creation and the meaning of our existence?

Some of our children are rebellious and fight the authority of their parents as well as the commonly accepted values and institutions. Some drag their rebelliousness into adulthood and even create whole movements that fit their personal ideas. This is how Communism came about, as well as the 60's movement and all kinds of offshoots. The issue of who we are and what we should do with our lives is in our lap to deal with; and one way or another, we do. Every thought and every decision we make is our answer to those questions and, our answers define the kind of existence we choose to have.

We have the legitimate desire to know as much as possible about life. We are life! If God is our creator, we cannot turn our back to Him and expect to be fine. How happy the prodigal son could have been! We are endowed with everything we need in order to find our way back to love and happiness. We only have to want it strongly enough to get involved and define our appropriate options in order to succeed. At one time, we decided to adopt different ways of living than God's Heaven, and drifted away from His intention for us. We are in a world of our own. Plainly said, "This [physical] world is not the will of God," (51) it is our will. To return to our worth, we have to reverse our choices and learn our way back to the perfection of our creation. Hesiod (700 B.C.), Isaac Newton (1700 A.D.) and other quality thinkers along history, found that humans, despite their physical achievements, constantly decrease in quality by constantly building opinions on top of the truth. Because we have our own creative minds, we've created the existing world as we think about it. We believe that our opinions about our world are reality and, our opinions became our reality. Different minds have different understandings of the world. Different groups of people built different cultures for themselves and established differing countries. Then, some desire what others built and assume the right to colonize other countries. Some want what God built, update their minds and join His Kingdom. Jesus came to demonstrate that this is possible. One cannot change his life unless he changes his mind away from what he used to think while confused. Tough job. Some even try, but we changed too much and too profound to succeed. It seems we have to physically die, clean the slate, before we rediscover the secret of life.

1.
ATHEIST ARGUMENTS

Trying to prove that God doesn't exist is as equally difficult as proving that He does. No one can prove or disprove the non-physical God using physical means. "Things that are seen had been made from things that are not visible." (Hebrews 11: 3) "Only the mind can create." (52) The fact that we see things is our proof of those things' reality. Things that are not seen or felt do not get our due attention and their reality could be contested. When Adam disagreed with God, was the moment when Adam wanted to be left alone. No more questions! From there, he got his independence by choosing his physical singularity over God's unified creation. He chose: his independent mind over God's advice, his feelings over trusting Him, his opinions over the unbending truth and he didn't want to be reminded of that incident. Once this step had been taken, the following steps became the consequence of his previous ones. Adam didn't lose his original quality; he only refused to have any revision to his decision. He already had God's permission to access everything in existence. God basically offered Adam the same freedom He had himself. Why? In order to know everything that can be known, of course. Learning is coming from knowing and all knowledge was made available to Adam and equally to those in his group. It is reasonable for one to know what is available before making his choice. One's value system comes with its own set of thoughts, consequences and ways; all are important in defining our development as humans. Adam became fixated on something existing beyond his known Garden of Eden. All right! He discovered what choices were available, yet once he made his choice, he settled into it and couldn't move-on away from that choice. He started to know it and it became familiar to him. Physicality is obvious to our senses and easy to explore. Knowledge, instead, is abstract and unseen; it can be known but, is unknown if not searched. Adam wanted to be separated from the abstract world of God. He wanted the satisfaction of the physical things he liked and the assurance they brought. Adam felt comfortable and accomplished. There is a feeling of pride in creating. He apparently wanted what didn't stand in his way, and that complimented his physical choices which stayed with him for life.

In any legal case, the only irrefutable proof is physical. Some hope that our eternal afterlife will be physical: "the resurrection of the body and the life everlasting." I have no doubt that some will find this kind of stagnation, in the pinnacle of their physical success, desirable. This is not what Jesus said but it is hoped to be by those humans who feel privileged and chosen. This may be the dream of some but it's not God's intention of wanting to bring each one of His sons back to the perfection of His creation. They don't realize that their physical success is lower than the success offered by God. They do not realize that feeling better off on earth, is their proof of selfishness and blindness to spirituality. Physically we want the pride of being special and better off than our brothers, while spiritually we are created equal and perfect. Equality is interpreted as making one feel average but being equal to God is the utmost one can be. As mentioned, challenges stimulate our motivation to grow. "Body is a learning device for the mind." God, in His awareness, did not cast us in a limited, slow-learning condition forever. We are a work in progress and sometimes this progress feels like a vague goal, while it is not. No one can be cast in any slow-moving or stagnating condition for eternity. Jesus himself came to help us change for the better: the free and independent owners of the universe!

How do atheists on earth deal with Jesus' theistic experience? There are only two ways they can and still maintain credibility. One is to deny Jesus' very existence. This explanation doesn't work because there are so many testimonies of His presence and of His desire to help us grow. Also, what He taught us is so meaningful and thought-creating that it cannot be dismissed. The other way is to accept Jesus as less than God incarnated: that He is not a divinity but a popular and influential philosopher who stimulated people's imagination. Jesus happened so long ago that we cannot know for sure how He was. We can only assume what we prefer to assume. Many have wanted to believe his extraordinary story and have hoped to be able to follow him. "The world is the belief that love [as God has it] is impossible" (53) on earth. The stories we have about Him are so incredible and impossible to duplicate that we cannot confidently know the truth. Even if we would know, we don't seem able to completely renounce the mentality that has served us all this time. We make some adjustments and accept some reasons but, we stop short in the face of major change. We had been as we are for so long, that we consider our way natural. The physical life is our reality!

Nevertheless, Jesus' message has something that satisfies our deeper needs of propriety. At the same time, we don't want our familiar ways challenged; we know how to operate our lives! It seems that Jesus is the answer to our desire for perfection but perfection seems to be an illusion. Jesus had not been understood well enough while living among us and, he is not well understood now: "When the Son of man cometh [again], shall he find faith on earth?". (Luke 18:8) Our condition is of our own making. We see ourselves as we believe we are and we cannot change what we have built for so long. Is it even possible? Truth is supreme and therefore independent of any belief. It is we who have to find the truth or we will never get it. How do we know if we know what we should know? We know because we are minds from God's mind. Our minds couldn't be created from material elements because the mind is not material and does not depend of anything material. It is not subjected to evolution either because it is perfect in itself. Minds see the Creation as it is. "Truth is God's will" (54) "Only the mind can create." (47) Again, "Worlds were framed by the words of God, so things which are seen were not made from things which do appear." (Hebrews 11: 3) In the beginning was a thought. Minds perceive the reality of our thoughts and program our brains to remember. The brain is acting like a biological computer that processes the information received. In our case, its programmer is God's given mind. The brain is a physical processor while the mind is the metaphysical power that operates it. When we physically die, the brain and its thought processing go to dust while our eternal, immaterial minds endure forever. Since we are endowed with complete freedom, at any mome we can adjust our minds and enact its perfection. Physicality is demanding the cooperation of our minds with our physical brains. This coordination makes physical living possible. Our minds thus become subjected to two very different influences: the spiritual mind and the physical brain making our awareness to temporarily compromise between mind and brain, God and ego, truth and opinions. In the end, our eternal minds prevail; no doubt. Once we are physically dead, our minds are free. Meanwhile, we constantly do our best to compromise between the two and keep mind and brain reasonably in tune. This compromise makes it difficult for us to follow Jesus.

So, we try to mix what cannot be mixed: our subjective ways with the objectivity of truth. We consequently cannot do what Jesus did unless we take control of our brain. Jesus didn't own anything and didn't have any physical goals or ambitions. He never claimed specialness. We do it all the time. Our physical thinking demands the pursuit of physical goods. Those goods are the only specialness that can be provided on earth. We pursue physicality for the specialness it can provide.

For our lifestyle, "truth" is too clear cut to be comfortable. Truth offers no room to explain, motivate, transfer, or ignore our responsibility, no room for the pride of having and winning. We cannot follow Jesus because we stopped at whom we chose to be. "The world of bodies is the world of sin." (55) Still, "Only the body makes the world seem real." We are spiritual beings exiled in the physical world.

From a materialistic perspective, what is not identifiable with our means of exploration is not real. Nevertheless, as our insights sharpen and our technology advances, we get closer and closer to the border between concrete and abstract. Albert Einstein believed in God, based on his knowledge of the world's perfect organization. This kind of balance must be God's work. There is no other intelligence able to harmonize everything that is and this perfect coordination cannot be the work of hazard.

For atheists, the problem with the imagined "beyond" is that it removes our attention from the obvious physical and invests it in what they call "empty hopes". Sure, on earth we have a difficult life but for atheists, this is not a reason to start dreaming of an Olympus, Valhalla, or Heaven. Per their understanding we have to fix what we have here and now and grow from there. For Michael Onfray, Professor of Philosophy at Free University of Caen, France, atheism is "restored mental health." For him, the concept of soul is meant to downgrade the body and eventually make it sick. He also believes that focusing on the immaterial turns our attention away from celebrating the body and enjoying everything the body likes, in order to achieve the salvation of the soul. Consequently, materialists see religion as an obstacle to embracing "reality." They believe religion invented the afterlife at the high price of willful neglect of the "only world we have." To them it is obvious that we should dedicate our attention to what is available and sustains life. For Professor Onfray, by offering the idea of eternal reward, religion failed to improve anything we already have here on earth. For him, religion appears to be a placebo that brings peace of mind without providing any substantial help. His conclusion is that religion is nothing but "perpetual mental infantilism." (Michael Onfray) As for the concept of Our Father which is in Heaven, "atheism rejects the existence of God as being a fiction devised by men, desperate to keep living in spite of the inevitability of death." If religion would be as valid as its supporters claim, the three monotheistic religions, believing in the same God, should not have three different eating requirements: the Catholics to eat fish on Friday, the Muslims not to touch pork and the Jews refuse shellfish. The Muslims don't eat any meat-eating animal nor any water dwelling creature that doesn't have scales. The orthodox Jews require food to be of a certain kind and prepared according to certain rules. Christians believe they can eat "whatsoever is sold on the market, asking no question for conscience's sake: for the earth is the Lord's." (1 Corinthians 10: 25, 26) If religion speaks the truth, then which one of those culinary requirements is the truthful one?

The indication that physicality is never too far from our interests, is the fact that even the monotheistic religions claim that, in the next life, we will be restored as perfected physical bodies in a perfected earth. This hope shows that even our highest spiritual goal is a compromise between physical and metaphysical. Physicality is what we know and cannot let it go.

Because monotheists' opinions do not make sense to the atheists, they, the atheists, value philosophers instead. For them, philosophers have the advantage of being independent thinkers, detached from any dogma. Their conclusions proceed from reason, intelligence and argument while the ordained clergy insist on faith and obedience. This is nicely said but still, are we created by God or had we developed spontaneously from the preexisting mineral world?

How do the atheists know that Heaven doesn't exist? They don't know; but it doesn't make sense to them and this seems enough to reject the idea. The lack of reasonable proof is considered an indication that Heaven is only an opinion and religion is a fictitious theory and seemingly an elaborate superstition. True or not, atheism only says that we have no physical evidence of a non-physical life.

Spinoza was condemned on July 27, 1656, for atheism. He was charged by the Jewish establishment for appalling heresies and dangerous opinions for which "his name had to be erased forever from the surface of the planet." (Michael Onfray) No one was allowed to come closer than six feet of him or be under the same roof with him. No contact with the twenty-three-year-old Spinoza had been allowed because he didn't agree with the theory of "chosen people" and considered Jesus a philosopher.

A well-known victim of the established church is Giordano Bruno, a Dominican cleric, who didn't deny God or the existence of the spirit but he understood that matter is made of atoms; each atom being a center of life. For having different opinions from the Catholic Church at the time, he was burned at the stake in 1660. The same fate would apply to Galileo for his opinion that the Earth is a satellite of the sun and not the unmoved and unmovable center of the world. He escaped the fire by formally retracting his statement. As he left the court, it is said he muttered: "Eppur' simuove" (still it moves). Nevertheless, he was placed under house arrest for the rest of his life. It is interesting that correct statements regarding the solar system had been made long before Galileo and Copernicus. "The Greek astronomer Aristarchus of Samos (319- 230 B.C.E.), published a brief work demonstrating mathematically that Earth went around the sun." Also "Phylolaus (470-385 B.C.E.), successor of Pythagoras, displaced the sun from the center of the universe." Intelligence, obviously, predated the age of Enlightenment.

"Tens of thousands of people had been executed by the Roman Catholic Church over the centuries for refusing to swear that God and Jesus Christ were one." How could they be? Jesus cannot be God incarnated because he was created by God: "Blessed be the God and Father of our Lord Jesus Christ." (Peter 1:3) He cannot be equal to God because "Christ doesn't know the future history of the world until he reads it in the scroll God will give him [see Revelation]. Because Christ doesn't already have the knowledge of the events of the end, which God possesses, he cannot be equal to God." Also, in Matthew 24:36 we can read: "that day and hour no man knows…but my father only."

Obviously the Christian churches wanted to spread Jesus' teaching and took the liberty to represent Him in a way acceptable to us but not entirely fair to Jesus. His crucifixion stopped his teaching and misinterpretation of his crucifixion damaged the meaning of the event: he didn't atone for our sins; he demonstrated the existence of immortality and the power of faith. As previously stated, despite their good intentions the religious experts relied on their human judgment. Consequently, the human interpretation of spiritual events introduced a materialistic contamination that derailed our understanding of the truth. This contamination affected the clerics also, as previously stated. They believe in God but, they're unaware of the whole truth about Him. Still, "Truth is God's will." (56) Jesus said. Their partial understanding made them use opinions to fill in what is not understood. As knowledge increases, the truth becomes more evident.

Atheists are helped by the fact that one doesn't have to go too far to find religion deeply flawed. In the Old Testament, God is described as "violent, jealous, quarrelsome, intolerant, and bellicose" to the extent that He "generated more hate, bloodshed, deaths, and brutality than it has peace . . . There is the Jewish fantasy of chosen people, which vindicates colonialism, expropriation, hatred, animosity between peoples, abuse, and finally an authoritarian and armed theocracy." (Michael Onfray) The Koran, the other monotheistic holy book, contains instances of hatred of non-Muslims. Theoretically, the Koran assures non-Muslim people of the book, of their right to exist and be protected. But this protection came only after the payment of a staggering tax, the Giza. The atheists reason that the precepts of any monotheistic religion are set by the people who wrote the holy books. This indicates that the religious standards cannot be accurate because they are written by humans and change from one writer to another. The atheists claim that each religion reflects the mentality of its writers and, therefore, do not accurately quote God.

It is an atheist opinion that religions prevent the fullness of the "real" life here, on earth, in order to glorify the afterlife. This is accomplished through aversion for anything that would allow a person to enjoy his condition: women, sexuality, our own bodies, desires, freedom, books, pleasures... Not being the least, the atheists believe "Monotheism hates intelligence." For example, the word "Muslim" means submission to God; meaning, not to think outside the Islamic Torah which has laws regarding every minute detail of daily life. In this way, the independent thinking is virtually eliminated in favor of obedience. The Jewish religion requires submission to their own set of laws. Christians also have the Ten Commandments that nullify our freedom of choice. For atheists, in order to come to God religious people need to ha a lack of awareness and a rote and dogmatic education.

Since medieval times, sciences had made strides with Jean Lamarck bringing up the idea of evolution in his book "Philosophie Zoologique" in 1809. Soon after, Charles Darwin published his well-documented discoveries in "The Origin of Species by Means of Natural Selection." (Nov. 1859) Darwin, being a believer in God and Jesus, was deeply troubled by his own conclusions but, science is science. It was left for later generations to make sense of it all. And, later generations did.

The atheists also seized the opportunity to question Adam and Eve as being the original couple, which the Jewish church believes had been created 5,777 years ago. The progress in anthropology and archeology indicated that first human-like creatures are much older than that. While this is true, we would never know the quality of their minds. Many animals are extremely intelligent but none of them master science, creativity or philosophy as humans have. Atheists claim that "Monotheism has no love for intelligence, books, knowledge, or science. Preferring the ethereal to the material, theism shows a strong aversion to man's instincts and basic drives. Thus, not only they celebrate ignorance, innocence, naïveté, obedience, and submission: the three religions of the book disdain the texture, forms, and forces of the world." Thinking objectively, "Preferring the ethereal" over science, doesn't mean that God is against knowledge. It only means that atheist narrowness is accusing the monotheist narrowness of narrowness. Books have been written to the glory of atheism and the fallacy of all monotheistic religions. In the end, atheism had the opportunity to prove its own value through the creation of Communism, an atheist heaven spread over one third of the world that implemented everything an atheist could dream of. This system that started by building on the healthy technological foundation created by previous societies, collapsed shortly after, under the weight of its own misunderstandings and inefficiency. How could atheism, the promoter of science and intelligence, fail at the feet of the "backward" Monotheism?!

2.

THE MEANINGS OF OPINIONS

In this world we need food to live, clothes to cover ourselves, a home to reside, cars to travel and so forth. The need for those objects doesn't make us materialists. We become materialists when we attribute to objects an importance they don't have, like considering that an object can make you happy. No object can produce any thought or emotion. Only a living being can. The Oxford dictionary defines materialism as: "The doctrine that nothing exists except matter and its movements; the doctrine that consciousness and will are wholly due to the operation of material agencies." In other words, for materialists physical matter is the only reality there is.

At first look, this may seem to be true but there are several observations that cast doubt on this theory: First, can temporary matter create the never aging and permanent minds? Second, if truth is unchangeable and permanent then the ever-changing and temporary matter is not true. Objects deteriorate, need repair, improvements and replacement. Third, that which does not change in time is immaterial. Love, peace, joy... do not change their meanings, cannot be improved, repaired or replaced, ever. The abstract does not alter. It can be subjected to interpretation but once interpreted, it loses its identity and becomes opinion. With this in mind, we ask ourselves what, then, is real: the decaying matter (the physical brain) or the permanent abstract (the spiritual mind)? Truth is God's mind; man's thoughts, in turn, are usually opinions. Mind is perfectly conceived by God and indestructible while opinions are self-satisfying thoughts to the body and changeable. What can make a decision confusing is the mixed use of the abstract mind and the physical brain.

For atheists, life's goal is satisfying the "body"; while for the spiritually minded, life is the opportunity to achieve excellence. The confusion may arise from the fact that mind is shared between its creator and the created.

(57). We have the difficult task to coordinate the two different value systems: the divine mind and the judgment of our physical brain. As created, mind is subjected to truth while the brain is subjected to physical perceptions. This mixed interaction prevents one to be consistently committed to abstract values and qualify for Heaven.

I remember a story told by Professor Dr. Mircea Eliade about the people from a barrack in the Siberian Gulag. In that barrack, the detainees decided to deprive themselves of part of their already insufficient food in order to make a full portion for an older lady detained among them. She was a good story teller and could make her audience dream of an ideal life beyond the Siberian labor camp. She was too old for the physical strain of hard labor in that freezing cold. If she would not work, she would have been denied that meager dinner soup. So those sharing that barrack agreed to trade a daily evening story for a portion of their soup. Her stories transported the detainees' minds to happier places, pure thoughts and away from their daily miseries. The strange and surprising result was that in that barrack the death rate was the lowest in the whole compound. "Man shall not live by bread alone." (Matthew 4: 4)

Mind is a power unto itself. It can motivate us to take physical risks, sacrifice for a cause, use our bodies beyond their limits, break out of our physical confinement, get out of a dreadful routine and dream of higher goals. Great Britain started both World Wars, the Boer's war and the Crimean War because it wanted to maintain its world supremacy. At the end of WWII, it gave Romania to the Soviet Union in exchange for Soviet abandonment of its support for Greek communists. This so called "the percentage agreement" (90% Soviet influence in Romania for 90% British influence in Greece) was meant to secure the safe traffic of the English fleet through the Mediterranean Sea for the price of Romanian enslavement to Russian communism.

For materialists, spirituality is a figment of one's imagination. They consider themselves advanced because they don't buy into religious "nonsense". They base this conclusion on opinions and opinions are of unlimited variety and of little substance. Truth, on the other hand, is one; unbendable and undeniable. It should be noticed here that top scientists like Albert Einstein and Sir Isaak Newton did believe in the spiritual concept of God while many smaller thinkers may not have. If atheists would truly use their scientific minds, they would find some scientific evidence to prove the opinion that body produces the mind. With their credibility at stake the atheists of today are trying to do just that, unsuccessfully.

I remember a patient of mine who had a stroke from which she recovered. I told her that my father recently had a stroke too. Her eyes got bigger and said:

"Talk to him. He cannot move or respond and may look like he's unable to understand a thing. He appears to just helplessly sit there. Nothing is more untrue. For as long as he does breathe, he is fully aware of everything happening around him. He hears and clearly understands everything. When I had my stroke, I was immobile but totally aware of what was happening around. Talk to him." It appears that because of a physical malfunction, her brain was temporarily unable to control her body but her mind was unaffected. If the brain stops working, it doesn't mean that one's spiritual mind also stops.

Being aware that God is in your corner, provides a significant help in dealing with life's challenges. With this awareness you know something very important: you are not abandoned to hazard. There is a higher reason behind what happens in your life. Even if one physically dies, he doesn't disappear. His physical body deteriorates but the spiritual self is unaffected. You are not abandoned because you have built in you a small fragment from your eternal Creator. Even in our physical creation, we have a small deciding fragment from our parents built in: a DNA molecule. "There is no separation between God and His creation." "the Will of God which is yourself," (58) follows you wherever you are. The will of God is the reason for our existence.

The general purpose of life is learning. Socrates said, "An unexamined life is not worth living." If one doesn't examine his life's experiences, he wastes his time. One cannot benefit from what he doesn't learn. Regardless if one is a materialist or not, successful or not, God still quietly guides you toward a successful outcome. Be smart enough to listen to Him.

If we accept that we are nothing but bodies producing things, then our unity as a race must come from dependency. If this is so, we need the others for what they can provide for us, and, learn ways to take advantage of them. This perspective may generate antisocial behavior, may justify the lack of love and can promote selfishness, specialness and disappointment. Obviously with this mentality, we cannot follow Jesus. As bodies, we see each other as separate entities competing for opportunities. Some are more selfish than others and consider themselves more gifted or more special than the others. This is the consequence of our physical understanding of life. As spiritual beings we do not compete because we have all we need; we don't depend on others; we depend on our minds. Being equally created, we cooperate, freely communicate and enjoy the others' interaction. For God, "giving is more blessed than receiving." He Himself only gives. God never asks us for anything other than to be as perfect as originally intended. God esteems Jesus for his commitment to his teaching. He endorsed His own words with his own life, thus being the most significant teacher we've ever had. He proved with his life, to those blinded by physicality, what couldn't be proved in any other way: life is indestructible, love is our best asset and spirituality is our identity. Body meanwhile, is the endorser of selfishness and the status quo. Even as bodies, we still have a built-in spiritual awareness: the need for excellence. Some are more spiritually oriented than others but we are all affected in different proportions by physical and spiritual concerns.

Matter is limited in duration, quantity and quality. It generates competition, comparison, envy, selfishness, pride and eventually conflicts. For materialists, competition is good. It brings out the best of humanity's abilities to produce and own. From a spiritual point of view, competition is a source of separation, selfishness, frustration, conflict, guilt, eventually hate. In our physical and temporal world, we believe that the rich are rich because they are somehow special, better, more effective, possibly favored by God than those less affluent. As a matter of fact, one's affluence is due to people's different kinds of interests, different characters and different opportunities. Spiritually, one "may believe that the gift comes from God to him, but it is quite evident that he does not understand God if he thinks that he has something that others lack." (59) God is fair. He shares with us all that is. Some who have less, may consider themselves the victims of those who have more and are prone to ask for "social justice;" a concept as poorly defined as it is emotional. Meanwhile, if we believe in God we should know we are all created equal and equally gifted members of one Creation. We should not depend on charity because by doing so, we lose our freedom, become contingent upon outside help and demand or crave for more. In God's Kingdom, we don't experience shortages and competition.

IV.
A Glimpse Of Truth

G od lives in a different dimension: He abides in his spiritual world while we live on physical earth. Regardless, we are not disconnected. He cannot be separated from His creation. "Ye shall know that I am in my father, and ye in me, and I in you.". . . "and he that loveth me shall be loved by my Father, and I will love him, and will manifest myself to him." (John 14: 20, 21) God created us for a purpose we haven't fulfilled yet. His decisions are forever; He continually takes care of us. His guidance is essential and always available in his unintrusive way. Most of the time we are not aware of it. The direct communication with God that existed in the Garden of Eden stopped once Adam and Eve chose to distance themselves from Him, become self-sufficient and drift to the seemingly independent, physical life. We started to communicate body to body and use our voice to express whatever we wanted. We also built our own understanding of reality; differing from truth (reality). Our understanding is based on opinions that we, most of the time, confuse for truth. Consequently, we are confident that we know God while we don't and we interpret Him as He fits into our understanding. Some accuse Him of being aloof, not interested and apparently nonexistent. Feeling disconnected and abandoned in our hard and perilous lives many times we seek prayers to Him for help. We built a personal system for dealing with our mistakes: a system where we find reasons for seeing our mistaken opinions in someone else, outside of ourselves; a place where we feel we can defer the responsibility of our doings. We claim to be victims, while we are perpetrators. In extreme cases, we used to sacrifice a perfect and innocent other as redemption for our "sins". For the last 2,000 years we were taught that Jesus had been sacrificed so we can be redeemed or forgiven. In the end, after so many convenient explanations and interpretations, we don't know any longer what reality is and expect God to save us from our world of confusion and peril.

Since nothing can be created from nothing, we must be created by the only existing being at the beginning of life and from the only existing source in the universe: Himself. "For in Him we live, and move, and have our being; For we are also His offspring." (Acts 17: 28) "There is but one Father, of whom are all things." (1 Corinthians 8: 6) We are therefore part of Him and can rightfully be called His Holy Children. "God dwelleth not in temples made with hands." (Acts 17: 24) "He dwelleth with you, and shall be in you." (John 14: 17) This means, He lives in our souls and minds. "He holds you dear because you are Himself." (60) In our material understanding of the immaterial, a child can come only from a sexual intercourse. Because of that, some assume there must be a Mrs. God somewhere. Well, remember that God didn't bring us forth physically. "Father did not create bodies" (61). Physicality is a human understanding of what we don't understand. We are His mental creation who became materialized as we see ourselves today and according to how we chose ourselves to be. We should never forget that, as He is Spirit, we are Spirits likewise. The confusion comes from the fact that sometime down the road we separated from Him and started to believe in our own reality that works our way, in our minds. Despite our separation, we still use the Minds He gave us. Our Mind, being divine, made us part of divinity. The Mind we have been given must coordinate with the thinking of our physical brain. In this situation, our abstract Minds are only temporarily influenced by our physical proneness. In our physical condition, the two (mind and brain) must work together. For this reason, we can say that we live by double standards. We are in a temporary exile here on earth (only until death). While our minds are eternal and make us who we are, the physical brain demands us to fulfill our physical needs. The bible calls our bodies "the temple of the living God" (II Corinthians 6:16) where His spirit dwells. If this is so, it makes sense to search for God's spiritual essence within ourselves, see Him as Us and hold us both, holy. If we would do that, we would return closer to the condition in which we had been created, and rejoin our Father and those Brothers who didn't follow physical fantasies. Jesus demonstrated this possibility when he lived among us. God is, after all, our Father, which makes us all a Sonship and natural part of His Trinity.

There is nothing out there but God and His creation which is also He. We generally believe that only Jesus is part of the Godhead but Jesus points out that we, all of us, are his equal brothers. The only difference between Jesus and us is our different levels of awareness. Divine awareness is truth. Truth, being a perfect state, is flawless, indestructible and consequently eternal. Human awareness is, instead, partial, incomplete, imperfect and temporary. Consequently, our perception of ourselves as bodies is also temporary. Our perfection is God's meaning for us. The perfect God can create only perfection. To our perfect Mind, everything is possible once it is free from the confusing thoughts of our brains.

    As humans, we indulge in our opinions and often miss the divine truth. We misjudge, misunderstand, are self-righteous and proud. Guided by opinions, we hit walls, get sick, accuse God of indifference and Satan of evilness and accuse others for confusing us. Consequently, we don't acknowledge our responsibilities for our thoughts and deeds. There is always others to blame! So, we don't do much to discover the truth about ourselves. We take this life as it comes. Only we are responsible for the opinions we built. If we understand our opinions as being "real", we automatically believe we are unable to change them. Our assumed reality doesn't change; but, we don't know what reality is. Regardless, we cannot deny what we believe. All guidance we receive from Jesus and the Holy Spirit bounces against the kind of mentality we built, trust and obey. We appreciate physicality so much that we imagine that even Heaven is physical (see our concept of redemption that is a reincarnation under better physical circumstances). Jesus, instead, focused his attention away from physicality to our real metaphysical nature which is the nature of God, and His Kingdom,… it is His Creation! By relying on our home-made faith, we replaced God's holiness with our opinions about it. And, our opinions prioritize our physical needs and fantasies. We come from the quantum world of infinite, causeless possibilities and behave like in the physical world of cause and effect. We don't comprehend the non-directional eternity or the absence of space and time and so we settle our life in the familiar small section of the infinite, that we call our world. Nothing that we accept on earth has any value in the immensity of the Kingdom of God. As we live our physical lives in our aging bodies, so we live on a physical and aging earth, in the middle of our physical and aging universe. This is the physicality where we confidently set our opinions, ways, and values independent of God's. Since we separated from Him, we live in a fantasy world of ours that is inconsistent, painful and vanishing. More to the point, the spiritual part of us doesn't vanish because it is divine and therefore, permanent; only our physical perception dies. We don't know what is beyond physicality. We don't know perfection because of all those beliefs, fantasies, observations and certainties that we piled on top of who we are. All of that will be discarded along with our bodies that carry them. Our Minds are sinless because they are of God's (62). Still, we live under the stress of confusions because our Minds must obey two masters: God, who owns them and us, who received and use them. (63) We may temporarily abuse and confuse our Minds by inserting in them our subjective judgments. Our mind became a cooperative venture with our brains. This creates some confusion but, we can never alter our minds. It is unavoidable at some point that we'll discard our physical interferences and return to whom we truly are. So far, we've drifted too far away from our Father to remember Him. We interpret Him as it makes sense to us, which is not who He is. It's generally agreed and assumed: "In the beginning was the word" (John 1:1). However, any word is the expression of a preceding thought. So, in the beginning, necessarily, was a Holy Thought; not "word". Thoughts are expressed in words and, here we are. We pushed our memory of God deep into our subconscious minds and forgot about it. Excited by their own success, humans charged ahead with their own "realities" that are not real. They seem real only because they are obvious to our senses but, our senses are both limited and perishable!

Anyway, why did He create us? The answer is: the only way God could improve His perfect state is by creating equally perfect beings with whom he could communicate. The only way God could share and expand upon what is already perfect, is by sharing His Mind with His worthy Sons. In order to access the quality of worthy partners, we have to return to the perfection of our creation. In any exchange, the values shared are returned to the sender; amplified with the added value of appreciation from the receiving partner. The exchange of Love between God and His Sons' is the only way to enhance what He already created perfect. We all are He. Because we are parts of Him, "God Himself is incomplete without me." (64) For that matter, He is incomplete when any one of us is unable to respond likewise. Since both God and His Sons are One, the creation is basically God's way to enhance His own wellbeing. Our way to Heaven is the love we share. Our nature is Love and Heaven is our domain. We must fulfill God's expectations of His creation of Us.

One may ask where is all that love? We don't feel it as described by Jesus. We don't because, at one time, we chose to have a physical identity which comes with a physical set of values and private demands. Those values are not God's. They do not have His intended perfection and, do not provide the quality expected. Therefore, we cannot fulfill His reality until we wake up, renounce the reliance on private opinions and live the truth. Until then, our connection with God is strained. "He holds you dear because you are Himself. All gratitude belongs to you, because of who you are." (60) We still carry His spirit but, influenced by our own thoughts, our understanding became increasingly fitted to our physical proneness. We see ourselves as being separated and special while we are equal parts of a perfect unit. We used our granted freedom to interpret and redefine the concepts of Creation. Through our understanding of life, we found gratification in selfishness and, in claiming innocence by projecting our guilt and responsibilities to someone else. We steal because others stole from us. We transfer our guilt and then criticize the receiver for having it, rather than seeing him/her innocent and worthy of love. We should love a sinner for the truth of his perfect creation even if he/she is temporarily imperfect. His/her imperfection is due to imagined and assumed to be valid, alternative thinking. Acknowledge one's perfect nature, not his imperfect choices and you will help both him and yourself. The way we live today is not Godly. Our values are not based on truth, but on opinions about what truth is. Reality is as He created it; not as we see it. His reality stays, our opinions vanish. Our ways don't fit in the overall creation of life. Nevertheless, we assume that our values are true and we keep going forward in this same direction. Our values fit our physical way of living. For this reason, we find it difficult to follow Jesus' 2,200 years old advice. Our physical choices include so many aberrations that it is a given that at some point in time we will willfully abandon them and return to whom we are. We live in a fantasy of our own, disconnected from God; a fantasy in which He doesn't intervene, out of respect for us and loyalty to His own promise of freedom. He won't take away what He once gave. We are not lost to Him. We are confused. Far from being a path to nowhere, our voyage through this physical dream world is our given opportunity to experience different alternatives that ultimately leads to the understanding of Reality. We must understand errors, in order to understand Truth.

God knew that we may misuse His given freedom but He also knows that only in freedom we can enjoy the full benefits of His Creation. If He would compel us to live in a certain way, that way, no matter how good, would not be our choice. Then, we may not fully appreciate its perfection and may not feel connected to it. Our trip through the fantasy land of chaos helps us to realize the difference between truth and illusion and to make an informed decision. By selecting the proper choice, we will reach the point where we can enjoy all the benefits of divine life. Some of us didn't need to take a detour through chaos, in order to understand holiness but, some do. God sees our troubles on earth and from His higher perspective, forgives our senseless mistakes. Past is the pit where all mistakes are dumped. He knows that how we behave is not due to a structural defect but to ignorant and temporary choices. Being enlightened, God doesn't compel us to take certain paths in life. He is advising only. Jesus came to us as a teacher. If we get his message or not, it is our choice and our responsibility. He knows that nothing flawed is eternal. There comes a time when we will understand truth. That event is the Atonement, the waking up to reality.

The crown jewel of God's creation is we human beings who, being of Him, share His love, Mind, and values. "His holiness is the power holding everything as one, the link between the Father and the Son which holds Them both forever as the same." "He holds you dear because you are Himself." (60) We are all connected by one love, one mind and one nature. We are equal parts of His one Creation. The fact that we all share His Mind, helps us to easily relate to each other. Sharing is, after all, the reason for Creation. Nothing real can be increased except by sharing.

The body is a limitation on any spiritual value; love included. "The body is a tiny fence around a little part of a glorious and complete idea. It draws a circle, infinitely small, around a very little segment of Heaven, splintered from the whole, proclaiming that within it is your kingdom, where God can enter not." (65) As Jesus did while living on earth, so we can do by maintaining our spiritual awareness. Obviously, our physical life experience makes it difficult but a change of mind is possible. Truth is all that matters! "Narrow is the way which leads to life, and few there be that find it." (Matthew 7: 14) Only in the physical mode do we compare alternatives and options, accept the existence of dichotomies and claim enlightenment. Outside of physicality, any statement is either true or not true.

Since spiritual and physical cannot be combined, we are in a situation where we have to separate them. The problem is that we cannot claim to be bodies because we are not, and we cannot claim to be spiritual because we are not aware of it. Because we combine the two, we finished confused in the troubled world we have now. For as long as we are confused about our nature, we will be confused about our values.

The first man, that might as well be the first group of men, lived in the heavenly place called the Garden of Eden where he communicated directly with God. He had three sons: Cain, Abel, and later Seth. We notice in Genesis 4: 17 that "Cain knew his wife" at a time when the only humans mentioned in the Bible were his parents and his two brothers. Obviously, in the Garden of Eden there was also a woman who became Cain's wife. She must have had a family from where she came. There also had been another family whose daughter became Seth's wife. Adam and Eve's story is, as a matter of fact, the story of all humans. We live, at least once, through the same kinds of experiences Adam and Eve had. We all chose at one time or another, to follow our curiosity rather than God's advice and, we all find ourselves in the same alternative world. Adam's story is the illustration of what physical choices mean. Adam marked the moment when humans adopted the mentality that made us those we are now. He passed around his ways of understanding life, of judging good and evil that, once adopted by the others, launched the "Age of Ignorance" we still haven't been able to shake-off. No one was created evil and no one is meant to judge the others. Adam's opinionated judgment broke the love and respect for his brothers, introduced separation among people, created the addictive feeling of self-righteousness and the sense of specialness. We ourselves introduced norms, laws, and restrictions. We created rules of right behavior and a hierarchy of valor. So, the harmony of Heaven was lost and love got interpreted as what we have today: judgmental, selfish, special and so forth.

Adam's son, Cain, seems to be the first follower of his father's judgment of good and evil. He became jealous of his brother for receiving a higher recognition from God and decided to kill him. His judgment was overrun by his emotions. Once you let your emotions control your thinking, you create a precedent that degrades your judgment for a long time to come. Cain chose to proudly hold high his anger and killed his innocent brother. His emotions made him stray from truth; he felt victorious.

This is the first time the Bible mentions sin. "Sin is at the door" of wisdom. For this reason, protect your wisdom by keeping the door to convenient alternatives closed. Those uncontrollable self-satisfying emotions that do not improve anything, hold one dependent on them: if one lets sin in, "thou shalt rule over him." Those emotions are the works of one's ego. Ego is not interested in truth. It is only interested in making you feel better. It creates a favorable perception without improving anything. No one handles the door that can allow sin in but you, the door's owner.

The First Couple seemlessly changed the awareness of the Garden of Eden to the awareness of the similar physical place called Mesopotamia and considered it their own turf. By losing his innocence, Adam could not see the beauty of Eden any longer and started to live as he saw fit. In this physical place of their choice, people could make their own rules, live as they wanted, judge good and evil and feel in charge. Once independent, they started to pass judgments, lost their innocent love for their neighbors and each minded his own business. We may assume they got along as they do today. Adam did not admit his mistake of disregarding God's advice and he pushed the awareness of who he is and of what he did somewhere into his sub-consciousness; as far back as he could. He was non apologetic and self-righteous: he preferred to live by his own decisions. Inspired by the discovery of good and evil, he and his followers stepped into a dream of their own making. They enacted their own opinions, started to till the land, raise their own food and the Garden of Eden became a parallel world where we live today, we call it Mesopotamia, and consider it real. We are who we want to be! In addition to the man called Adam, God created other persons who, when Adam ate from the forbidden fruit said: "behold, man is become as one of us." (Genesis 3:22) This suggests that God's kingdom was already populated at the time by people that already partook from the tree of Knowledge of Good and Evil without succumbing to the kinds of temptations that sidetracked Adam and Eve. These others also became aware of "good and evil" and of the infinite choices available but, didn't lose sight of what is good for them.

1.

THE KNOWLEDGE OF GOOD AND EVIL

In the Garden of Eden, Adam chose to partake from the forbidden Tree of Knowledge of Good and Evil against his Father's advice: "Of every tree of the garden thou mayest freely eat; but of the tree of the knowledge of good an evil, thou shalt not eat of it; for in the day that thou eatest thereof thou shalt surely die." This means the adoption of his new way of living: material (physical), clear independence, physical detachment from God's and humans' interference and, of course, being subjected to aging and ultimately death. God's creation being eternal, human death means the disappearance of his physical image but not of his existence. Adam's appearance changed from ethereal to physical, as desired. He wanted to be different, independent and self-sufficient; and so he did. We don't know if he enjoyed his decision or not. He no longer had to simply pick fruits that had been provided. He had to cultivate them. His access to food and goods required work in this new kind of life. Also, his relationship with the other people took a different approach. People surely make mistakes when they assume they know. Adam could easily get confused by the maze of the "Knowledge of Good and Evil" that suddenly opened up to him. He suddenly found himself in the physical world where everything rested on his shoulders including the consequences. Opinions are personal and, usually, satisfying interpretations of truth. But, truth is too overwhelming for inexperienced people like Adam and other materialists like Karl Marx, I. V. Stalin in Russia and Nicolae Ceausescu in Romania who ran as fast as they could to fulfill their chance for "leadership" that communism suddenly offered in their countries. Private opinions, particularly those offered to inexperienced leaders, are real ticking time bombs. If somehow they get in control of what they thought they knew, their control usually collapses due to their ignorant excitement, combined with their pride, of the victorious ways that propelled them to leadership. It helped that their Communist movement, was the deepest sink-hole into physicality. In the middle of war shortages, destruction and confusion, such a simple and promising idea like communism seemed like a major discovery. Many thought that this new economic system may be the final answer to the world-wide economic inequalities and crises. It was the right time for a reevaluation of how our world works and an opportunity for the white middle class to finally take the lead they always wanted.

Physicality offered the physical solution of monetary distribution across society for preventing poverty.

Simple! But, simplicity is good for advertising but not for success. The biggest problem was that serious thinkers had been purposely avoided. Serious thinking must be included to implement any solution for its success. Communism left the process of building a new life in the hands of the working class. And, the working class didn't have a good answer. "Comrade doctor," a communist official who also was my patient, said during a friendly chat, "I don't know what is wrong with you intellectuals. Our communist policies are so simple and still you make it so complicated. Where there is a group of intellectuals, there is popping up all kinds of other ideas." For heaven's sake, where did he expect ideas to come from? Since I was intending to emigrate from our Romanian heaven of simplemindedness, I avoided the answer. Creating effective policies is the crux of the matter. And, the working class didn't see the complexity of leading the country. They relied on simple instinctive solutions encouraged by our massive and "progressive" "political education" program. Karl Marx, who had a legal license, was unable to effectively interact with people and had a hard life of being unemployed. Communist ideas were not new. They had been circulating around for some time. Marx only offered it a pseudo-scientific appearance: the world had developed throughout history with revolutions that replaced one social system with a new and more efficient one. This is what happened when unmotivated slave laborers were replaced with more productive paid laborers and later, advanced from agriculture as the main way of survival to industries. From Marx's perspective, the "time" was ripe to move from private industries to communal industries run by the "majority". Who is doing the creation of new technologies now? The community? Industries had been developed by intelligent people who invented technologies and procedures. During World War II, capitalism, under the stress of winning the war, supplied the primitive Russian industries with new technologies that allowed them to win the war. Their victory created the illusion that Russian communism may be a good idea. But, creativity requires freedom, while communism is anything but. In the middle of the excitement of winning the war, it was misunderstood that the communist victory was not a political development but a political accident that turned into an economic nightmare. A communist country is led by one supreme leader who is politically selected but not democratically elected. Historical characters like I. V. Stalin, Nicolae Ceausescu and others, ran highly publicized and politically preconceived "elections". Unfortunately, the communist idea of election became a disaster. Sin draws its motivation from ego; not from truth. If we don't accuse, we don't have a reason to fight. So, communist leaders fought fiercely to safeguard their leadership and got what they deserved: communism. Communist leaders fighting for their recognition find useful this idea of judging their political opponents as evil. Only our perception as bodies can justify this line of thinking. Spiritually, the idea of evil has no value. God didn't create any negative entity that needs to be identified. Physicality instead, does; the enemies of the "righteous" ones are evil. So, evil should be simply eliminated. We only need to know what makes life successful, avoid misjudgments and mistakes. It seems, the "Tree of Knowledge of Good and Evil" was placed in the Garden of Eden to allow us to see what the alternatives to truth do. "Know the truth and the truth shall set you free"! (John 8: 32) Yes, but under so much confusion, we failed to see the truth. While truth is love, accusing others is not. Accusations provide a false sense of self-satisfaction that can be confused for wisdom. Again, God created knowledge and not choices. Only physicality is interested in the glory of separation, criticism, abuse and personal victory God offers certainty only.

Good and evil are a consequence of physicality's need to evaluate people. Because life is created to fulfill a high purpose, the judgement of good and evil is not a fair practice; it is ego's way of doing business, of avoiding responsibilities and claiming specialness, wealth and convenient explanations. This is our world of separate beings that practice a new way of living, as it fits one's physical desires. The introduction of judgment created in our materialistic culture has some unexpected effects:

First. If we judge each other of good and evil, we cannot love as God sees it: "Thou shalt love thy neighbor as thyself." (Mark 12: 31) It is impossible to equally love one's "evil" neighbor. We love selectively those whom we find worthy to love. Judging another means that we all have not been created equal; and heaven then, may not be accessible.

Second. Judging each other is not a human prerogative. For reasons of competence, judging belongs to God and not to His inexperienced son. Humans cannot know all details of a case, all circumstances and all consequences of their "judgement". Also, we cannot anticipate the negative effects of uncalled-for criticism. The only One who has full knowledge and fairness, is God. His abilities prevent Him from errors and regrets. Besides, if we all are created perfect and, of equal value, there is nothing to criticize. If so, why do we judge anyone else?

Third. The judgment of good and evil is harmful for the one who judges, too. Jesus' advice is to "Lay down the cruel sword of judgment that you hold against your throat, and put aside the withering assaults with which you seek to hide your holiness." (66) Judgment piles negative thoughts on the mind of the one who judges. By perceiving one as guilty, the judge perceives himself guilty also. He didn't do what the one being judged did but, because he easily understands the mental dynamics of the other, his innocence is tarnished. He sees himself as if he can do the same. If one accesses another's thoughts, he is contaminated by the other's reasons. Notice the breaking of the law by law defenders and, the breaking of the rules of a company by a company's employee hired to protect those rules. They know how to abuse their powers and, they are tempted to do so.

In addition, if there are any mistakes in one's judgment, his mistakes bring regrets that needlessly burden the mind of the one that judges. So, "Why do you judge your brother?" . . . "for we shall all stand before God's judgment seat." (Romans 14:10) God is the only one qualified to judge and the only one in charge. Otherwise, if you try to take His job, besides trying to unduly limit your Father, you confuse your judgment with wisdom, totally unaware that you have no consistent criteria to determine what's good and what's bad. People are not our creation and, not our responsibility.

In the Book of Enoch, those angels that came down to earth to enjoy "iniquity with the daughters of man", brought with them the knowledge of "all kinds of sin" and of metal technologies among other things. After they begot "thousands of children", they desired to return to Heaven but they could not. They had been contaminated by the physical mentality on earth. Their minds could not fit any longer the place of purity they abandoned. They evicted themselves by being touched by the alternative judgment of good and evil.

Fourth. For God, evil is a nonentity. He didn't create it. Evil's purpose is to justify one's desire to hold someone else responsible for his own selfish thoughts. Apostle Paul said: "God has shown me that I should not call any man impure or unclean." (Acts 10:28)

Fifth. By judging, Adam and Eve certified the destructive concept of guilt. As a matter of fact, the one considered evil is not evil nor guilty. Sure, people make mistakes. But those mistakes require correction and not accusations. Accusations require punishment and punishment is the confirmation of guilt. Again, God is not a punisher. He offers correction through learning from life's experiences. This temporary physical life is our creation where we decide what we should and shouldn't do. But, if one's sinful thoughts are corrected, he is not guilty any longer. In this situation, where is the sin??? God forgives our fantasy of sin as one forgives a bad dream. He created us perfect, sees us perfect and we are perfect. For this reason, sin and guilt don't exist.

Sixth. Being judged of good or evil makes a human uncomfortable and makes one look around for others to whom he can project his mistakes. If one makes a mistake, one assures himself that likewise anyone can do the same and "he probably does". Passing around the thought of sin is ineffective but appealing. It helps us feel clean while we are not so.

Seventh. Judgment of good and evil introduced the concept of dualities and dualities are a human concept. As mentioned, God's statements are singular, definite and true. God's words are meaningful and, for Him, evil is nonexistent.

Eighth. By judging others, one avoids introspection. Once the other is found guilty, he cannot be forgiven because the judgement of good and evil came to a conclusion that separates the winner from the looser. Judgments give us the right to categorize others and, create a scale of worthiness among equals that doesn't exist. God didn't create it.

Ninth. By judging good and evil, we separate those meant to be loved from those that don't. The separation between those we love and those we don't is possible only in the physical world. Only on earth we sharply divide our judgement between good and evil. This means that our way of judging is not universally valid and consequently, cannot be true.

See the perfection in another and, you will see the perfection in yourself.

Tenth. The expression of one's guilt lays in his condemnation by another (67). All of us are recycling among ourselves the same thoughts and feelings. If we focus on somebody else's negative thoughts, we understand him and our minds become contaminated by negativity. Even if temporary, thoughts carry weight and responsibility. "Anyone who hates his brother is a murderer." (1 John 3: 15) It is a mistake to judge others. No one can be hated unless, seen (judged) guilty. If we judge another guilty then we judge ourselves guilty too, for recycling his perceived thoughts of guilt in our own minds. Even if not physically implemented, a thought you adopted becomes part of you for a while. This kind of dynamic, makes physicality the lair of sins. Guilt affects your thoughts and your thoughts are the only things that can defile you. God asked Adam and Eve not to eat from the Tree of Knowledge of Good and Evil for their own good. "Judge not, that ye be not judged. For with what judgment ye judge, ye shall be judged" (Matthew 7: 1, 2).

Eleventh. Judging others as evil makes the world appear as a dark place; darkened by people's own judgments. As humanity expands and the projection of guilt becomes a wider practice, the whole world will seem to appear dark. Remember: "By one man's disobedience many were made sinners." (Romans 5: 19)

Twelfth. By setting laws to judge by, we downgrade ourselves from Sons of God to servants of the law. As sons we are free and allowed to create and enjoy the son's rights while as servants we are bound by external rules and laws created by ourselves. Jesus is quoted in the Gospel of Mary: "Do not lay down any rules other than what I have given you, and do not establish law, as the lawgiver did, or you will be bound by it." Our laws are not the will of God but, the will of man. God's law of love, which is the same as truth, is an internal law written in our identity.

Thirteenth. Judging good and evil violates God's unity. Love and wisdom are the only powers that unite us.

Fourteenth. Judging others justifies the physical concept of inequality and specialness. Our desire to be special justifies our desire to have more possessions and of taking advantage of others. But, people are of equal value. "Specialness is the idea of sin made real." (68) and, "sin is lack of love" (69). Specialness is not a compliment and neither is it a Divine privilege.

Fifteenth. Judging good and evil doesn't include forgiveness and forgiveness is the only precondition for love. Therefore, judgment of good and evil is not fair.

Sixteenth. By introducing the judgment of good and evil in our lives, we trapped ourselves in this physical world. On earth, we cannot be seen good because we commit sins; so, we must have evil traits. If evil, we are set for a physical life with no hope to see Heaven. Consequently, some believe in their own physical haven. For as long as we believe in sin, we cannot believe in love. "If you are sin, you lock the mind within the body, and give its purpose to its prison house, which acts instead of it." (70) As crafty as people are, we figured out that we can create a mentality that makes us feel sinless without upgrading anything. We think we only have to change our opinion about sin. The architect of this opinion is our faithful way of thinking called ego. Ego's only role is to protect our image from negative associations. It can transfer your perception of guilt to someone else. It provides subjective explanations, excuses, projection of personal guilt to another and imagines a deceiving evil outside of us. The most absurd tactic of all: requires the atoning sacrifice of an innocent other on our behalf. All this takes place in a way that doesn't inconvenience the creators of ego. No learning, no correction, no self-evaluation, no growth, are required. Also, no mercy and no love are involved. Just believe that you did the "right" thing, whatever that may be.

Seventeenth. The concept of evil requires pay offs; this is an aggression. Judgment of good and evil, as mentioned, not only attests to the reality of evil, it attributes this evil to someone else which raises the need for a defense against him. The absurdity of this thought is that the "others" are innocent people to whom we have projected our flaws. This way, we deny to ourselves the access to happiness.

What makes ego wildly acceptable, almost untouchable, is the fact that it doesn't require any effort on our part; it doesn't change anything, except our perspective. This way, sin is not denied; it is motivated and eventually overlooked. Once one incorporates ego into his thinking system, suddenly, he sees the world differently from what it is. It is no longer an innocent world. It is a world of independent sinners; a parallel to the Original Couple's decision, made long ago, to avoid, justify and display their mistakes rather than to acknowledge them in themselves and correct them. Ego created the idea of judging others of good and evil and hold them responsible. This fictitious separation between one and his sins is ego's job fulfilled through explanations, dismissal, accusations....

"By one man's disobedience many were made sinners." (Romans5: 19) That man was the trend setter. The introduction of sin into our thinking was cautioned by God in His exchange with Cain: "if thou doest not well, sin lieth at the door. And unto thee shall be his desire, and thou shalt rule over him." (Genesis 4: 7) Instead of realizing that his performance was of low quality, Cain became angry for his brother's better performance. He allowed his emotions to overcome his thoughts "and [his emotions] ruled over him." Once one feels the satisfying effects of self-gratifying emotions, he will never let them go. This is the victory of emotion over reasoning and of opinion over truth. Cain didn't expect that with this kind of "victory", he is losing his innocence and, bringing his own worth down. He never even cared! And, the sinful thought that "rule over him", changed the world.

Eighteen. If judged guilty, one's sin is confirmed. For Jesus instead, sin is "a strictly individual perception, seen in the other yet believed by each to be within himself." (70) In other words, "Sin does not exist" (71) independently. It is a perception, a vanishing thought available to anyone interested. Why be interested? To justify some personal opinions, to prove yourself right, to create reasons to exist, to be in control of your opinions, ... this is life! Since we like the comfort of doing nothing we, instead of going through removing the undesirable thoughts, would rather transfer them to another who is unaware and we assume to be a suitable candidate. In more important cases, if we imagine sin to be a foreign intervention, we may deny our responsibility of dealing with it and transfer this duty to God. Then, we depend on the church for help and the church depends on us for relevance. This way, both we and the church are winners: the church wins importance and we win the comfort of "innocence". Nevertheless, sin is the center point of the Abrahamic religions. "A major tenet in the ego's insane religion is that sin is not error but truth" (72). If sin is an error, it is easy to be eliminated through one's correction of his thoughts. If so, it is under the control of mind's owner and, it is our duty to deal with it. Nevertheless, if we try to transfer the thought of sin, we deceive ourselves: we blame God for miss-creation, become unable to believe in Him and, we are lost in space. If somehow one may assume it's appropriate to punish the sinner, one contradicts the very meaning of Creation as a perfect act. It remains to conclude that we should accept responsibility and correct our judgment. But, do we?

Nineteen. Judging others has the negative effect of stimulating our emotions in counterproductive ways. Those excitements become the, "open door" to subjective interpretations of reality. The emotions become people's unreal reality that deceive and ruin their awareness of holiness. Emotions that replace wisdom are the downfall of democracy. Excite the mob, and you win… an assumed importance.

Twenty. Judgment of good and evil is a strait jacket while at the same time God gave us the wide freedom of choice. On earth nothing is either black or white but a wide variety of shades of gray. Gray, by not being white or black, is not truth. Life becomes a swimming pool filled with illusions. We still accept our judgement as being almost white, as all our thoughts are, and we consider it acceptable. How dire! It only made us accept compromises that are common ways for our "normal" life. Our physical experience is therefore a failure. We all live Adam's experience!

"Because strait is the gate, and narrow is the way which leadeth unto life, few there be that find it." (Matthew 7: 14) The access to Heaven is not a matter of divine mercy, but a matter of a personal walk on the right path. God does not take sides.

While we make many mistakes, we are still created pure. We only wrapped ourselves in layers of misperceptions, mistakes, opinions, transgression, selfishness and errors that make us who we are. What we built on the top of our creation is a deceiving facade that is not us. We are not the ones we believe we are. We are as created. The whole life on earth is the choice of Adam and Eve in their eagerness to have the kind of independence they wanted. It is up to each one of us to return to whom we are. Since you receive what you give (73), forgive your brothers' mistakes and, abandon the damaging judgment of good and evil. Reconnect with your brothers. If you don't forgive them, you cannot love them and you cannot apply to yourself the only law Jesus left to us: "love your brother as you love yourself and love God with all your heart, all your mind and all your soul." This is the proverbial narrow road to perfection. To love your brothers means to love the Creation and the One who created it. To love God means to love everyone, you included; everything is love. We all are of God and consequently, part of Him. By loving us, we love Him.

Only our minds can restore our awareness of Heaven. See the beauty in your brothers/sisters and you will see the beauty of the whole creation. One is what he thinks. By accusing another, we finish accusing everybody, ourselves included. Seeing evil, degrades us into isolation, selfishness, hate and claims of unjustified specialness backed by self-righteousness.

One can only correct his own thinking. So, one's own mind is the answer to humanity's fulfilment of joy. "For I have given you an example, that ye should do as I have done to you." (John13: 15) Only by correcting our judgment can we return to the perfection we are. Jesus didn't come to atone; he came to teach us how to atone.

Judgment is a dishonest act of pointing fingers that follows a dishonest thought of evilness. In any condemnation of another lies the conviction of your own guilt (74).

According to the Church teachings, sin being the cause, its effect is our demise. (Romans 6:23) From here comes our belief in the existence of time. So, we will depart from this earth hoping to leave all this mess of pain, frustration, sickness and war behind for others to pick up and, enjoy. As a matter of fact, "In death is sin preserved, and those who think they are sinful must die for what they think they are." (75) We don't trust what we don't know. If we don't fully trust Him, we are bound to trust what we think. And, what we think is off the mark. Perfection is indestructible. "God is all in all in a very literal sense." (76) We are created by Him and are part of Him. (77) We are the Sonship that completes the Trinity. In order to fit the place reserved for us, we have to return to our perfect self and enjoy its rewards. The universe is ours.

It is interesting that in our physical understanding of the world, every occurrence has a cause or it doesn't exist. But then, what is the cause of love? Love simply exists as we simply exist, for no cause. That means that we come from outside of space and time, where no cause and effect rules exists. We come from the thought of God. The non-physical manifestations have no cause. Thoughts are desires of our minds that manifest as desired. Abstract realities exist outside of physicality. Physicality works according to the Newtonian physical laws, while spirituality works according to quantum physics. We live in two different fields: the field of cause and effect and the field of instantaneous mind travel which is the realm of possibilities. Again, possibilities have no cause. In the domain of potentiality, "no signal is needed for communication; everything is instantaneously interconnected. By contrast, in space and time, signals, always moving with a speed no greater than the speed of light, mediate communication which always occurs in finite time." (78) "The domain of potentiality is our higher consciousness in which we all are one. The higher One consciousness is empowered by Downward causation, to choose among the many facets of a wave of possibility." "It is conscious choice that transforms waves of possibility into particles of actuality." (79) It seems that conscious attention selects its physical manifestation. The transition from wave of energy to particles is seamless, instantaneous and takes place the moment it is observed. Also seamless is our transformation from spiritual existence to the physical awareness as Adam and his group subconsciously decided to do so. This transformation is reversible, once we return to our original, spiritual condition. This transformation, takes place in both directions, instantaneously. This shift is a choice, taken at a certain level of consciousness, above and beyond physical access. This possibility shows that Adam was not expelled from the Garden of Eden. He simply made a conscious choice of having a different way of living, a decision honored by God. Since then, we experience consequences. His change of mind from eternity to the awareness of space and time, changed the way of perceiving our existence of adopting different values and living different outcomes. Spirituality became a distant memory; a dream that doesn't fit our physical choices.

God does everything perfectly, better than we can do. This is why He doesn't delegate his works. He wants us to discover and teach the truth because this process is beneficial to all involved. Trust Jesus, who subjected Himself to physical abuse in order to prove to us the nothingness of physical bodies and the permanence of our spiritual selves. See where He put His trust, with no hesitation! Albert Einstein concluded one time: "Imagination is more important than knowledge." Knowledge works within our physical limits. Imagination penetrates the infinite.

Enoch's fallen angels, according to the Book of Enoch, brought with them to earth the freedom of enjoying whatever the physicality may offer. This is the atheistic paradise, but, to what avail? In the end, this physical "reality" didn't matter any longer and those fallen angels wanted to return to the ideal place they left. Happiness comes from love and truth, neither one being of a material nature and neither one is the result of knowledge of good and evil. Divine qualities can be enhanced only by sharing them.

2.

Salvation Is Escape From Guilt

The Garden of Eden was a place of unity between God and man until Adam and Eve decided to go their own way and rely on their own decisions. This act was their declaration of independence and their mental distancing from their divine family. No more guidance and questions! People started to evaluate each other according to their usefulness, physical needs and abilities but, all physical considerations are inconsequential for the spiritual side of life even if essential for our physical side. Physically, one depends on his environment while spiritually, one's environment depends on him. Physical resources are limited and require skills and hard work to get what's needed. The spiritual world is different; it freely offers everything. We only need awareness. One's spiritual living means independence from physical possessions and dedication to knowledge and creativity in perfect harmony. The only concern one has is to maintain his clear-mind, as given to him/her at inception. This means to base our lives on love, truth and creativity, with no contests. On earth, the concept of love and truth seem related to physical needs, and lose their abstract purity. They become for us unavoidable parts of life. Human interaction becomes a form of collaboration enhanced by our practice to refer to another some of our concerns. The observation that, "You never hate your brother for his sins, but only for your own." (81) appears accurate.

The world we see is the only world we know. Physically we compete for goods and feel successful when we get them. Spiritually, there is nothing to compete for. There, everything is available to everyone and we can fully enjoy everything that is. Jesus healed and made food appear when needed.

The difference between the spiritual world and the world in which the Original Couple died is the difference between being and having and between truth and opinions. Jesus disclosed this sharp difference when he said: "give to Caesar what belongs to Caesar and to God, what belongs to God" (Mathew 22: 21) Give to Caesar the due physical things (the tax) and to God the due metaphysical love. Physicality separates people, makes them self-centered, pursue having and avoid giving. Separated humans can freely judge, interpret, accuse, and take advantage of each other. Judgment of good and evil introduced the concept of sin and the feeling of guilt. If sin exists then the ensuing guilt must exist as well.

What the Tree of Good and Evil offered was the awareness of infinite alternatives to the singular Truth. After partaking from the fruit of that forbidden tree, the Original Couple, tempted and confused, tried to conceal themselves "amongst the trees of the garden." They felt guilty and the guilt diminished their confidence. As told, sin started to kill them: if you eat of it, "thou shalt surely die". (Genesis 2: 17) "And the Lord God called unto Adam, and said unto him, where are you? And he said, I heard thy voice in the Garden, and I was afraid, because I was naked; and I hid myself." Adam was naked before and it never bothered him or God. But now, his cover of holiness had slipped away. "And He said, who told thee that thou wast naked? Hast thou eaten of the tree, whereof I commanded thee that thou shouldest not eat? And the man said, The woman whom thou gavest to be with me, she gave me of the tree, and I did eat. And the lord God said unto the woman, What is this that thou hast done? And the woman said, The serpent beguiled me, and I did eat." (Gen 3: 9 – 12) When asked by God, Adam tried to project his guilt of disobedience in two different directions: to Eve, who gave him the forbidden fruit to partake, and to God, who gave him Eve as a companion. Eve, in her turn, projected her guilt to the serpent; the early symbol of Satan. Those explanations were pointing to the origin of sin outside of themselves; so that they could claim innocence. Regardless of their reasonings, the guilt stood where it had been produced. Both Adam and Eve felt responsible and tried to hide themselves behind the trees. Thus, a vicious circle started to spin and it is still spinning today: by feeling guilty, one blames himself and, by blaming himself he feels guilty again. Then, the one feeling guilty, tries to shake off his guilt by projecting it onto others. Regardless, the guilt belongs to the guilty. The guilty ones may try again to defer their guilt only to have it returned back to them. From here a full world of accusations started to roll.

Instead of recanting and stopping their slide, Adam and Eve allowed themselves to be carried away by their misplaced sense of pride and accused those around them. Each such judgment was another step further away from their Father and another step toward humanness. If God is life, the alternative to Him must be death. "In the day that thou eatest thereof thou shalt surely die," God warned them. The Bible claims God said: one day is like a thousand days and a thousand days is like one day. God allowed Adam time to fully experience his physical choice of living. Interestingly, Adan lived a thousand years. This death is not a curse, but the consequence of the Original Couple's foolishness. Their death is not their disappearance either. They are as eternal as their Father is. Death is only the disappearance of their physical fantasy.

What is generally understood as being an expulsion from the Garden of Eden was, as a matter of fact, an understanding gap that opened-up between God and those children of His who shared Adam's physical choices. Their new garden, called Mesopotamia, is the place where our recorded history began. "The Lord sent him forth from the Garden of Eden" was, as a matter of fact, the man's change of life. Physicality comes with its own values attached that put life in a different perspective. Adam's whole life became different. He got his colorful opinions, his new understanding of truth and his new knowledge of good and evil. With this new understanding came a different kind of life. Among other things, human harmony collapsed. Lack of harmony created guilt and guilt creates fear; a new feeling in Adam and Eve's arsenal. Fear made them withdraw within themselves and raise selfishness to their defense. Feeling fearful, one takes some defensive precautions, loses some of his freedom and changes his understanding of love into something which borrows only some elements of real love. One even imagines a guilty entity outside of himself called devil: a thought, not a being. Adam's thought of devil, "died" when Adam "died" (God could not create an opposing force). But, the idea of devil had been found useful by others who borrowed it from one generation after another and it is still used. Devil will linger around for as long as the humans find this concept to be a useful escape goat. Because Satan, known as devil, is seen by many as an entity outside of us, apparently immune to human rejection, the humans assume it is God's responsibility to deal with it.

By accusing others, humans created another novelty: the separation of those that were meant to work as a unit in perfect harmony. This unnatural separation due to accusations, implies guilt once again. Separation is weakening the unity of Creation and raises and spreads the thought of guilt. Among other things, the guilt projected on others allows men to further convince themselves of how firm and insightful they are because they can think differently than God does: He doesn't believe in guilt while we do. While God created us all equal, some sons discovered that they are better than others and special. In the process, they dismiss the fact that when God created us, He gave to all of us small parts of His own mind to use. Those parts are of equal value. So, the differences between us are due to our different choices and not to different creations. But, ego does not endorse the existence of God. It suggests that our minds have different levels of development. Again, human mind is not the product of our physical nature and is not the product of physical evolution. The brain is. Because each one of us thinks with God's mind, explains why we so easily understand each other's thoughts and emotions and why He knows everything we all think and feel better than we know ourselves. We all share His mind. The common source of all minds allows us to work as a unit even if physically separated. As a unit of equally well-built fellows, we freely communicate and communication is a wise mechanism to upgrade what is already perfect: the creation. If, instead, we get physically separated our communication is scant and our union is deteriorated by selfish concerns; we cannot fully exchange a wide diversity of thoughts, cannot fully love and our mentality deteriorates due to recycling old personal thoughts stored by our brains. This continuing decision to remain separated is the only possible reason for the life we have now.

If anybody asks himself: what is the big problem with biting from a fruit one was told not to touch? The answer is: guilt. Feeling guilty, one sees the others guilty as well and this opinion further enhances separation and all its consequences. Separation brings a person to a tough and lonely alternative that can create selfishness. So, we built for ourselves other vicious circles: as guilt causes separation, separation causes guilt and one tumbles into specialness, elitism, abuse, conflict, selfishness, fear, projection ....

"God created beings who individually have everything, with the intention to share their happy thoughts and to increase their joy. Nothing real can be increased except by sharing. That is God's reason of creating you. Divine Abstraction takes joy in sharing. That is what creation means." (82) Obviously, our new physical identity created new kinds of demands and our new reality of inequality, isolation and confusion about our nature and meaning. Our highest duty we assumed and misused is to judge good and evil.

Spiritually, the future doesn't exist. God didn't create time. He lives in eternity that can be imagined as permanent sequences of the present. Time is used to understand the physical passage from birth to death, from sin to punishment and for understanding the future as a consequence of past deeds. This sequencing depends on seeing time as a one-dimensional mover from past towards the future. God is aware of our concept of time but He is outside of it. He can freely and instantaneously travel between past and future. Eternity includes time but time cannot include eternity. Time's relativity makes the concept of atonement possible through erasing one's past mistakes. The past is basically a dumping ground of all negativity, thus allowing anyone to renounce his mistaken judgements and live a clean life. This constant resetting should not be regarded as a divine favor or a divine mercy. Mercy is exceptionalism; it contradicts God's system and, consequently, it can only be a human assumption. Asking God for mercy is nonsense! God works in an organized way that cannot include exceptions. Exceptions are human assumptions that never materialize. We should atone for our mistakes instead of asking for forgiveness. Atonement is the willing return of one's mind to the flawlessness of his creation. One's return to his awareness of perfection is not a Divine favor, but the way life is set to work; it is the truth. The sacrificial atonement is a need that only a mistaken person can have . Also, physical sacrifice cannot pay for a non-physical error!

Once we adopted the concept of time, we locked ourselves in a "reasonable" chain of events. We see the need for future reparations for damages we did in the past. While we see the need for reparations, God sees the need for correction (atonement). The reparations cannot reverse the damage done and cannot compensate for it. The past is gone! Leave your load of mistakes in the past and live an honest life now. This is the only correction you need. "God is not angry." (83) "He holds nothing against anyone." (84) "God established no sacrifice," (85). Through correction done in the present, one's misjudgments are eliminated and his honor is reestablished. Realize that God trusts you so much that He gave you custody of your brothers so you can project on them your holy perfection: if you are holy, you see your brothers holy. Those "whom God has given you to save are but everyone you meet or look upon, not knowing who they are, all those you saw an instant and forgot, those you knew a long while since, and those you will yet meet, the unremembered and the not yet born. For God has given you His Son to save from every concept that he ever held." (86) Saving them means to see them all as pure as created, not fooled by personal and passing opinions disconnected from reality. By seeing the others as being pure, you save yourself. You and they are built equally well; if you see them well, you are well. Thus, we are all saved from the illusions of imperfection and sin. Each one of us has the messianic role of saving his brothers by seeing the perfection in them. Truth excludes guilt. We all make mistakes, but the mistakes are not who we are. Mistakes are removable; we are not.

The fabricated idea of one-dimensional time, among other things, doesn't allow one to understand eternity. Guilt introduced the perception of future consequences of past actions which suggests that eternity casts you in one place and one condition forever. Meanwhile, eternity simply allows you to be, create, interact and enjoy life in peace and freedom without getting old and sick. Eternity is not stagnation in an eternal now; it is the exposure to limitless possibilities. God is living outside of time. Time applies only to human thinking, born from the physical concept of cause and effect. "Truth takes no part in all the mad projections by which this world was made." (87) "Truth is God's Will" (88)

Our concept of time is a quirk in our idea of physicality. It supports our assumption that God decides our purpose, our quality, our deeds and our lifespan. We often believe that each one's life is predestined and elected for certain functions. Meanwhile, God doesn't ask us to do anything for Him. All we must do is for our betterment. If predetermined, we cannot have freedom of choice, there's no opportunity to learn and grow and no forgiveness. The confusion about predestination comes from our assumption that God knows what the future holds for us. He knows it because He knows us. He also knows that if we change our mind, we change the outcome and He doesn't interfere in our decisions. We must experience the consequences of our thoughts or we will never learn the truth.

Guilt, the consequence of thinking evil, ruins one's life. If you accept your guiltlessness instead, you learn that past has never been more than a dream and that future is needless. (89) You never sinned because you are not created a sinner and because all your mistaken decisions had been made while in a state of confusion that is not You. Sin is your inconsequential dream that can only be imagined. To atone for our past "sins" means to abandon them to the past, and freely enjoy the life we have. Atonement is our self-realization of our divine nature. When holy, we have no unsatisfied needs haunting us.

The proper answer to our idea of sin is not its dismissal, but the dismissal of the thinking that created it; so that we would not do the same mistake again. Satan cannot be, because God didn't create such a thing. "What is opposed to God, does not exist." (90) Only humans think in terms of opposites. There is only one way that guides one to perfection: God's way, the dismissal of imperfection. Obviously, the consequence of imperfection is guilt. Guilt is something we cannot easily accept as originating in our thoughts; only our thoughts can imagine it. We consequently imagined several convoluted ways to disconnect from guilt:

1. It is not me who sinned but the others. I got caught in their ways. It's a crazy world out there.
2. It is not me, but the devil with its deceiving influences that mess-up things.
3. If I have any part in this sin, I paid amends, confessed and asked for mercy and forgiveness.
4. God offered his Only Son as an atoning sacrifice for the forgiveness of sins, forever.

In all these scenarios we see ourselves as being either victimized or saved by others. By believing so, we expect to be saved from the others' interference by Who else, but God. If sin is not of our making, it is not our responsibility. This is our ego's perception. The only question is: is sin true? Are we simply powerless bystanders in what happens to us? Accepting ego's tactic of avoiding responsibility is comfortable but, prevents our own growth.

This way, we condemn ourselves to being less than what we can be and, truthfully, less than what we are meant to be. We cannot go through life like a dog goes through water! If we err we should be aware of it and correct it. Our mistakes are ours's to deal with. Their projection to outside of us is of no value beyond comfort. "The purpose of projection is to get rid of guilt" but, this way one cannot get rid of the mistaken thought that produced it. This projection is a sin. If we see no need to correct our mistakes, we may consider it practical to use this tactic of guilt projection, again. Regardless of what we may believe, the truth is that for as long as we don't recognize our misjudgments and don't renounce them, we cannot access the perfect life we are created for. Truth is a straight mind, awareness and no excuses. Humans do not want to abandon their prized selfishness secured by ego and its self-righteousness. To improve our minds requires an effort. So, should we follow Jesus? With the Church's blessing, we call our interpretation of holiness, holy: Jesus came to offer his life as an atoning sacrifice! That is hard to believe. His sacrifice is another external solution for our internal problems. Jesus never claimed that he came to atone. It is we who interpret his life that way. Meanwhile, the only requirement for our salvation is the correction of our mistaken thoughts. If we don't eliminate the cause, we cannot eliminate its effect. Because we decided to stay put in our mental boxes, we cannot correct our minds and are unable to perform any of the miracles Jesus assured us that we can perform. By the way, miracle is not exceptionalism. It is the removal of the misjudgments and the illusions we accumulated on top of our pure nature. Miracles are a natural return to who we are. We cannot perform them because we moved away from our awareness of truth and stay with our opinions instead.

Guilt doesn't stop with a confession. It stops when the mistaken judgment is annulled, eliminated from our minds. Anything short of that, will steadily lead to failure. Also, projecting your sins to another with the purpose of relieving your conscience, never works. If you succeed to understand the other's mind, you can no longer transfer to him your sense of guilt because your line of transferring your opinions to him is interrupted. Then, you understand his reasons, you know that his mind doesn't allow room for your transfer of guilt. Here we find that the one who said: "to understand someone means to forgive him," makes a lot of sense: you cannot transfer your guilt to him. Then, we know that his mind is not open to our opinion. Then, you either forgive yourself and atone or, look for another recipient for your sin; someone you don't really know. In a nutshell, if you believe in guilt you see the world as we customarily see it today: delusional, fighting wars that shouldn't be, accusing each other and failing to behave like the Sons of God. Guilt makes us blind: while you see the world, you will not see the light in it. If another is a criminal, he may hate you for what he believes that he is not. If you hate him back, you have a relationship made in hell. If you believe that guilt is true, you cannot believe in God. God and guilt represent opposing values that cannot share reality. Guilt hides Christ from your sight. (91)

The happiest moments in one's life are those of a successful relationship. Tons of books have been written to the glory of those precious encounters and others about their painful dissolution. The million-dollar question is why something so beautiful can fail so miserably? The answer is, because of guilt. In our world guilt is so ubiquitous that we don't even notice it most of the time. Ego creates certain needs that we feel are important to satisfy. Those needs could be simply overspending, building a "good" image, collecting things or could be the association with a person who has the qualities one misses in himself. We choose a relationship based on the assumption that that person can provide us with what we need in order to feel more accomplished. But, there are two problems here; both related to the guilt of assuming a quality that is not yours:

First, no true relationship can rely on guilt or even hold one spot of it for that spot mars the relationship's purity. If the desired partner is seen as able to make you complete, it means that you don't see yourself as complete, thus harboring a sense of guilt. Those relationships are motivated by selfish reasons. If used for patching you up, the relationship loses its value. A proper relationship requires total commitment, which implies faith in your ability to offer guiltlessness. Of course, this kind of commitment is impossible if the one involved carries guilt. For that matter, the moment you can accuse your partner of something that may not even be in him/her, but in you, the relationship is spoiled and no longer real.

Second, love is a giving process. What you give returns to you. If you demand anything from your partner, that demand is returned to you and the relationship is ended. Projecting guilt is nothing but an attempt to get rid of it and that, as a matter-of-fact, is not possible.

The only way of getting rid of guilt is the atonement, the correction of the illusion that made you feel guilty. Your awareness of your brother's / sister's guiltlessness is the awareness of your own guiltlessness. Be sure you understand that atonement means your guiltlessness or enlightenment. Embrace the truth of your creation: sinless among sinless brothers. Sure, your brothers do crazy things but those are only misperceptions of what they may mistakenly consider to be not significant. If one considers cheating, he should know that he will win something insignificant but obvious to his senses, and, loose something not physically obvious but far more important: his integrity. God created us pure and He doesn't see us any other way despite all our missteps. Missteps can be and will be corrected and we will be back to where we truly want to be. In the end, our proper choice is too obvious to miss. Nothing is like fine quality!

Remember that by seeing another guilty, you fail the Son of God who is your guiltless brother and your equal. Your brother is your way to Heaven. If you don't see him as he truly is, you are not fair. If unfair with him, you are unfair with yourself and you both loose. The alternative is to "know the truth and the truth shall set you free." (John 8: 32) We should remember here the story of Jesus accepting to have a dinner in a tax collector's home. The apostles were confused: tax collectors had been known for dishonest practices. Jesus, instead, saw him as a perfect creation of God, who, even if incorrect for the time being, had been created holy and the holiness of his creation justifies respect. Holiness is his nature while his misdeeds are his errors. Should Jesus reject that man's offer and uphold his own superior morality? If he would do so, he would show disdain and confirm the tax collector's sin. Instead, Jesus chose to overlook the tax collector's misdeeds and honor the holiness of his nature. The tax collector knew himself. Should Jesus display proud contempt rather than love? If he would, he would enforce the belief that the tax collector is a faulty being. Jesus came on earth to save people from their own misunderstandings; not to condemn them. Any rejection is a recognition of sinfulness. In a way we all manifest a lower quality than He but, because He values the truth in us, He came to have dinner with us all and talk to us as equal to equal. He doesn't judge anyone of good and evil, He doesn't compare and doesn't accuse; He brings a spot of light.

A frequent question people have is: where is God when we suffer and need Him? Where is He when we need His help? He seems indifferent! If we believe that, we question His love and values and we feel hurt. We transfer to Him the responsibility for our errors. We use the same projection of guilt we apply to our fellow humans and to the imagined Satan. This time, we see Him guilty of indifference. Where is His love? It may be convenient to accuse Jesus, who never retaliates, but it is we who are responsible for our ways and values. Why don't we change direction? God is aware of our beliefs and ways but He doesn't interfere in our decisions out of respect for our freedom and our ability to find our way back on track. He helps us at every opportunity but He doesn't do that which we are supposed to do. If He would, He would state that we don't wave the needed awareness and dignity. This cannot be true! His creation of us is well thought. It is possible that by following their alternative ideas, some humans will fall into a psychological downward spiral from which they would be unable to recover. Then, God would have no choice but to step-in and save the day. This is what the Bible calls "The day of the Lord". Obviously, I don't know what that "day" means, but it will clean the slate.

Ever creative, people came up with a defense system for their status quo rather than grow to the task. We call this defense of self-righteousness, ego. It makes us feel right while ignorant. It interprets our idleness as the way of life. Let life follow its course. Sadly, we prefer to use the effortless and meaningless ego than to follow God's advice and rise to the challenge. In a way, this is the difference between physical and spiritual.

What we live through, is the consequence of the values we choose to live by. We get what we deserve. God doesn't take into consideration our mistaken judgments; "God answers only for eternity." He created us able to be aware of our condition and capable to correct our judgements. He even shows us the way to get back on track. Can you see any unfairness in this arrangement? Would you rather give up your divine rights as Son and be treated like a pet instead? Would you give up your dignity and ask Him to do everything for you? Some may prefer to be taken care of (the pet scenario) over reviving their given quality. God made you better than you may believe you are and He is not going to downgrade you. Time and wisdom are on His side and implicitly on ours. We will, one time or another, wake-up and finally take our due place in the Creation.

It is important to notice that God didn't punish Adam and Eve for their transgression known as the Original Sin. He doesn't punish anybody. People simply shortchanged themselves and lived the life they chose. "Your will be done, you holy child of God." (92) God openly shows us the way to return to our original quality: renounce guilt, atone our misjudgments, regain your wisdom. Our salvation is in our hands, now.

Guilt is more powerful than we assume it is. Guilt precludes relationships, precludes you to see the light of love in you, precludes your fair communication and prevents you from knowing the truth. Guilt makes you blind. For as long as you see guilt, you cannot see the light and by projecting your guilt on others, the world seems dark and shrouded in your own guilt; you cannot see God. If you believe in guilt, you see it in others. Guilt is a decision against your own happiness. For as long as you believe that guilt is justified, you will be unable to find the atonement within yourself. You must define your choice. In order to return to your original frame of mind, you must discard the thoughts that brought you down. If you see guilt as justified, atonement cannot take place. Guilt cannot be removed by a pardon. Like any convenient surrogate, the pardon only confirms someone's sin and praises the sinner for admitting it. At best, pardon pushes your guilt in the background, overlooks it but never denies its presence. And, if let in, guilt "shalt rule over him." (Genesis 4: 7) Guilt creates the delusional world in which we live.

Guilt's importance consists in the fact that it makes sure that sin is not "confused" for a mistake. The interpretation of sin as mistake is the end of guilt. Mistake is a temporary lapse that can be easily corrected with a change of mind while guilt, as we understand it, stays. Truth is that guilt can be equally dismissed and replaced with confidence, as it happens to mistakes. When you see others as guilty, then, have no doubt, you see guilt in yourself too. What you give is what you receive in return (93). You will never see the end of guilt for as long as you believe there is a reason for it. That reason, comes again, from identifying guilt through the judgment of good and evil. Nevertheless, guilt can be denied if you understand it as a transient opinion of a confused saint. Salvation is the escape from guilt through the awareness of truth. Guiltlessness is invulnerability. Guilt instead, is the consequence of sin and sin, no matter what kind, is the result of a mistaken thought. This means that it is within our ability to dispose of it through a change of mind.

Can one be forgiven because Jesus was crucified? Not likely. The idea of paying for our sins is a human transaction and not a spiritual reawakening. Atonement is strictly a personal rise of awareness, not a pay-off. The physical killing and the spiritual atonement are two different and unrelated acts, operating at two different levels. Jesus never mentioned the need for sacrifice. Spiritually, we are how we think. Physically, we believe that we are what we see. Notice that the old practice of "sacrificing" an innocent other, on the sinner's behalf, does not require self-examination, no correction of the sinner's mistaken thoughts, no concern for truth and no consideration for what the victim has to go through.

What a story! The Bible is written by humans for themselves. How can we claim personal absolution from sin through killing an innocent man? We don't even have the decency to question the thoughts that lead us to this practice. The Bible claims that we cannot correct our mentality: "For by grace are we saved through faith. Not of works," (Ephesians 2; 8&9) Doesn't this also suggests the uselessness of the work of sacrificing? Well, I do not know how they go around killing the innocent and feeling holy at the same time.

We show no recognition of the fact that God created us able and holy, "in His image". "Be ye therefore perfect, as our Father which is in heaven is perfect." (Matthew 5: 48) What we consider guilt, is a temporary confusion amid those infinite choices. The dreadful final judgment is only a review of one's life in the light of truth. It is a wakeup call: one's exposure to a reality he didn't previously consider, an experience shocking enough to make one change his life. Some of those who went through a near-death experience and got a glimpse of the "beyond", go through major changes in their lives as they reevaluate their choices. In our present condition, we cannot qualify for Heaven. We will, when we get our minds straight. We should review here Apostle Paul's story. He was convinced that Jesus and the Christians were a nuisance diverting people from Jewish orthodoxy; basically, a destructive force. Based on this belief, he persecuted Christians with conviction. But then on his way to Damascus where he knew the apostles were gathering, "suddenly a light from heaven shined on about him: and he fell to the ground, and heard a voice saying unto him, Saul,

Saul, why persecutes thou me? And he said, Who art thou, Lord? And the Lord said, I am Jesus whom thou persecutes"…"And he trembling and astonished said, Lord, what wilt thou have me to do?" (Acts, 9: 3-6) What sin can be deeper than the one against God, Jesus and the Holy Spirit? Was Saul (Paul) punished for that "sin"? No. He was made aware of his mistaken judgment and he atoned on the spot. Notice that he atoned by his own will. He changed his mind because he instantaneously understood the foolishness of his previous convictions. He renounced them and became the most effective apostle. Apostle Paul's experience had been duplicated ever since through near death experiences as documented by Dr. Bruce Greyson, Professor of Psychiatry and Neurobehavioral Sciences at the University of Virginia, in his book "After." This is what will happen at the "final judgment": no punishment and no imposed transformation; simply exposure to the truth in an undeniable way. You, like Apostle Paul and everyone else, have been created perfect and nothing short of perfection is expected from you. To believe in guilt means to deny the truth about yourself.

Guilt is the root of condemnation and condemnation is the cause of attack against another. If you see one guilty, you believe he deserves punishment. Aggression is not God's way to solve problems. He creates life for the purpose of learning through personal experience. He doesn't kill, sacrifice, abuse or revenge. In the beginning years of Christianity, some religious leaders wanted to drop the Old Testament from the Gospel because it presents God as a punishing murderer totally different from the forgiving God upheld by Jesus. Who better knows the Father, than His holy Son?

Because guilt is a human emotion, it cannot be a Divine reality. Any thought that conflicts with God's creation is not real because outside of God there is nothing. "Father judges no one," (John 5:22) implies that your confession of sin is an aberration whose only value is a wakeup call for change but is, obviously, not the change itself. Change is one's personal responsibility. All that matters is your straight mindedness.

Guilt starts with you and ends with you. Guilt is one's attempt to separate himself from his brothers. Again, one does counterproductive things due to selfishness and ignorance but both selfishness and ignorance are the product of one's opinions that do not reflect his nature. One's nature is the will of God while, what one believes is his own private choice having no eternal implications. We are rejecting unity due to our desire to uphold our personal opinions and personal pride. Since personal opinions are not the truth, we feel guilty.

The idea of being individually separated is supported by our perception of inhabiting individual, physically separated bodies. The belief that we are bodies, justifies comparison, specialness, opinions of superiority, judgment the and abuse. My body helps me write this book, but the decision to write and what I write are entirely my mind's decision. However most of the ideas written here are not solely mine, but borrowed from other minds who have deeper knowledge than me. We are in constant union and communication. No human is limited to one person or another. We are closely related, understand each other and lovingly share thoughts to everyone's advantage. We don't compete, we cooperate. Our open communication is our source of knowledge and happiness. "The minds are joined, but you do not identify with each other. You see yourself locked in a separate prison [your body], removed and unreachable, incapable of reaching out and being reached." (94). So, free yourself from your confining thoughts!

3.

THE DEVIL

Where, in the picture of God's perfect creation, can a character like Devil or Satan fit? The answer is, nowhere. Everything is of God and, in Him there is no room for the Devil. The Bible writers go around this common belief by claiming that God created him as an angel of light (Lucifer) who turned bad by his own will. This transformation took place in people's minds only and not in the essence of God's creation. Confusions are personal and ephemeral, "Salvation is for the mind, and it is attained through peace. This is the only thing that can be saved and the only way to save it." (95) There are many enticing choices that are not beneficial. Those choices are not created by an evil genius and are not suggested to us by anyone or anything outside of us. They simply are decisions that we find useful for saving us in some difficult situations. So, where is the Devil here? Nowhere. When we die, the idea of Devil dies with us. The fact that the idea of Devil persisted for so many generations is due to the tempting desire of every generation to project their errors to an evil entity, outside of themselves. This is convenient but, useless. It is an excuse only; therefore a fantasy. If we don't face our mistakes, we cannot correct them. So, why do people avoid facing their mistakes? Certainly, embarrassment is a reason. It is certain also that Devil is an ideal target for guilt deferral: . . .'it is not my idea, it's the Devil's. . .' Also, if Jesus' sacrifice does atone for our misjudgments why should we even be concerned about evil? Religious experts came up with the idea that God allowed Satan to exist for the reason of testing us; but, God doesn't need to test what He already knows. God has one Creation, performed with one purpose, working one way, according to one truth. This is the uniqueness of the principles on which a solid life can be built. Once truth is incorporated, an endless field of higher possibilities opens to us. Then we know all that can be known and enjoy our life.

We prefer the comfort of our opinions over the immensity of truth. Among those opinions is the idea of Devil that we don't particularly love but, it became part of our physical life. We learned to live with it to the extent that we made evil just another opposite of God. However, both cannot be simultaneously true. Interestingly enough, in our thoughts both God and ego, in different ways, point to the same conclusion: we are sinless. God created us perfect and therefore sinless. Ego, in its turn, claims that we are just victims of the Devil's works; therefore, blameless. If crafty enough, we can justify everything we want. Nevertheless, for as long as we accept the concept of sin, we are responsible for its consequences. What we adopt is ours. God wants us aware of those thinking traps so we will be able to choose our thoughts wisely. In our earthly life, everything can be motivated. There, in spirituality, everything we need is available with no competition, no social ranking, no supervisors or range of values. The Kingdom of God is the infiniteness of free and pure minds and opportunities while on earth, we have access to limited physical choices that imply competition, inequality, restrictions, etc. If so, why don't we do the best we can to get there?

"I beheld Satan as lighting fall from heaven." (Luke 10:18) "And his tail drew the third part of the stars of heaven, and did cast them to the earth."(Revelation 12:4) Is it possible that some of us could be members of the "third of the stars of heaven," cast on earth?

God's central message, and the answer to our struggles, is love. He doesn't blame, suspect, manipulate or accuse. He knows. Satan, like any other human concoction, cannot exist beyond our humanness. It simply is an alternative value like so many others we use, all of them imagined and, for this reason, all of them are perishable, meaningless and dependent on our willingness to have them. The truth is that sin is not part of our essence. We can mentally create and justify everything we want. For as long as this concept or any other concept serves our immediate interest, we find enough reasons to justify it.

The creation of Devil is a central player in our psychological games. We didn't find it difficult to argue that we need the Devil to test us, to separate wheat from chaff so that in the end, we, the faithful and obedient winners against temptations, may shine like gems and earn God's generosity. Thanks to our invention of Satan (or Devil), we assume we can transfer our negativity to another and feel OK. In order to resolve the issue of Satan's awkward presence in God's creation, we decided that in the end, God will… "cast into the lake of fire and brimstone, where the beast… shall be tormented day and night for ever and ever." (Revelation 20: 10). What a picture! Is this what God will do or, it is the creation of the scripture's writer, again? If we think that God may forever torture his confused son who turned evil, as the Bible claims, then we don't know Him. God tries to rehabilitate people. He is not a killer.

Can the story of one thousand years of peace, when Satan will be bound, be true? Providing that Satan independently exists, the Bible says that during that time Jesus will rule and the world will be at peace. The message of the church is that what we need in order to have peace and prosperity, is a righteous leader who, once again, is someone outside of the human group. This idea means that our happy existence doesn't require as much of a personal awakening, as it requires an awakened leader. Again, we dream of another one to rise to perfection and do what we should do for ourselves. Because we believe that everything bad originates outside of ourselves, we believe that everything good is also outside of ourselves. This interpretation suggests that we are pretty much helpless peons on the table of life. The church claims that what is missing in our ways to success is not an inside (personal) awareness, but an outside enlightened (non-physical) leader. It is sad to see that we don't trust our ability to properly conduct ourselves. We dream of help coming from outside of ourselves. All right, but we had the most powerful righteous leader in the Garden of Eden where humans communicated directly with God and still, we followed our own minds lured by colorful ideas and lack of self-control.

Can a righteous leader make people think better? Will people, under the expected future rule of Jesus, be any different from who they presently are? We had Jesus among us once, and we killed him. With him gone, we now methodically kill his legacy by interpreting his meanings according to our acceptance level, and then call this philosophical crime: holiness and professional wisdom. Remember Jesus' prophetic words: "Nevertheless when the Son of man cometh, shall he find faith on earth?" (John 18: 8) Yes, He will find faith, but faith in human opinions. It is a good time to remember that our rising to the occasion can happen only through our personal, firm commitment to truth, or it will not happen. As it is, we want to validate the thinking we already have and not to achieve a "higher" one. So far, we want to be considered victims overpowered by outside forces and, be brought back on our feet by the supreme God. We don't want to abandon our convenient mind-set and, ignore that we are the only ones who can decide which path to take. We do continually try to change our physical ways and miss the mark each time. Will we be in such awe when we'll see Jesus at his second coming (provided we will recognize him), that we'll drastically change our minds according to His guidelines? We will probably be impressed, but not fundamentally changed. We spent many life-times with our minds; enough to settle to the way we are. Jesus came to teach us how to succeed; not to achieve success for us. His first coming caused a commotion but not the needed uptick. Look where we are today! We may believe we love our neighbors but, how do we understand love? Can it be political correctness, communism, socialism, progressiveness or something else? What can make us believe that we will take charge of our own transformation at Jesus' second coming? Why didn't we do that the first time? He pointedly asked us to follow his example. We did, a little, as much as we had accepted to do before feeling like strangers among our own kin. We reverted back to our "normal" ways again.

We are not meant to obey rules concocted by others. We are meant to follow our dreams, enjoy them, love and exchange our happiness with others, cooperate and take charge of our lives in total freedom. The trick is, the future starts now and now, we don't show any signs of progress. Artificial freedom and politically correct wisdom we now have, are our graves. If we don't improve, grow, take charge, unleash our own dreams, we cannot get out of our swamp. As Einstein said, we cannot solve our problems with the mentality that created them. The ones who created the problems, hold on tightly to their control. The thinking that brought us to this point, cannot bring us any further; we need a better way of thinking. Faced with those problems we did create a way out, the only way we could: we built a self-satisfying, stagnant system called self-righteousness:. . .'if this is what our powerful leaders want then fake cooperation and live in peace, why try to change the unchangeable, and, the next big change will probably be flying to another planet to be free and start over again'. Well,

Adam was free once…. and exchanged it for self-righteousness. By the way, our general education doesn't teach critical thinking any longer. Why?

If Heaven is within us, "behold, the kingdom of God is within you." (Luke 19: 21) then God did provide us already with all that we need. If we would decide to improve ourselves we have everything needed. It is up to us to take charge, acknowledge our abilities and search for answers. I did, once I emigrated, and I felt so good! Other Romanian dentists who came to the United States under similar conditions as mine, preferred to return home. A question is, should someone really want to do that: to return back to familiarity? It seems our slow and limited advancement on earth, created already a low expectation for change. Self-righteousness is only a placebo. Still, we are in charge with who we want to be. The deciding step is ours to take. People's apathy under coercive laws of political correctness proves to be disastrous. Apathy comes from lack of freedom, limited creativity, social manipulation, expecting God to take charge of our lives. President Abraham Lincoln said: "no man is good enough to govern another man without the other's consent." But, this is what we do. It is not a righteous leader that we need in order to have what we seek , but a righteous self. God did His part. He equipped us with all we need to succeed. We just need to want it. Keep in mind that guilt stays where it is produced. Success means to create and achieve. Do not deprecate yourselves to the level of wimps who oscillate between the influences of Satan and Jesus while not understanding either one. Build your life with your personal given abilities!

I always asked myself, could Satan, for all his brilliance, have chosen self-destruction? Can defeat be a "success"? If "God is all in all in a very literal sense," (96) then, "what is opposed to God does not exist." (97) This means that Satan is a fiction, that we can dismiss any time we want. We are not impacted by nor bound to its decisions, its presence, its influences.

In the Garden of Eden, once feeling guilty, Adam started to slip into an interpretation of reality that separated him from his Father. He tried to defer his guilt to Eve, Eve deferred her guilt to the serpent (the early version of Satan) and, the serpent stood mum. We still use guilt transfer today. Guilt made the original couple accuse God of punishing them, which is an old attempt at guilt transfer. The fact is, not only that He didn't reprimand Adam and Eve but respected their freedom and dignity by "clothing them" with "coats of skin" to protect them from their newly acquired shame of nakedness, before He let them go their way. All along, He offered to them and their descendants, His guidance so we can see the right way ahead. He cast no blame because He sees no guilt but only temporary confusion.

Freedom is of the mind. Our physical choices are basically an opportunity to have an overview of what life can offer us so we can make informed decisions. But Adam understood what he wanted to understand: his new reality. We need each other but need is not love. Love is of the spirit, as is the truth. As bodies we mainly provide for our body's needs and, neglect our minds and hearts.

Like any other human concept, Satan rose gradually from a benign role to the enemy of God. Elaine Pagles found, "the figure of Satan, as it emerged over the centuries in Jewish tradition, is not a hostile power assailing Israel from without, but the source and representation of conflict within the community." (76) "As he first appears in the Hebrew Bible, Satan is not necessarily evil, much less opposed to God. On the contrary, he appears in the book of Numbers and in Job as one of God's obedient servants, a messenger, or angel. The Hebrew word for messenger is translated into Greek as angelus. Elaine Pagles noticed, "that while angels often appear in the Hebrew Bible, Satan, along with other fallen angels or demonic beings, is virtually absent. But, among certain first-century Jewish groups, predominantly the Essenes (who saw themselves as allied with angels and the followers of Jesus), the figure variously called Satan, Beelzebub, or Belial also began to take on central importance." Thus, "Job's Satan takes a more adversarial role" and later "Satan stood up against Israel, and incited David to number his people" for the purpose of taxation. Taxation feels always evil. Isaiah (14:12-15) increased the status of Satan with the story of him being a fallen star, translated in Latin as Lucifer (light-bearer). Then, different stories converged in calling him an "intimate enemy" meaning an enemy involved in the internal conflict among Jewish groups. "The gospel of John, like many other gospels, associate the mythological figure of Satan with specific human opposition, first implicating Judas Iscariot, then the Jewish authorities, and finally 'the Jews' collectively." The today "vision of cosmic struggle, forces of good contending against forces of Evil, derived originally from Jewish apocalyptic sources and was developed by sectarian groups like the Essenes as they struggled against forces they saw" opposing them. Then, "Christians have turned the same political vocabulary against a wider range of enemies. In the sixteen century, for example, Martin Luther, founder of Protestant Christianity, denounced as 'agents of Satan' all Christians who remained loyal to the Roman Catholic Church, all Jews who refused to acknowledge Jesus as Messiah, all who challenged the power of the landowning aristocrats by participating in the Peasant's War, and all 'protestant' Christians who were not Lutheran."

4.

EGO

The Bible points to duality in one person's nature: one side is carnal, or physical, and the other is spiritual. People consider both sides had been created by God, even if the two are mutually exclusive. God the Father is exclusively spiritual. The simultaneous acceptance of the two sides of human nature justifies our acceptance of dichotomies and, our attempt to validate simultaneously those dissimilar opinions. God's creation, meanwhile, is based on one truth and one meaning. God is not a duality nor a trinity and, neither a multitude. He is One; the whole creation is He.

Physicality shapes our lives around simple, tangible values. From our perspective, life is achieving physical goals that satisfy our physical needs. The other humans are our means for progress, our measuring sticks for success and our cheer leaders. We want not only to cooperate with them but to compare favorably, to project our insufficiencies to them and to use their abilities for personal purposes. This allows us to feel special. Here the judgment of good and evil becomes handy. Alongside with right and wrong, people can be qualified either guilty or innocent, common or special, dumb or smart, selfish or generous, loving or hateful, knowing or assuming, judging and feeling, love and hate, and so forth. If judged to be better, we deserve more consideration and assume the lesser others can be used and abused. Because physicality means having, we are largely selfish and because we share physicality, we share the material evaluation of success. Even our mental capabilities are evaluated according to how much we can physically achieve. Our different abilities to physically produce, prevents us to consider ourselves as equal. For us, on earth, quality has a physical face. Ego is loveless and selfish; it believes that our existence is defined by separation and rewarded by possessions and responsible positions. "Whatever you accept in your mind has reality for you." (98) If you want to feel special, adopt an ego. Ego can raise our bodily importance to the highest levels possible even if this importance is only a thought and therefore, a fiction. The thought of ego creates the glory of specialness. "The body is the ego's home by its own election." (99). Ego is one's stout defender of one's beliefs. As we approach the end of our physical lives, we step closer to the metaphysical unknown and closer to the answer to the old question of, who we are. We become less concerned with righteousness and strength and more willing to know the truth. For as long as we rely on the concept of ego, we cannot fit into God's Kingdom; we linger in our physical dream. We stay physical because we created the powerful idea of a private and protective ego that can exist only in our physical understanding of life. Obviously, if we believe we are equally created, we cannot claim singular individual values; so we use ego to give us what God doesn't: the sense of specialness. As special, we feel justified to dominate those less special. If special, we cannot love everyone the same, as spirituality does.

In the apostle Paul's opinion, "the carnal mind is enmity against God: for it is not subject to the law of God, neither indeed can be. So then, they that are in the flesh cannot please God." (Romans 8:7& 8) The "flesh" has built a way constantly justified by ego: a person can feel successful or at least neutral in all situations. This specialness allows ego to supersede God's perfect creation of us. God created us equally gifted while ego provides us with the feeling of specialness that is one notch higher than equality. Again, perception of specialness is achieved through judgment of good and evil. Meanwhile, in the realm of truth there is nothing that can be judged. We are all created perfect and equal. "Judgment is symbolic because beyond perception there is no judgment." For ego, even pure divine love is interpreted as a reward granted to the "better" ones. We assume no one can love everybody. "The ego does not regard itself as part of you. Herein lies ego's primary error: when God created you, He made you part of Him; while ego considers you to be independent of God. That is why, any attack within the Kingdom [of God] is impossible, while outside of Kingdom, comparison, which is a form of attack, is a way of life. You made the ego without love and it does not love you. You could not be in the Kingdom without having love so, you, who customarily misunderstand love, believe that you are outside of it. This enables the ego to regard itself as separate and outside its maker, thus speaking for the part of your mind that believes you are separate and outside the Mind of God." (100) This tactic of separation is a creation of ours that makes room for the belief of ego. The presence of ego in our minds is helped by our poor understanding of God. If confused about truth, can we really see the need of loving everyone? A church bishop said once: "we are supposed to love even those who don't deserve to be loved." An associate pastor said during his sermon: "we cannot love those we don't know." Having such opinions, can we follow Jesus? God cannot abandon us to our ignorance. If we cannot save ourselves through "works", we assume that God will save us through His "grace". We are neither confident nor aware and not willing enough to straight-up our minds, so, we believe that only God can do it for us. Thus, salvation is, according to our monotheistic churches, a waiting game. According to Jesus, salvation happens in the moment when we upgrade our minds to the understanding of truth (remember Apostle Paul's conversion). Some minds did and do upgrade but many still trail under ego's influence. Still, mind is our best hope of getting out of this rat race. Nevertheless if we cherish salvation, God will show us the way so we can do the correction that will bring us back on track. This process already happened to some people who went through a near death experience. Dr. Bruce Greyson, M.D., "clinical chief of psychiatry at the University of Connecticut and at the University of Virginia," had a rather drastic change of opinion on the issue of brain and mind: "I had been raised by a no-nonsense skeptical father, for whom life was chemistry, and I followed his lead in forging my own career as a main-stream scientist." But then, after studying thousands of near-death experiences he couldn't deny that patients' physically dead bodies, who had no function in their hearts and brains, could see, hear, and clearly understand things he/she couldn't in a physically alert state. He quotes his patient, Tracy, who said: "I did not see this Presence of Light and Sound so much as I simply, totally knew and loved IT, within and about me, as IT knew and loved me. There was no space, no time, no separation, no duality of anything, as every cell of my being was flooded through and through with knowledge of how it all is, just is; of how it all makes Divine sense, of how all is in Divine Order. Of how loving one another is loving self and loving the Divine, of whom each of us is an atom. Like a hand is part of a body. . . though it is not the body, and though the body is not a complete body without a hand.... I knew in that moment, and for all time, that I was a unique atom-aspect of this wondrous being. In a quickening of awareness, I felt illuminated with an understanding of how each individual is an aspect of The Source. Words do not do that experience justice, any more than they could experience what the yellow-pink-gold of this morning sunrise looked like, or felt like, to one who has never seen a sunrise." There are 200 pages of quotations and analyses of near-death experiences in Dr, Greyson's book, "After".

We cannot believe both our human opinions and the spiritual truth, at the same time. Our human-created church asks us to beg for divine mercy while God patiently helps us to understand who we are and claim higher values. Apostle Paul was saved on the spur of the moment when he understood the truth of Jesus; and so can we. Notice that God provided us with all we need to succeed. We only have to use His gifts: mind, faith, common sense, love, forgiveness.

Albert Einstein observed once: "We will not solve the problems of the world from the same level of thinking we had when we created them." We either grow mentally or we linger where we are. We have the potential of God's sons. We have also created our perfect formula for stagnation, controlled by our egos, and feel comfortable with it. Some people even imagine an eternal bodily Resurrection meaning: a physical reincarnation on an improved earth, in a privileged position, forever. If so promised by God, as some human scripture writers claim, it must be eternal! "The Lord is not slack concerning his promise." (2 Peter 3: 9) "According to all that he promised: there hath not failed one word of all his good promises." (1 Kings 8: 56) This is desirable for those who assume specialness. They leave out of the picture the impossibility of being stuck within the narrow limits of a physical environment forever. Can they reproduce forever in that limited space and not overpopulate it? It would be unlike God and unfair to have people stuck in a permanent condition with no space to grow. This is contrary to God's decision of giving us freedom of choice so we can figure out what our best interest is and thus being able to return to the spread of Creation. We are all built equally well and deserve equal chances.

Many wait for Jesus to come again and, do what he didn't do when he came the first time: change us for the better. On this subject, I quote Jesus: "My mission was simply to unite the will of the Sonship with the Will of the Father by being aware of the father's Will myself. This is the awareness I came to give you, and your problem is accepting it as a problem of this (physical) world. Dispelling it is salvation, and in this sense, I am the salvation of the world." (101) Jesus is only teaching us how to better ourselves. It is obvious that God wants us, once we experience physicality, to realize the indescribable value of truth and, return to the fold. It is fair to allow people to grow and reach their potential, by their own will.

Change is our responsibility. It is not that difficult after all. Jesus already provided the answer: "love your neighbor as you love yourself". This decision eliminates the validity of ego because ego depends on inequality, judging and accusing. If there is no one to judge, we don't need ego. It is clear then that ego is the promoter of comfortable self-righteousness, of comfortable no growth; justifies the stagnation and the illusion of the specialness of special love that fits our physical understanding. Again, the choice is ours. Jesus promised to always be with us and offer his guidance when we ask for it. "Lo, I am with you always, even to the end of the world. Amen." (Mat. 28: 20) He doesn't change our minds for us; he helps us change them ourselves, by our will, when we will understand the meaning of life. Walking the walk was and is our decision and the proof of our commitment to return to whom we are created to be. Doing what we should is our nontransferable part in the process of living.

We seem to be reluctant to move out of our cozy mental boxes. We are complacent in having egos on our side. We also prefer to believe that our lives are preordained so, we cannot do anything about it. What separates us from Jesus is the level of awareness and the acceptance of truth. Truth, perfection, love and holiness are something we long forgot. We'd rather use the knowledge of good and evil instead! When we judge we compare, criticize and classify enough to feel good about our judgements. Very exciting but by accepting the idea of evil, we miss the truth. God could not create an evil opposition to Himself. Is this statement simple enough to understand?

The more successful persons may believe they are more gifted than others. This evaluation applies physically only, because it can be used by physical people only. Separation is an idea, dependent on one's evaluation and evaluation is physical. Separation may seem real in time, but doesn't exist in the eternity beyond (102).

As separate persons, we lose the safety of togetherness and try to compensate for this loss with ego's perceptions and fantasies. A thorough definition of ego would be, "a wrong-minded attempt to perceive yourself as you wish to be, rather than as you are." (103) In other words, ego is an idea, not a fact, nor a being; it is the belief that it is completely on its own (104) and separated from God. Ego is part of one's identity and of his precious version of truth. One can see himself as special, only if separated in an individual body that compares and competes. Ego didn't exist before we adopted the physical perception of ourselves and, will cease to exist when we return to the awareness of oneness. Ego never acknowledges our spiritual dimension. It regards the body as its home, tries to uphold its truthfulness and satisfy itself through it. Our physicality is ego's birth certificate and it is not likely to let the concept of physicality change, because its own existence depends on it. We should remember that ego is only a belief, a thought system that complements our wish of specialness. It is the higher identity we assume and defend at every opportunity. It finds reasons and means to assures us at every opportunity of how right and special we are. It has a "precious" self-gratulatory quality that it makes hard for us to dismiss.

Ego confers to us a self-awarded dignity, it offers to any experience we have a reasonable advantage makes us feel in control, and right about our beliefs. Self-righteousness is the bedrock of our claim of specialness. We understand our reason for every action we take and, this understanding validates our righteousness. All beliefs are real to those who believe them. Egos made the otherwise disastrous communists to run for victory until they could not run any longer Because Lenin, the founder of communist Russia, believed in his Marxist ideas, he declared that his communist party, which was a minority in the Russian political system is, as a matter of fact, a majority (called "Bolshevik"). He called, instead, the majority party, a minority ("Menshevik"), based on his wishful opinion. He forced-fed communism to his country. If you believe your ego, you live by its standards. In return, your ego takes care to prove at every opportunity that you are right, different, unique and special. Ego is your defender and protector.

Ego is the strongest supporter of our physical nature. It is obvious that ego cannot live in the spiritual world. If one lies or exaggerates, he cannot be spiritual.

The thought of God is unacceptable to ego because this thought clearly points to the ego's nonexistence. Ego is a way of thinking that either distorts or refuses to accept the truth of our divine origin. Ego is the wrong minded attempt to perceive yourself as you wish to be, rather than who you are. The reason for the mandatory monthly "political education" lectures we had been subjected to in communist Romania was to support the truthfulness of communist ideology. Because this ideology could not be trusted, the politicians used their ego to "justify" their beliefs and tactics. Ego is a line of thinking that makes one feel more justified and successful than he is. It supports a precious personal opinion. "Sane judgment would inevitably judge against the ego, and must be obliterated by ego, in the interest of [its] self-preservation." (105) We value the perception of pride that ego gives us. I mention again that ego is only a way of thinking that defends your physicality. Only as physical bodies we can compare with each other and prevail. Ego is the thought that uses our bodies for attack, pleasure, and pride (106). It makes life exciting so, how could we renounce it in favor of truth which, we don't even truly know? Ego gives us what we want: the feeling of superior uniqueness; thus making us aware of its usefulness. This way, ego appears desirable to the extent that we become unwilling to renounce it, not even in exchange for Jesus' knowledge.

The body's brain induced its mind to accept the idea of ego, that otherwise is an aberration. Our brains find ego useful to justify our bodies, a function our divine minds cannot. It preexisted the body and it will outlast it. As mentioned, our minds are small parts from the only Mind that is. Consequently, it cannot accept opinions and interpretations of truth. No wonder, ego cannot accept the existence of God!

The brain receives its information from the environment and concepts from the mind; it memorizes, combines them with other data and comes to conclusions. The brain is the user of information received but, it doesn't create concepts. Once the body dies, the mind regains its full freedom. Practically, if the brain is our biological computer that we discard after a while, mind is its lasting programmer. Because our minds are small parts from Divine mind, they connect and are eternal. The unique source of minds justifies the unity of creation. Minds are joined, immortal and sinless. Consequently, salvation is not for the body, but for our strained mind (107) that, in our case, had to function in the stressful, physical environment. Through death, mind gets dissociated from the body and discards its load of limitations and compromises. Again, one is not a body but the idea of being one. Body is nothing more than an illusion. You are unharmed by death because the truth cannot be harmed. Jesus proved it by moving from life to death and back again in front of the apostle's eyes. His statement is: "Be not afraid of them that want to kill the body, and after that have no more that they can do." (Luke 12:4) No one can damage a mind. The kingdom of God is in your mind! (Luke 17:20, 21)

Of course, you may find this hard to believe because you choose to believe your opinions. I remember from my childhood the saying, "what's in your hand is not a lie." It is a catching straightforward statement that struck me, not because I believed it but because it is so powerful. Like all materialist slogans, it is catching and deceiving. If one doesn't succumb to the strong imagery of this saying, then he realizes that things do not have to be in your hand to be true and that what is in your hand may not be true after all. What's in your hand is a display suggesting to your physical senses that truth is physical. Things are not under our physical control because the nature of things is not physical. Everything is accomplished through life and life is of the mind. (108) Only the mind is real because only the mind can be shared. "Nothing real can be increased except by sharing", Jesus said. No object can be shared but only borrowed or given. The purpose of God's creation is to share because only share and communication can increase the joy of living for all participants. "This is why God created you." As a matter of fact, the whole "Creation is in complete and direct communication with its Creator. Creation and communication are synonymous. Communication is the will of God." (109) What is in your hand cannot be shared; only abstract values can. At the same time, ego is a wrong-minded attempt to perceive yourself as only you wish to be rather than as you are. Your ego is meant to serve you only. Consequently, one reacts to his ego with love and protection; we consider our bodies to be our identity, basically we believe we are our bodies. This makes it difficult to accept your identity, as presented by Jesus.

Your choice to believe your own ego has multiple consequences, all of them detrimental. Let's look into some of those consequences:

A. Separation.

Ego is the part of your mind that believes your existence is defined by separation from everybody else. Only by being separated can you compare yourself with the others, judge them, take from them and blame them. For maintaining this belief, ego offers you the prized sense of being better than others, more prosperous, more gifted and special; proving its physical usefulness.

B. Avoid responsibility.

Ego denies the existence of God because God doesn't recognize specialness which is ego's prized gift to you and its main value. Ego is one's private cheer leader that finds ways to protect his creator (you) from inconveniences. Among them, is one's protection from being accountable for his "sins". It claims that the physical sacrifice of another on one's behalf, is an effective pay-off. It is obvious that to punish a body for the mistake of its mind is nonsense but, the ego chose to consider it valid and the guilty one accepts it. Ego is a thinking process born from the need to protect the sinner from responsibility. Ego does that by confirming the sin, usually by attributing the responsibility to another and, eventually, sacrificing someone else as a pay-off. Notice the Old Testament mention of executing ones' first born for absolving their father's sins. Also, see the execution of Jesus.

C. Guilt.

Guilt is the consequence of a misjudgment that can be corrected by the awareness of truth. But, truth means the denial of ego. Ego in its turn, by covering up for guilt, is the denier of truth. "The spirit of truth; whom the world cannot accept because it sees him [God] not, neither knoweth him: but ye know him because He dwelleth with you, and shall be in you. I will not leave you comfortless: I will come to you," Jesus said. (John 14:17-19) Truth is denied by the judgment of good and evil. Meanwhile God denies the existence of evil and makes truth the foundation of His world. The thought of sin is a source of guilt, while love takes evil and its guilty verdict out of the picture. God denies the existence of evil. He didn't create it and neither could anyone else. Evil is only a bad thought.

Believing in only convenient values is a sturdy reason for guilt. Guilt and separation run a small vicious circle whose victim is you: the acceptance of guilt is the beginning of separation among brothers, and separation maintains the feeling of guilt. Feeling guilty is an unavoidable consequence of violating the divine law of unity.

D. Selfishness.

Being created to satisfy its owner, ego wants to prove his owner's specialness; ego's existence is dependent on that. Its usefulness has to be constantly justified by providing a feeling of success endorsed by physical achievements. Those achievements are best proved by accumulation of things, collectables, properties, money, status, . . . through unfair means, if it has to. Selfishness is not concerned with justice. It is concerned with having and considers having to be a legitimate concern. For that reason, materialism cannot be fair. Communism, which is based on materialist assumptions, claims that it replaced the capitalist upper class but, created instead a lower quality communist upper class.

E. Atonement

Sin cannot be atoned if continuously brought up. Not surprisingly, ego doesn't want atonement to begin with because atonement means ego's elimination. If no sin, ego doesn't have anyone to save from anything. If properly atoned, one has the chance to love, see his brothers as his equals and joyfully communicate; no competition, no defending, no sense of superiority and no guilt. If love, there is no reason to sin and ego is not needed. Ego recommends instead, its own kind of atonement which doesn't atone at all.

In case guilt is perceived in you, ego is readily used to find "reasons" for your exoneration; it denies your sin and accuses someone else of having it. In extreme cases, ego asks for a substitutional atonement (someone else is to be blamed and punished). In this way it gives you a sense of relief and ego fulfills its purpose. We should notice also that ego plays a subtle game: it denies sin while it depends on it. Sin has to be saved in order to allow ego to repeatedly show its usefulness. At the same time, sin has to be dismissed, in order to uphold the sinner's image of integrity. This duplicity is accomplished by a double play: First, sin is interpreted as an objective fact of life so it cannot be dismissed. Second, the sinner cannot be considered guilty but a victim of guilt. So, ego dissociates the perpetrator from his sin (it is not my fault/mistake; this is life) and exempts him from punishment. However, . . . people like the freedom of doing whatever they want, sin included. Ego is quite useful!

There are some problems with the way atonement is understood. First, the desire to atone confirms the "reality" of sin. God didn't create you sinful; neither did He create sin. Sin is an improper thought. (110) Second, if sin is true, it is also impossible to remove. Truth is forever. We understand atonement as forgiveness, or an overlooking, but, no matter, all interpretations do nothing to renounce "sin". Third, the survival of the thought of sin secures the survival of ego, whose job is to protect you from blame. Fourth, atonement through Jesus' sacrifice is not only a gratuitous crime, but an insult to God. God already forgave us. He "forgiveth all thine iniquities" (Psalm 103: 3) A true atonement requires the annulment of the thought that produced the "sin". This annulment implies a responsible introspection of the sinner, leading to a better understanding of life. Truth, eliminates the value of sin. So, the kind of atonement recommended by the Bible (the execution of an innocent other) is not only ineffective, but it protects and perpetuates the recognition of sin and its attached ego. In addition, who in their right mind can give to God as an offering, the body of His most brilliant Son? Not to mention, what is already forgiven (Psalm 103: 3), does not require an additional form of "forgiveness".

God and "the Holy Spirit will never call upon you to sacrifice anything." (111) Also, Jesus said: "Those who disengage themselves from Sonship, are disengaging themselves from me." (112) Do not try to transfer your responsibility to another; it cannot be done!

The sacrifice, as devised by ego, secures ego's importance, doesn't inconvenience the sinner and confers a sense of salvation without saving anyone. Amazingly, it makes the guilty one feel vindicated while not vindicating. All is about opinions, semantics and emotions. Also, through sacrifice the status quo is safe and this physical "atonement" is meaningless. It is time to remember Jesus: "God established no sacrifice, and no use of strain is called forth" (113) "The sacrifice of the wicked is an abomination to the Lord." (Proverbs 15: 8) Real atonement is the nonphysical act of repentance performed by the one who needs to repent.

Despite all negative consequences of sin and guilt, the Bible claims, "If we say we have no sin, we deceive ourselves, and the truth is not in us" (1John 1: 8) Why? Because, with no sin there is no guilt and, no protection is needed from the Church and /or, from ego. So, the Bible claims that we are not truthful if we claim to have no sin. Both Church and ego, "protect" the idea of sin while formally condemning it, both doing it for the same reason: to justify their own usefulness. From a different perspective, sin is the denial of your nature as sinless Sons of God: if sin is true, God is not. The important question is: are sin and guilt real, or not? Because guilt is a human thought that fails the test of time, it is not true. "You are not guiltless in time, but in eternity. You have sinned in the past, but there is no past" in eternity. (114) Time is a human invention that allows us to project truth in the future by revising the past. "Atonement is but the way back to what was never lost [your innocent creation]. Your Father could never cease to love His Son." (115)

F. Fear

Any violation of truthfulness is a violation of God's way and, creates fear. "Before the separation the mind was invulnerable to fear, because fear did not exist. Both the separation and the fear are miscreations that must be undone for the restoration of the temple, and for the opening of the altar to receive the Atonement." (116) "You are the temple of God, and the spirit of God dwelleth in you." (1 Corinthians 3: 16) Humans are the temple that has to be restored. If we forfeit the security and certainty He offers, we are left with insecurity. By not recognizing God, we don't recognize love and from having no love comes suspicion, criticism and fear of the unknown.

Ego's purpose is fear because only fear can make one to desire ego for protection. Selfishness (product of ego) creates desires for more personal power and, fear of the selfish others. All negative thoughts have negative outcomes that promote some degree of fear. Also, ego believes in the so-called "battle for survival" which is basically ego's struggle to preserve itself and overcome fear. One's desire to be right, implies the fear that he may not be so.

G. False projection of truth.

Truth is a major inconvenience for ego because it denies ego's validity. Ego is an interpretation of truth and consequently not the truth. It is a "feel better" strategy that, conveniently, doesn't require truth or growth. It thrives in justifying the status quo. It avoids introspection because it doesn't want you to discover that what you need is to improve your mind. Here we run into another dilemma: on one hand we value ego for its contribution to our sense of safety; on the other hand, safety is truth, not ego. In order to know the truth, one has to grow over confusion and, over convenient opinions. Consequently, ego avoids truth. This means that, with an ego mentality, one will never be able to reach Heaven.

In order to resolve this impasse, ego managed to create an interpretation of truth that is not true. That interpretation is the self-righteousness that, obviously, means no growth. Ego does not enlighten; it reassures. If we want to be "right" by any means without engaging in the demanding work of introspection, (means no progress and discovery) we must interpret our opinions as truth.

Ego's concern is its self-preservation, while Jesus' concern is self-improvement. We want to be right about what we believe and, stay there. This means to rely on our convenient perceptions, knowing that perceptions are personal choices, not the truth. (140) This is the tragedy of our way: ego helps everyone to feel good without promoting truth, objectivity, or growth. Stay where you are and, don't worry! To solve mind's confusion between the demands of ego and of the Spirit, you must make clear to yourself if you believe you are the follower of your ego or of God. Pursue the knowledge of truth and ego will disappear, or at least subside, if you don't go all the way.

H. Avoid knowledge.

Once decided to break away from God, the Original Couple started to live by perceptions. We are the only creators of perceptions because they have no meanings outside of what one can accept. This reminds me of the massive and constant indoctrination people were subjected to, in communism. Verbosity is used there to justify perceptions, not the truth. God cannot be part of this perceptions game and, as a result, our direct communication with God, subsided greatly. Communism denies religions, obviously.

Ego is unable to perceive knowledge and it's not even concerned with it. Its concern is exclusively focused on pleasing its owner. In order to stay with our opinions, our minds must avoid knowledge. Growth is a threat to the status quo that, in turn, is defended by self-righteousness. For this reason, we would rather use convenient opinions versus thinking.

Moreover, because Jesus is the bearer of truth and knowledge, ego is trying to convince you that itself is real while Jesus is not. In the matter of enlightenment, our choices are as clear as they are limited: to be or not to be, self-righteous. One either stays with his thoughts, or searches for the truth beyond. If ignorant, we create illusions, justify anger and see sin, disease and death, as ego does. This happens because ego doesn't have access to knowledge. "God holds nothing against anyone." (117) The concept of punishment is nothing but ego's attempt to separate us from God. The world God built has the ability to purge itself. Otherwise, He wouldn't tell us: "Be therefore holy as your father in heaven is holy." (Mat. 5: 48) In God's creation everything is love. Sin is mistakes we build on the top of our holiness.

I. Judgment

If the brothers whom we "judge" are perfectly created, there is nothing to judge. Their mistakes are not they, and besides, we are not qualified to judge because we use perceptions instead of knowledge. "Judgment has no value [in our physical world] unless the goal is sin." (118) No one is wrong; all who seem wrong, are confused. One misjudgment induces other misjudgments and, creates this culture of errors. This is the life on earth.

"The sting of death is sin; and the strength of sin is the law." (1 Corinthians 15: 56) Why? Because the law proclaims a mistaken person guilty, and a guilty verdict endorses sin. Judgment of another, always involves the acknowledgement of sin. Ego is by definition partial. "Ego cannot survive without judgment" (119) because if it doesn't judge, it is losing significance. With this in mind, on what grounds do atheists pass judgment on God? On their opinions?

Based on what is said, should we close our justice system on earth? Sadly, not. It is an imperfect system, no doubt, but it is all we can do in our physical attempt to control our imperfect physical lives.

J. Anger

The Bible claims in several places that God was angry. How could He be? He is perfect and His creation is perfect. The only possible imperfection on this issue is man's opinion that He is angry. God gave us the freedom to choose our thoughts from the unlimited choices available. The purpose of this freedom is to know what choices are available, so we can make an intelligent selection. Nevertheless, the Old Testament writers claim that God became angry when people made some decisions they, the writers, consider wrong. "Anger is nothing more than an attempt to make someone feel guilty". "Guilt is the only need the ego has" (120) in order to display its usefulness. God can be saddened by some decisions we made, but never angry. God is peace, and His "peace can never come where anger is." God knows what to expect from our freedom and never regrets awarding it to us. There is nowhere we can run. We necessarily face our mistakes and, hopefully reach a truthful conclusion.

Humans promote the idea of anger because it makes room for ego's protective role. As mentioned, ego generates soothing excuses, defends our existing thoughts, defers our guilt and justifies anger.

"Anger cannot occur unless you believe that you have been attacked, that your return attack is justified, and that you are in no way responsible for it." (121) Remember, Jesus was never angry. If angry, ego makes you feel superior to the one who angered you. While doing that, ego doesn't help with any of your problems. It only makes you feel righteous, keeps you in bondage to your present condition and secures its perceived usefulness.

"As stated, anger is nothing more than an attempt to make someone feel guilty, and this is the only basis ego accepts for special relationships. Guilt is the only need the ego has, and for as long as you identify with it, ego will remain attractive to you." (122) Anger induces the separation of those meant to be united. In turn, separation gives your ego the opportunity to make you feel the special person you always loved to be: better, more gifted, preferred. Anger justifies ego's existence. You don't realize that "attack on him [your brother] is enemy to you, for you will not perceive that in his hands is your salvation." (123) If you love him as you love yourself, you are both holy (therefore saved).

K. Pride

Pride is another one of ego's creations meant to promote its self-preservation. Be proud of yourself, keep your head up and march to success, claims ego. Of course, pride doesn't confer any success and doesn't provide any quality. It only boosts confidence and, it is assumed, it makes a good impression. Pride creates an image not a quality. Also, pride supports the feeling of specialness.

God created you as the "Light of the World" while pride prevents you to see any connection between your world and you. Pride is a self-congratulating invention.

L. Failed relationships.

By not being interested in others, ego is loveless. Pretty bad, because "Love is the basis for forgiveness" and forgiveness makes room for love. Ego, instead, sees love as a condition in which ego itself is not needed but most likely an inconvenience. For this reason, love is the power which ego must deny in order to assert its own.

Ego accepts the flexibility of our morals, accepts opinions and doesn't get too concerned about our mistakes. No wonder it is likable! Ego's main disadvantage is its promotion of self-righteousness and the resulting stagnation. It doesn't improve anything. It fits our physical demands and it is the main obstacle in adopting a higher mindedness. If our minds are acceptable to ego, why should we even try to improve them?

In the case of relationships, ego sees love as the acquisition of something precious that he/she is missing and, the other has. That "awareness" can make one possessive and jealous. The loved one's independence is a source of concern and of constant alertness that easily degenerates into suspicion. As a taker by excellence, ego is unable to love; love only gives. Even the most giving relationship we have, takes a selfish turn under ego's guidance because, for ego, the idea of completion means triumph, not union. Ego regards others as a source to borrow something that you don't have but your partner does, and you want. Meanwhile, as created, one is complete and has no need to search for completion outside of self. In the physical world, where completion is never complete, ego is using special relationships to attempt to join Heaven and hell in a fantasy of both. It mingles love (heaven) and selfishness (hell) while unable to perceive either one as it truly is. One cannot possess another person whom he "loves", even if he tries. This "loved" asset we see in the other person may be a physical appearance, a moral quality, beauty, wisdom, an image of success, wealth or anything else one may imagine. Regardless, this unnatural union between love and want cannot succeed.

In the final analysis, this ego-sponsored relationship is nothing more than the triumph of confusion: a union that rests on the exclusion. Two unite because of what they desire from the other, while excluding what does not interest them. It seems surprising that the special one we meet and makes our toes curl, brings us into a relationship that is the outcome of confusion. It seems difficult to understand how anger can produce love. Managed by ego, it can. This is how:

First, people feel something important is missing in their life and they hate themselves for that. What they are missing is their awareness of God being on their side. People do not go to God when haunted by their emptiness. They go instead to their ego, the trusty and intimate product of their own thinking. Then ego advices them to seek a substitute for God, something we call idol.

Secondly, this idol is the other person's quality that can sooth one's pain and fill his emptiness. The ability to satisfy his need by associating to the one who has what's needed, becomes his relationship. You love your provider of completion, that he/she may offer.

Thirdly, this matching doesn't heal one's original need; it only masks it. Your need is still there under the cover of the relationship you have provided. Any change in priorities on either side of the relationship leave the hidden need exposed and you "grow apart". Then, you search for another special relationship.

Both sides in this special relationship are unable to perceive the other as he or she is. You are in need for something and the other is seen as the provider of what's needed. One gives of himself what he or she can do without and tries to take in return what she or he would prefer to have. On a subconscious level, the one feels guilty for the sin of taking something he/she highly regards and of giving something of lesser value in return. If both parties see this special self in each other, the ego sees "a union made in Heaven." Neither one will recognize that he or she has asked for hell and will keep going for the illusion of Heaven until either one will realize that the transplant of qualities is not possible. Each must build his own sense of completeness. A true and lasting relationship can be established only between two wholesome people that esteem each other and, do not have any personal lack to fill.

The special relationship is not exclusively established between persons. It can be created with items. It is known that dependency on alcohol, drugs, overeating, shopping, collectables, status, making money and everything that one feels she/he needs to be happy are all attempts to compensate for personal insufficiencies. From this disclosure, you can see that what we celebrate as "love" usually is not love at all. Love is the way God created it: a quality feeling that embraces the whole Creation. "Love your neighbors as you love yourself." Obviously, we do not expect to love everyone the same way but we should look at everyone with the same amount of love.

M. Mental illness.

We are created to collaborate and exchange, to enjoy each other's love, happiness, creativity and wholeness. By adopting an egotistical mentality, the interaction with other humans cannot be fair any longer. To ego, people are a little more than a source of whatever one needs. Physicality and ego, both being interested in personal fulfilment, have different concerns than the spiritual world has: physically one takes in order to have, trades rather than share, criticizes to claim specialness. Spiritually, we don't take anything. Spiritually everything is equally available to all.

This reminds me of a lady who gave to her church a certain amount of money under the assumption that the money, as suggested by the priest, is going to be returned to her multiplied. After a suspenseful waiting period, the money didn't miraculously return to her and, disappointed, she asked her minister for the money back. There is a difference between physical money and spiritual blessings. It seems that the woman and the priest had in mind different kinds of values. The priest invoked spiritual rewards while the woman understood physical money. Well, many believe that God physically rewards people for spiritual needs and qualities. Read in the Old Testament: Jews received many blessings and promises for obeying the rules the scripture writers detailed for them.

If a person feels ignored he may start shouting in order to be heard and prove that he can make a difference and that he has power and significance. If used and abused, we either get angry and retaliate or become submissive, withdrawn, lowered self-esteem, poor performers, loose our self-confidence, blame others for our lack of success, become emotional burdens, prone to abuse drugs and alcohol, and many other problems. Politicians came up with the idea of laws as a solution to mental health problems. In this "developed" society we live in, where we communicate electronically, loneliness and quality of emotions suffer more than it ever has. We try to control its effects rather than its cause (mental health).

Let us focus instead on returning to our creation where love and all its purity reign. Let spiritual values return to its rightful place within us all. Let us tap into the perfection God gave us.

N. Sin

"Whosoever is born of God does not commit sins; for His seed remained in him: and he cannot sin, because he is born of God." (1 John 3: 9) Despite this clear statement, sin is the most important invention of ego. "Sin is the idea that you are alone and separated from what is whole." (340) Separation is ego's goal. Only if separated you can compare better, take advantage of others and feel like a winner. Separation, in turn, is the main feature of the physical culture. Sin's importance comes from giving to ego the opportunity to prove its worth. And, ego's worth comes from relieving one's feeling of guilt that had been created by his assumption of sin. As mentioned, sin is a mistake generated by our physical's overrated desire of having things. For this reason, physicality is incompatible with spirituality. Sin as well as the thoughts that conceived it, are the perceptions of disturbed minds and therefore unreal. Sin is not created by God. If detected, ego has his work cut out: it either proves that the sin is not yours, that you have a good reason to sin or, eventually, that somebody else atoned for your sin.

Sin justifies the importance of both Church and ego. While both "fight" sin, in the process, both affirm sin's reality. Sin can be instantaneously annulled with a change of mind but, why should we do this while we perceive it as useful? Sin is the foundation of a whole philosophy that justifies not only our physical lifestyle but, the need of Church for protection. Because of its serious implications and, the difficulty to renounce its entranced acceptance, we will deal with sin, in a more detailed way, in the next chapter.

In conclusion, ego is an illusion that tries to deny the reality of truth. Instead, it offers comfortable feelings that do not disturb one's self-righteousness; does not require the effort of mental development and offers no renunciation of selfish specialness. This is ego's field of action. God and ego are two value systems intertwined at the foundation of our time on earth. During Jesus' life on earth, the mob wanted physical means handed to them, while Jesus tried to improve their mentality to the level where they would be able to materialize themselves all they needed. Once Jesus was silenced, the mob dropped him. He "couldn't" provide people with what they thought he would. More than that, He could not prevent his own crucifixion either. Between the Holy Spirit and ego, the mob chose ego. Ego helped them fulfill their physical dream of enjoying what physicality could offer.

On this subject, books can be written. I am not a scholar and I don't intend to exhaust the subject either. I only want to present religion in a valid way and eliminate the confusions we have. Religion is a unique tool for our development, if we only use it properly. "Religion is the recognition that the irreconcilable cannot be reconciled." (125) There is only one truth which is the only way to eternity. "Knowledge cannot come down on a mind full of illusions, because truth and illusions are irreconcilable." Therefore, life offers a way to learn from our mistakes, and grow. Salvation is self-discovery. If we don't understand where we are, we cannot figure out where to go. From what we've found so far, ego is the closest we can come to evil and this world is the closest we can come to hell. It is certain that God didn't create it. We did, in our miscreation mode introduced by Adam. "By one man sin entered into the world, and death by sin." (Romans 5: 12) "Aren't you sick, if you deny to yourself our wholeness of life? Your savior waits for healing, and the world waits with him." (126) "Healing will be one or not at all, its oneness will be one or not at all, its oneness being where the healing is." (127) "Miracle does nothing. It only undoes. It cancels out the interference in what has been done" (128). Miracle is not receiving something from God, but removing the misconceptions we piled on the top of our pure Creation. We should be aware that all beliefs are real to the believer. So, be careful of what you choose to believe.

5.

Sin

As darkness is lack of light, sin is lack of love. If we neglect love, we misunderstand our nature and consequently we are ignorant about the meaning of life. Is life possible without love? Sin is as dangerous as it is fictitious. We should remember that "Father created you wholly without sin, wholly without pain and wholly without suffering of any kind. If you deny Him, you bring sin, pain and suffering into your own mind. Your mind is capable of creating worlds, but it can also deny what once had been created, because it is free." (130) We used this freedom, to say: "In the times past,"... "we were by nature the children of wrath." (Ephesians 2: 3) The fact that we observed that we are sinful "by nature" shows that we either had been created sinful or, that we became so, by our own will. Is this possible? We are "created wholly without sin" means that we are the only other creators in the world, who did interfere in God's work and turned ourselves that way. We assumed this identity when we decided to have a physical, independent life. We are small creators ourselves, in private matters. Today's churches will say without hesitation that sin is very possible and we should constantly pray to be protected against it. The apostle Paul mentions in the book of Romans 7: 17, the "sin that dwelleth in me." If sin is built in our physical nature, it is only lasting for as long as our bodies last and, only considered true for the time being. In order to alleviate any apprehension, the Church presents God as a forgiving Father. This relief brings to our attention at least two Bible hesitations:

First, is sin a reality that stays, or an opinion that goes? Since sin is our idea, its existence depends on our decision. Forgiveness only pardons a sin, it never removes it. Forgiveness is only a relief from the due restitution and prevents resentment against the sinners. Through this concept, sin is only pushed out of the way for a while but it remains indefinitely untouched. Ego is saved!

Second, Sin is the consequence of ignoring the meaning of our creation. If this is so, why had no-one tried to dispel this form of ignorance? Why is sin so easily accepted? God forgives our sins but the Bible doesn't seem to deny it out-loud. God doesn't create anything negative that interferes with His Creation. He pardons our mistakes but, pardon is not a denial. It's only the admission that sin is a non-entity that our ego finds useful. Far more beneficial is to have an end to our physical life and of everything it entails. Sin has an image of permanence for being used by one person after another. It is a self-serving temporary human invention. It is no wonder that Gnostics consider a fundamental problem of human life to be ignorance; not sin. Sin is created by ignorance.

We validate the selfish thoughts propelled by ego by suggesting that sin is a law that runs our bodies. "With the mind I serve the law of God; but with the flesh the law of sin" (Romans 7: 17). We should admit that both flesh and its external (legal) laws, point to the existence of sin. God, who gave us freedom, could not contradict His own decision, and change our selected laws: "All things are lawful unto me" (1 Corinthians 6: 12). So we use our private laws and concoct sin, in our time on earth. We should stay with God's internal (spiritual) laws that are built in our nature, versus the new and private (physical) laws that we, the owners of our bodies, brought in. Ego is a thinking process not concerned with fairness. Its only concern is the protection of its creator's (human) self-image. As a matter of fact, ego, being created without love, doesn't love you (131). It doesn't even regard itself as part of you (132). It is seen only as a protector of the thinking process that created it. It believes that you are separate and outside of the Mind of God (133).

Ego, is a justifier of whatever can makes us feel good for the time being. No moral concerns. Some people perceive sin as the law "of the flesh" which is basically a self-justifying opinion. Nevertheless, we are not hopelessly bound to our creation of sin. Remember, "Be ye therefore perfect as your Father which is in heaven is perfect." (Matthew. 5: 48) This means that we have control over our minds and consequently over choices. We have the ability and the duty to handle any one of our choices. We only need the desire to be fair.

As mentioned, God doesn't even consider sin because sin is not a divine creation but a human short lived fantasy lasting for as long as a human physically lasts. Only our ego can claim the truthfulness of sin because sin offers to it a protective job. As a bonus, sin can be reactivated any time one desires.

Guided by ego, we respectfully evaluate Jesus' teachings, praise him and incorporate some of his advice, adjusted to our understanding. For different reasons, both Jesus and ego are defending us from sin. To Jesus sin doesn't exist, while for ego, we should push the awareness of sin into our sub-consciousness so that we may forget about it for a while and feel free of blame. Ego doesn't demand anything from us; not introspection, not growth, not truth. "Through the grace of the Lord Jesus Christ we shall be saved." (Acts 15:11) This transfer of atonement from a personal duty to Jesus is our ego's idea and, to no surprise, it is convenient.

As stated, Jesus was executed for dogmatic reasons; He was not sacrificed on our behalf. On the contrary, he was sacrificed to our detriment by the Jerusalem religious leaders. He came on earth to teach the way to salvation; not to perform salvation for us, as interpreted by the "experts" years after the fact. Jesus never claimed to atone for our sins. He was executed for teaching the truth that didn't match the teachings of Jerusalem's Temple. Jesus called us to eliminate our regard for sin. This means, again, that sin is not true but a fiction and within our ability to eliminate. When we do that, we make the definite statement of where we are on this issue. Because love and holiness are the truth, they "give the Son of God the power to forgive himself of sin." (134) This is the divine perspective: sin is a human creation whose elimination is a human's duty. Nevertheless, since we find it difficult to renounce sins, the Church assumes that God will do it for us, His way. "Not by works of righteousness which we have done, but according to his mercy he saved us." (Titus 2: 5) The book of John has a different angle: "Whosoever is born of God sinneth not." (1John 3: 18) Aren't we all born of God? "Before I formed thee in the belly, I knew thee, and before thou comest out of the womb I sanctified thee." (Jeremiah 1: 5) So, because we've been created with no sin attached, we are able to get rid of sin from our lives, and we should. No doubt, but we want to please our body's ego also! Sin is only a convenient opinion that endorses the concept of evil. God did not create evil. Sin is an opinion that separates people, justifies ego, and creates the concept of inequality and specialness. Ego does everything in its power to get justified. Ego justifies separation among brothers, creates a hierarchy based on human values and influences the kind of life we have on earth, run by selfishness and conflicts. Separation is a fantasy that replaces love's meaning with self-satisfying meanings. It can also be called "the decision not to know yourself" (135). Unless we reject the thoughts that ties us to failure, we will never see Heaven. "What plans do you make that do not involve your body's comfort, protection or enjoyment? These plans make the body an end unto itself, not a mean for a responsible interpretation of life, and this always means that you still find sin attractive." The purpose of life, as created, is not to satisfy your body; it is to free yourself from physical restrain, "that [physicality] cannot have been created by the Father, for the world is not as you see it." (137) The physical life is what we safely may call hell. What is not true, must be wrong. For us, salvation is an opinion and an opinion is not the truth. Salvation is "what the Holy Spirit has saved for you, because it is the recognition that reality is only what it is true." (138). "Salvation is a collaborative venture. It cannot be undertaken successfully by those who disengage themselves from the Sonship, because they are disengaging themselves from me," (139) Jesus said. We must break the boxes that contain our thoughts, or those boxes ill incarcerate us for a very long time. The Church of ego unconvincingly covers the dismissal of sin with soothing words like forgiveness, absolution, repentance, remission, reconciliation and even divine atonement. All those words point to the avoidance of truth but, none of them explicitly deny sin. "I will confess my transgressions to the Lord; and thou forgaveth the iniquity of my sin," (Psalm 32: 5); but, does not dismiss it. The denial of sin must be accomplished by each mind that entertains it, not by God. God never recognized it. You don't have to confess your sins to the Lord. Confession is your recognition that a fantasy is existing in your mind. What you confess is already known to God, and familiar to you. Sin is your illusion that has to be dismissed by you. King David is another man who believes: "Blessed is he whose transgression is forgiven and whose sin is covered," (Psalm 32: 1); but not annulled. Forgiveness only avoids the feeling of responsibility. Sin is accepted by our religion as a weakness "that dwelleth in me" (Romans 7: 17&20), suggesting that it is unavoidable. "By one-man, sin entered into the world, and death by sin; and so, death passed upon all man, for that all have sinned." (Romans 5: 12) Sins are part of human thinking. The Bible's teaching is that sin can be washed away with blood only, which allows one to call for a sacrifice. "Without shedding of blood is no remission" of sin. (Hebrews 9: 22) But, is it true? God didn't create blood to be spilled. This statement is made by a man who pretended to represent God and not by God himself. As mentioned, we are told that sin enters our minds when, in an emotional moment, we lose control of our judgment and allow sin to prevail. (Genesis 4: 6,7)

God doesn't "forgive" sins because they are nonexistent in the world He created. Sin is a human thought that vanishes along with any other human illusion. God wants sin erased from our minds through the awareness of truth. Once we know the truth, we cannot lower ourselves any longer to speculations and opinions. His Son was created guiltless and is guiltless. Ego's interpretation is certainly different: guilt is real in our world. In order to make it unreal and forgivable, ego requires an atoning sacrifice. In our physical world, sin has a physical significance that requires a physical cleansing. At this point we have to make a choice between the two different and irreconcilable perspectives: God's, and ego's. Are we perfect and sinless minds located in flawed and sinful bodies? Are we the way He created us or the way we see ourselves? Do we trust God or our thoughts? Even if we are God's creation, the way we see His creation of us is our opinion. The confusion between our supernatural nature and our physical interpretation of truth is so profound that it became literally impossible for us to know anything. The unfortunate decision Adam made is transitory as our physicality is transitory. Ego, the sponsor of those decisions, is not permanent either. Again, monotheistic Churches, created by ego driven people, consider sin real and the crux of salvation. Here, on earth, our minds built familiar illusions that cannot stand the test of time. With a change of mind, we can renounce sin and return to the perfection we had been given. With a change of mind, we can remove all the mistaken ideas we piled in our minds. Our salvation is in our lap, now; a change of mind away. "Know the truth, and the truth shall make you free," (John 8: 32) instantly. The man Jesus stood attached to his spiritual root and, asked us to do the same. The decision is ours.

In ego's religion, the same incident that for God is a mistake, is considered as "sin". Ego does so because, if sin is a feature of one's character, it cannot be removed, therefore the man is sinful and imperfectly created. This way, ego can claim that God is fiction. For ego's religion, the son of God is guilty (see 1John 1: 8), and therefore, an imperfect creation of God. By claiming that God's creation is imperfect, ego implies that God himself is imperfect and, therefore, He cannot be eternal! Also, the Bible claims that the wage of sin is death (Romans 6:23), while the immortal son of God cannot die. Jesus was physically killed (crucified) and he appeared healthy among people three days later. Several dead people, according to the Bible, had been brought back to life by Jesus, thus proving that they had not been dead; only their physical perception was removed. Therefore, for God, we are not sinful. What dies is the physical image of ourselves. We must make this fact clear to ourselves! Only our physical image dies.

God created us from himself, because He is the only source of everything that is and, He is eternal ("in Him we live"). The truth is Son of God cannot sin, cannot have flaws, and cannot change his own reality (143). We, the humans, can change only our thoughts, beliefs, and opinions, but we cannot affect what God did and who He is. We are as created, not as we see ourselves. Jesus may come to earth again, but not to "judge the living and the dead." He was not sent to us to be a judge. He is aware of our confusion and, He came to teach us the truth. God knows us; He doesn't need to pass judgements and dispense penalties and, He doesn't. Does any penalty improve one's minds? Our deeds are out in the open. What the writers of scriptures have to say in addition, are superfluous opinions.

We, again, have to deal with ego's interpretation, so popular these days, that sin is true, it has to be punished, and the belief in innocence is deceiving: "If we say we have no sin, we deceive ourselves, and the truth is not in us." (1 John 1:8) It appears that for us, one's admission of sin is a sign of holiness. No punishment can eliminate our sins; only the awareness of truth alone, can. Only one's awareness of his misjudgment can annul his sin. Sin is a product of our confused interpretation of facts and can be eliminated only by correcting the thought that created it. Confusion can be corrected only through the understanding of truth. The problem is that this straight forward solution is denied by the Church of Ego. For Ego, our claim of purity is arrogance. This reminds me of the story that puzzled my wife when, as a second-grade student at a Catholic School, her class was brought forward for their first communion. She faithfully attended her religious education, as required and, when the priest asked her to start confessing her sins. She confidently answered,

"I have not committed any sins."

"It's not possible, everybody does. Maybe you don't remember them. Take your time."

She took her time, sweat bullets and, in all honesty, she couldn't find any. Still, intimidated by the deep significance of the moment, in that impressive church, and the presence of God's representative, she broke down and listed all the sins in the book. The priest smiled conciliatory and blessed her. Only then she became sinless, according to the Church of Ego. As a matter of fact, she was sinless since inception and forced by her own priest to lie about it. For ego's religion, the admission of sin is perceived as the dignified admission of truth and is therefore, holiness. Can the confession of innocence of a young girl be regarded as dishonesty? On what grounds? "A major tenet in the ego's insane religion is that sin is truth, and the claim of innocence deceives. The claim of purity is seen as arrogance, and the acceptance of sin is perceived as holiness. Is this humility?" (144)

Luckily, it is not that difficult for one to reset his thoughts. The difficulty is to find the truth under the pile of opinions and grasp it. Once found, can truth overcome the wave of misperceptions that carry us nowhere? It seems, what makes truth identification so difficult is ego's accepted dichotomies and plurality. This lax acceptance of opinions makes truth hard to discern. Sin gives legitimacy to ego; it justifies ego's intervention to "save" your reputation. One misperception justifies the other which is accepted by another and so forth. And, keeps on going!

So, one thing entails another. For some, their claim to dignity and valor depends on holding up their stifling self-righteousness. They claim their dignity by holding firm to the opinion they consider accurate. The problem is that opinions are, most of the time, inaccurate. Next, self-righteousness is used in their defense: if one's opinions are considered valid, why change?

With ego's blessing, we run another vicious circle: if we believe we are right, we believe we are knowledgeable and, if knowledgeable, we must be right. Ego is our private cheerleader that offers a sense of valor. Ego is so important to us that not even the thought of Heaven can separate us from it. People's egotistical opinions crucified Jesus two thousand years ago. Since then, the egos of titled religious employees do their best to kill what is left from Jesus: his legacy. We have many teaching institutions that show how to adjust spirituality to our well established opinions. For ego's thought system, sin is wholly sacrosanct and, should be protected. Because we consider both truth and sin real, we hold them closely associated. So, we interpret sin as a deep flaw, assume it is impossible for us to correct and, we call God for help. But God helps in a different way than we, in our physical thinking, understand helping: He doesn't do it for us, He helps us understand the need to do so, ourselves. Regardless of our opinions, sin is still a mistake, a belief imbedded in our awareness. Sin is the most "holy" concept in the ego's system: powerful, upheld as holy for being perceived as truthful, and protected with every defense at ego's disposal (145). For ego, sin is precious because it supports the lasting idea of ego's usefulness. Ego is the promoter of the kind of sacrificial atonement that leaves sin unaffected. "Yet I had planted thee a noble vine, wholly a right seed: how then art thou turned into the degenerate plant of a strange vine unto me? For though thou wash thee with nitre, and take thee much sope, yet thine iniquity is marked before me, saith the Lord God" (Jeremiah 2: 21,22). This accusation attests that sin is an early error that created the need for ego's endorsement through accusations, crimes and "atonement."

Sin has changed the human perspective of creation from the idea of God to the ideal ego. We see ego as more reassuring and more personal than God – it is our creation, afterall -. It changed our reliance from the abstract, loving God, to our mindless, concrete bodies run by desires (sins). Our world is compatible with corruption and decay. It is overseen by a judgment based on good and evil and relieved by the transfer of guilt. In the extreme, we believe our sins can be forgiven through another's crime; see the substitutionary atonement by killing an innocent, pure other, as a pay-off.

Any mistake can be corrected if confronted with truth. But if the mistake is considered the truth, then its correction is impossible. More than that, even if one can evaluate his thoughts, taking charge of his own salvation requires an effort that most people refuse to engage. People prefer their cozy status quo, protected by make-believes and self-righteousness.

Nevertheless, in the short run the only run we are interested in is where sin and ego reign.

There is no stone in the ego's entire embattled citadel that is more heavily defended than the idea that sin is real. Sin gives legitimacy to ego because it allows ego to claim its usefulness by "saving" you from your "sin". Ego becomes an irreplaceable, free of charge, effortless, personal savior. If "sin" is recognized, God is sidestepped and ego becomes necessary. If sin exists, it entails that God created a negative character and this creation disqualifies god to be the God. In this situation, ego is the only other way of alleviating our feeling of guilt, (I did it because…) Nevertheless, not ego and not sacrifices can generate enlightenment or denial of sin. Only the truth of God can.

While upheld, mistakes are harmful but easy to remove. If repeated, they may generate a thinking pattern that makes atonement virtually impossible. Regardless, the Kingdom of God is within you; a thought away from where you are. You have the intelligence you need to access the higher value, above any mistake: change your mind away from your errors. It is you, who have the custody of your Heaven.

The world is the product of thoughts and, having no thoughts is an impossibility, as it is having no opinion. Every word we utter and every act we perform, no matter how careless, is the product of our opinion. You may not want to take responsibility for it but the responsibility is built in. And, the Holy Spirit or the ego are the only choices we have. Regardless, no one can fight something that does not exist. By thinking of sin, one gives it an importance it doesn't have. So, all that one needs is to change his mind away from sin. Your lines of thinking called ego and sin are entirely dependent of your will. Love offers the only awareness that sin is an illusion. Therefore, ego would never renounce sin; only your mind would.

In order to justify its existence, ego requires a formal recognition of sin through a guilty verdict, certified by a subsequent punishment. Communists sacrificed the upper class, ancient Jews sacrificed on occasions the innocent first born, Islamic jihad sacrifice the "sinners". For God meanwhile, all that a "sinful" person needs is to correct the mistaken thinking that brought him where he is. With a higher intelligence, one's performance can be improved. As one's opinion improves, his sinful thinking subsides or disappears and the man is not a sinner any longer.

One is how he presently thinks. God enables you to return to your perfect mind, if you want. People, in general, prefer to be right as they are; their egos tell them they are right so no change is necessary. Ego is irreplaceable for one's self-righteousness. If comfortable with his mind, one doesn't see the need to change it. Sure, we admit that Jesus is right but, we also believe that we must "adjust" his advice to our specific circumstances. Of course, it is error-proof to have God do the change of our minds. It is not only comfortable, but we assume God can do everything. Except, that, we don't know that He doesn't take back what He once gave: freedom of choice. The freedom of choice is ours to handle. He gave us the custody of our beings. He trusts our given quality; He counts on our ability to find the truth among so many temptations.

In case sin is perceived in your action, this is an opportunity for your ego to step in and provide a solution: sin is reconciled and ego shines as your protector. This way makes punishment a great preserver of sin, guilt, and ego. All our tactics are stout preservers of status quo.

This practice of paying-off is born from a mercantile mind. You pay for a product, you own it. You pay for forgiveness, you have it. All right, but how fair is the price set for forgiveness? Nobody can set a fair price for what is priceless; not to mention, the way we set this system, one who pays is not the sinner. Neither the sinner nor the victim are even consulted. The guilty party manages both sides in this decision; both to the convenience of the sinner. Is it fair to call Jesus' execution, redemption? His killing can never be justified, never fairly evaluated, and should never be considered a pay-back (redemption). A killing, for any reason, cannot be a justifiable pay-back.

If God "forgives all our sins," (Psalm 103: 3) why should a pay-off for our sins still be required?

The difference between sin and mistake is a matter of interpretation. Both are consequences of mistaken decisions and both require the same basic treatment: correction of the thinking that produced them. Those corrections are atonements. Both situations require responsible, personal attention. Both, mistakes and sins, are human creations and consequently under human control.

"Sin is a mistake you keep hidden, a call for help that you keep unheard and unanswered." "Sin has changed creation from the Idea of

God to an ideal the ego wants." (142) Sin is the belief that your belief is untouchable, and that your mind must accept it as true. If the mind does not, the physical world judges it as insane. And so, your mind, the only power that can correct our perception, is kept impotent, held to the body by the fear of change.

Sin, is not only doing something inappropriate; it is the belief that that something inappropriate is the truth. Sin has life changing effects and, believes that those changes had been meant to be; that they are facts of life. If sin is this belief, we must wearily check if this is true. Our happiness depends on it.

The opinion that sin is a human concept, is not new. Quoting from The Gospels of Mary: "The savior replied, 'There is no such thing as sin, but you create sin when you mingle as in adultery, and call this sin." Because sin is a human idea, one can be healed of sin in the instant he stops giving it any recognition. "Sin is a mistake that you keep hidden." (129) "Sin has changed creation from an idea of God to an idea the ego wants; a world of rules, made up of bodies, mindless and capable of complete corruption" (136)

6.

LOVE

We love Jesus because of the quality of his mind and the purity of his Spirit. "Who is drawn to Christ is drawn to God as surely as Both are drawn to every holy relationship," (140). This is the love that pervades the Kingdom. This love can also turn earth into Heaven if we turn holy.

People cannot create and enjoy life if they don't lovingly relate to each other. We are meant to love. We are the outcome of our Creator's love and we are meant to amplify the beauty of the Universe by loving Him back. "There is no love but His, and He is in everything that is." (141) Love, like any creation of God, being truth, has no substitute. If interpreted or adjusted to personal acceptance, it's losing its original intention and, it is not any longer significant; its perfection is tarnished. If you want to consider hate as the opposite of love, realize that everything that is not love as intended, it is not love. Love, being perfection, is eternal, while its variants, being human interpretations, are as temporary as humans are. No creation can outlive its creator. Love is used by God as the foundation for a fulfilling life, while its human version is meant to satisfy our physical desires, for the duration of our existence.

As intended, love is the most rewarding form of cooperation. Love is the power that unites the creation. Harmony and fairness cannot be achieved without it. Meanwhile, life on the physical plane, sidetracked by ego, guilt and sin, manages to replace it with what we physically have. We understand love as an emotion that includes attraction, desire, devotion, adoration, all used in a personalized way. Emotions give us the feeling of freedom; freedom is truth, love included. Emotions can easily get out of control. We easily confuse love with desire, admiration, possession and so forth. The main difference between the holy love (love as created) and ego's (special) love is the difference between love for the whole creation and the selective love for selective persons. Most of the time ego's love is motivated by personal interests like sexual attraction, emotional balance, or security concerns. Because we do not love all creation, we interpret love as something that is not as intended and, therefore, it is not love. As usually, we subject truth to our personal interests, rather than adjusting our personal interests to the truth. Emotions give us the feeling of freedom, while our freedom is our universal acceptance of truth. In our opinions, physical freedom is limited by restrictions while true freedom is a limitless field of creative possibilities. We compensate for our physical limits with illusions of freedom so that we may feel free, while limited. What is not of God is not real!

God's offers are indestructible and never disappoint. God chose love as the bedrock of his creation. Love is a whole culture, the reason of being and the meaning of life. "The Holy Spirit is part of you. Created by God, the Holy Spirit constantly accompanies God and His creation. He is both God and you, as you are God and Him together." "Nothing real has ever left the mind of its creator. And what is not real was never there." (146)   In our on-going state of confusion, one may believe that love is nothing more than what he experienced, one time or another. Truthfully, love is life itself. Nevertheless, we interpret it as what it is not, because we, as physical persons, have a physical, transient and selective understanding of everything. "The body is a limit on love," as it is a limit on mind, consequently an attempt "to limit the unlimited." "The body is a tiny fence around a little part of a glorious and complete idea. It draws a circle, infinitely small, around a very little segment of Heaven, splintered from the whole, proclaiming that within it is your kingdom, where God can enter not." (147) For materialists, the emotional aspect of love has a physical foundation: procreation. Not surprising, the physical attraction gives to ego the opportunity to prove its importance: "everything is fair in love, war, and business!" Nothing physical has any connection with spirituality, nor is it intended to have by our Creator. Spiritually love is understood as perfection, untouched by selfishness. Physically, the goal is to gloriously succeed. As a physical creation, ego motivates you to succeed by any means, prevail over competitors and savor your victory. It makes you feel great for a while, special, remarkable and victorious while, love is not victory; love is enlightenment, appreciation for life. If we are all equal, none is victorious and none is defeated; we are equal and perfect partners.

When Adam and Eve started to judge their kin in terms of good and evil, they lost their love. One cannot accuse his brother/sister, if he has love in his heart. There is nothing to accuse. We are all perfectly built and temporarily confused by our, imagined and unlimited opportunities; not all being good. We may think differently, which is stimulating, but we are meant to look on all as one (148). We all are created by the same creator, from the same source, having the same quality mind: His. This is the unity of the creation. My two physical brothers and I, we are different. They approach life in ways I wouldn't but, their ways work for themselves and their partners. They balance their lives differently than I and make it work. I would never criticize them for not using my "better" ways. If I would, I would destabilize them and weaken our union to no avail. The consequence would be resentment and separation. We all learn by observing our loving brothers and complimenting their success. Judgment condemns, love unites. My brothers are equally accomplished as I am and, I am as they are.

Our physical world, based on judging in terms of good and evil, has an opposite understanding of love from what love is. To my observation, there are four main differences:

First, in our physical perspective, love has a physical, practical meaning, while, spiritually, love is universal and as perfect as God. Physical understanding implies a physical purpose, while love implies a deep appreciation of what all our brothers/sisters are. All are creations of God.

Second, the unions we celebrate on earth define love as a partial union born from physical interests. It is a union of two persons who see each other as special, based on what each one has to offer. They exclude everybody else. In Heaven meanwhile, love is the equal union with all creation: His total "love is given to all alike." (154) All are perfectly created. There is no one to judge and, everyone to trust. All fulfill your expectations, in different ways. On earth, we see love as a special relationship between two people; born from the hidden wish to be associated with the one who has what you need. That one is, for you, special: love conquers all. This specialness cannot be real in the place where all are equally well created. "There is neither Jew nor Greek, there is neither bond nor free, there is neither male nor female, for you are all one." (Galatians 3: 28) There is

"One God the father of all, who is above all, and through all, and in you all." (Ephesians 4: 6) His "love is incapable of exceptions." (149)

In order to enjoy their fantasy of specialness, humans created an accommodating line of thinking: the judgment of good and evil. This identifies a range of worthiness that contains what one can see as specialness. Specialness is possible only in the physical world because only there do we use a critical view of our equals. This gives to ego the irreplaceable importance of physical evaluation: it picks and chooses what makes one feel special. As mentioned, one cannot go to Heaven alone. He either goes with love for all his brothers/sisters or he/she doesn't go. Special love is ego's chief tool for keeping you away from Heaven. In Heaven, while having more than we can dream of, all are accomplished and no one is special. Special love is ego's most boasted gift it can give you. For those unwilling to relinquish guilt, special love has the most appeal (150). The guilty is the one who needs the most the support of a loving other.

Thirdly, the union we celebrate on earth, and call it love, as previously explained, is a combination of hate and love. We love what we may borrow from our "loved" one and, we hate what we miss within ourselves. We love what the other can offer, but are not too much concerned about him/her as a person. Once we discover that what we borrowed from the "loved" one cannot be transferred to us, and that we are still incomplete, our special relationship, interpreted as love, is finished. True love comes from our awareness of wholeness. If whole, we don't need anything; we only give. Love is the happiness of loving that returns to us, amplified, with the love of our partner. Meanwhile physically, love is a transaction.

Fourthly, we interpret love as victory; we get what we want. As bodies, we look to love as a precious acquisition that makes us happy. Our specialness is confirmed in our opinion by this special acquisition. As mentioned, this interpretation of love is not love and, it doesn't work. So, if one cannot go beyond special love, he cannot expect more than what he/she gets from it: a temporary, partial relief. Physicality doesn't come with high expectations, because it doesn't understand love. It understands having.

In all its forms and sizes, ego interprets specialness as Heaven. Knowing that Heaven is generally seen as completion, ego gets on the bandwagon and agrees on this. But, it is in complete disagreement on what completion means and how it is accomplished. The Holy Spirit knows that completion lies in union with all creation. For ego instead, completion lies in the individual triumph over the others. More than that, it extends this "victory" all the way to the final triumph over God; meaning, that you can achieve the specialness that God refused to offer. Nothing can make you feel better than personal victory! If you believe that you are successful, this is your ego's idea of Heaven. This reminds us, again, of atheism that regards divinity as a concept that limits one's freedom through listing what one should and shouldn't think, say, and do. In the Old Testament, the Israelites considered themselves preferred over all others due to the virtue of one of their ancestors. Obviously, ancestors are not responsible for their descendants' performances. The descendants themselves are responsible for their opinions; not their ancestors. The writer of the Old Testament, unaware of this situation, is quoting God: "And I will establish my covenant between me and thee and thy seed after thee in their generations for everlasting covenant, to be a God unto thee, and to thy seed after thee in their generations." (Genesis 17: 7) What about those who are not "thee" or "thy seed after thee in generations"? Are them to be treated as "lower" because they do not belong to the club of seeds? If ego is "right", no one can interfere and introduce love, forgiveness and growth as a condition of success. As understood by ego, special relationships are a triumph achieved through selfishness and consequently, is unrelated to holiness. Ego tries to join hell (sin) and Heaven. For ego, hell is heaven. It sees this self-gratification as desirable. This odd union between selfishness and love, not surprisingly, can be called utmost confusion, because Heaven and hell, being of opposite values, cannot be combined. They have separate meanings that point to different consequences. This situation can be described: "The scepter (symbol of utmost authority "from on high") shall not depart from. . . . nor a lawgiver (human ruler) from between his feet." (Genesis 49: 10) This odd union of the spiritual (scepter) and the physical (lawgiver), being opposite value systems, can be appreciated only separately, according to one's opinions, but not simultaneously. This situation can best be described as seeking the right thing in the wrong place: it seeks one's fulfillment (the right thing), through the other's qualities (the wrong place). Obviously, the "right place" is the achievement of quality through the improvement of personal awareness. A balanced mentality provides one with everything he/she needs, thus making one independent of outside gratification. The awareness of truth is the completion of our needs. When complete, one enjoys everything while needing nothing. Then, love is the appreciation of a beautiful partner. Truth is fulfillment that can come from one's mind only. Also, be aware that, as God created us, "separation is impossible." (151)

The search for a special relationship is a sign that you equate yourself with ego; for the special relationship has value for your ego only. Ego perceives all love as special; focused only on one subject: the need that has to be fulfilled. By fulfilling this need, ego proves its usefulness and secures the appreciation of mind's owner. Yet, this is not natural for it is unlike the relationship between God and His Son. God gives his full love to His Sons and, doesn't ask for anything in return. Ego instead, takes but doesn't return. Return, is the perfect love He gave that comes back to Him, enhanced with the receiver's love. The quality you give is the quality that returns to you. "The measure you give will be the measure you get." (Mark 4: 24) Consequently, many feel guilty for the "sin" of giving little. Therefore, having no love is a source of guilt.

Eben Alexander, MD, who detailed his near-death experience in his book "Proof of Heaven", describes the love he felt while meeting on "the other side" a beautiful girl that came to be his long-gone sister: "She looked at me with a look that, if you saw it for a moment, would make your whole life up to that point worth living, no matter what had happened in it so far. It was not a romantic look. It was a look of friendship. It was a look that was somehow beyond all these ... beyond all different types of love we have known here on earth. It was something higher, holding all those other kinds of love within itself while at the same time being more genuine and purer than all of them." Love has no meaning except as its Creator defined it. It is impossible to define it otherwise and understand it.

How then, does ego see love? It does as we customarily see it. We "love" a person and desire his or her company for a while, until we start feeling unfulfilled; then, we glorify our departure from it with the excuse of "growing" along different paths. Sometimes we are unable to renounce that relationship once the initial interest is gone, and live in an abusive relationship. In the most fortunate situations, we fall in love again before we "grow" again or, before a relationship becomes "second nature". Ego's "love", which can be more accurately called special relationship, arises from the conviction of littleness. A more concise definition of special love would be: achieving an illusion of completion with what a partner has, and you need. If one is convinced of having no needs, he doesn't search for special love. Only a deprived person can value the acquisition of what he misses.

In this charade run by ego, one can never see himself complete because he is not. Ego notoriously values lack of completion because, lack of completion makes room for the display of ego's feeling special. In the case of love, ego offers a sense of completion by associating one who has a missing trait with another who owns that missing part. The brain that is aware of its imperfection is not going to renounce ego's service and gets involved in that relationship; something to be had. In order to enjoy freedom, one must renounce his dependence on outside help, resurrect his own awareness of completeness, and regain control of himself. Only then, he does not employ "love" to fill his personal void. Only then he can truly love.

Where disillusionment is possible, there is no love but selfishness. Being an illusion, selfishness is a temporary value while love, being truth, is eternal. Love is more than an emotion, it is a fact. Everything created by God is an eternal completion. In order to have joy, you simply must be your complete self. Love is built-in at your creation. Uphold your proper understanding, above any other understanding. Your completion is your rise of awareness to where truth is. If you don't upgrade your thinking, you cannot join the Kingdom; the only choice you can hope for is the mercy of God. God gives you all the time you need to wake-up and claim your worth. His mercy is His offer of the knowledge of truth and patience until you wake up to it.

The very reason for your creation of ego is to provide for yourself the feeling of being "a cut above." For ego's own importance, it is essential to one's ego to believe that the specialness it offers you, is a gift from Heaven. "The search for the special relationship is the sign that you equate yourself with ego, not with God's perfection." The special relationship highly values ego. Ego perceives all love as special. Yet, this specialness is not perfection but ego's assumption of having it. As understood on earth, love is subjective; therefore, ineffective. "The only true love is how God defined it. It is impossible to define it otherwise and understand it," Jesus said. Special love is selective and based on selfish needs, while holy love is universal, with specific affinities and, based on truth. Therefore, love is freedom while special love is bondage. "The real world is attained simply by the complete forgiveness of the old." (153) Forget all the improper thoughts you have had and, wake-up. Salvation is forgetting your past and the discovery of the true self. Realize that there is no union in separation from Creation, or freedom in the thoughts you assume you have, but you don't. In our physical understanding of reality, love must be physical. If we see it as a form of personal victory, a glory only ego can esteem, it means that we don't know God any longer. We only imagine Him in ways that satisfy our hope. We don't know who He really is and, we cannot comprehend its spiritual greatness. What we know, is what we see. The special love we cherish is a form of building obligations, while real love involves no obligations and no compromises to quality; only happiness. Forget this not, or love will be unable to comfort you. Since every special relationship is based on taking, it entails that only the deprived person could value it. Meanwhile, the deprived remains deprived until he/she grows to completion that truth offers.

To summarize: in the special or unholy relationship, two come together, each to complete himself with what the other has and, they stay until they realize that there is nothing that can be taken and then, move on. And so, they wander through a world of strangers who perceive themselves as bodies that live with other bodies, maybe in the same room and yet a world apart. It is not a mistake to have a limited physical life. One's special love cannot usually survive longer than that.

A holy relationship starts from a different premise. Each one is aware of his/her own reality and have no unfulfilled needs that require soothing. This state confers to him or her, freedom from ego and guilt. When all feel complete, the belief in differences is undone and conditions are set for peace and freedom for eternity. They see nothing to take from each other, but seeking the pleasure of togetherness. When we realize that we are perfect creations of a perfect Creator, we find that this is all we need to find that perfect love. Then, we see it as a reality that makes up the Kingdom, the place where we belong. Love is the rule of the universe, the power that makes it work in harmony. This power is what ego must deny in order to save itself.

When Jesus said: "Love your neighbor as you love yourself and love God with all your heart, all your mind and all your soul." (Mark 12:30& 31), He mentions love as an entity undivided by kinds or degrees. There is only one love, the one given by Our Father "to all alike" (206) or, there is no love. It is impossible for the child of God to love his brother except as himself and it's impossible to love God unless one loves wholeheartedly his brothers/sisters. God's holy creation is built from Himself. The whole Creation is HE. If you know yourself, you know your brother/sister and, you know God. You can then knowingly share it with others and, thankfully, return it all to the One who created this system. Only by loving God's creation, you love Him. You are love; a part of the universal love. If you see your brothers holy and love them, you see peace. For this reason, God made you a messenger of peace and love.

Love is the same as truth, forgiveness, atonement, and holiness. They serve the same meaning.

Love is the key to coming back to the Kingdom of God. One cannot return to God alone; he must bring with him the love for all his brothers/sisters. We all are love created by Love.

Love depends on forgiveness, which is a higher understanding of life. If one doesn't forgive all, he cannot eliminate all his negativity. Unless one loves others as he loves himself, he cannot access Heaven.

Love has no degrees. There is no special love. You can love only as God loves, or you deceive yourself.

V.
Our World

If we accept that our minds are parts of the Universal Mind, then our enlightenment is a universal gain. For our own good, we have to contribute to the universal quality by improving our own quality. We cannot do this by criticizing and continual fighting among us. We must improve our minds. It is doable! Start by knowing the universal truth, as presented by God. We know the damage of selfishness, specialness, materialism and so forth. Don't project any insufficiencies to others, don't accuse them and then retaliate against what we claim they think and do wrong. First and foremost, wake-up from our physical dream of ignorance. Can you do that? The most comfortable thing to do is to do nothing, as we already experienced for centuries. This is the age of ignorance, after all! Should we continue trotting down the same sorrow road? Can the spiritual way make sense to you? This is the only solution I can see, providing we understand it properly. The accurate understanding of ourself, is the purpose of this book. I hope you find it useful!

For Jesus, the choice is simple: elect knowledge, uphold wisdom and protect its purity. The solution to our problems lies in our minds, no matter how much we like to point our problems to external agents, outside of self. Jesus always stood for meanings over displays: love by loving. People instead, like to solve our problems by obedience to external laws, rituals and customs as the way to "please" God, so that, once again, it will motivate Him to do what we should do: love, be truthful. It doesn't take much to show respect for quality, adulation of and subjection to the laws designed by us and assumed to be of His. The problem is that we do not have to show Him anything; we only have to be loving: no abuse, no killing, no specialness. If you don't love and try to cover-up your selfishness with ceremonial customs, you miss the point. Outward displays do not raise your inner value and do not impress God. Thoughtfulness does. Quality doesn't need to be displayed; it is obvious. Quality is love, truth and wisdom. God's "equal love is given equally to all alike!" (154) Follow the love in your heart and you will be fine. If you choose to follow outside (written) laws and rules instead, you downgrade yourself from son of God to servant of your laws; and a rebellious one on the top of it. The fact that one believes Jesus' words and honors Him, doesn't provide one with the inner quality he needs; not until he learns and incorporates Jesus' teachings. You either follow His guidance or settle for your ego.

How can Jesus' death be interpreted as a sacrifice that results in the remission of your sins? It cannot! "No one can die for anyone else, and death does not atone for sin." (155) If sin is God's creation, it cannot be removed. But, if it is a human creation ("Do not let your mouth lead you into sin,"- Ecclesiastes 5: 6) then, you had better stay away from it. If one doesn't practice love and wisdom, he is wasting his life. It is within human ability to renounce their mistakes that lead to sin. You created your mistaken thoughts, you can remove them. Nobody is in charge with your mind but yourself. Jesus' execution cannot straighten up the bystanders' minds. Our awareness of ourselves is strictly ours to deal with. God is also aware of our condition but, His intervention in our life would diminish us and He would never do that. Instead, He gave us all the time we need to wake-up. You must reach your holiness in order to enjoy your divinity. You pay for the consequence of your misjudgments customarily called "sins", every moment of your life. Everything you do, has a consequence. You are the creator of your sins, so you know better than anyone else how to eliminate them. You show your quality through the efficiency of eliminating your selfishness. This task is not transferable. Jesus' thoughts and deeds are teaching lessons that guide us to salvation but they are not salvation itself. "To this end I was born, and for this cause I came into this world, that I should bear witness unto the truth." (John 19: 37) Jesus' physical death does not pay for our mis-judgments. He only tried to enlighten us so we can be aware and avoid being mistaken again.

For God, your thoughts are not a secret. We think with His mind that He,God, gave us; to use as ours. For this reason, "my mind is part of creation and part of its Creator," Jesus said. (156) Private thoughts "do not exist, and so they mean nothing." (156) The influence of our brain only clogs our communication with God. God knows our thoughts and understands us intimately. We are our thoughts and, the world is our thoughts about it. Our future depends on the quality of the thoughts we have. For this reason, it is always a good time to evaluate how we think. Our only mistake is that we prefer to evaluate the others' thoughts. We decided long ago to judge others of good and evil; so, we don't disturb our petty self-righteousness.

The value system we use on earth is not able to fix our lives. Without improvements, we will continue to downgrade ourselves to beyond the hope of recovery. The time will come when the Lord will have no choice but to pull us out of our swamp, and help us understand what we do not. Again, He won't change us. Change is our duty. What we built here, based on opinions and run by egos, can be called hell. It is natural to desire a happy life, based on truth that God built in us. That happy life can be ours only if we return to the mindedness of our original selves. We can enjoy Heaven only as we think holy thoughts and only if we love our fellow humans as we love ourselves. No one can save himself alone. Because we are all built the same way, if we see our brothers/sisters innocent, we see ourselves innocent too and, we are all saved. Dealing with all kinds of patients in my dental office, for half a century, I learned to see their perfection behind their antics and assumptions. We should see ourselves as puzzles that perfectly fit into the spread of Creation. If we don't fit, we cannot be a part of it; but outsiders longingly looking in. What makes this situation sad is that we have Heaven itself (the God-given love) built within us from the beginning. We only have to access it: "Kingdom of God is within you." (Luke, 17:21) Return to love, truth and wisdom, so you can fit into the holy place, reserved for you. As created, holiness abides in us and is subjected to our unencumbered acceptance. If we look for alternatives to perfection, we will find imperfection and settle for whatever we make of it. We call this approach: "that's life!" It would be reasonable to check your minds. If we don't improve, we cannot expect a better life. We receive back what we give. Our lives are the expressions of our mentalities. To be transferred to Heaven simply because we physically die, or through God's grace, is impossible because "death does not atone for sin," (155) and, God's grace does not improve our mentality. Death removes us from physicality, but doesn't automatically correct our thinking. It takes time to recover from our physical fantasies. If we are not holy, we cannot share Heaven.

God being perfect cannot be improved, and still, God found a way to do just that by creating us from His own nature: love from love, holiness from holiness, and wisdom from wisdom; co-creators and partners in peace and happiness. There is nothing outside God that could create us. As already mentioned, because we are organic parts of Him, we are part of the divine Trinity. We and the Father are One. We had been created in order to make possible the gift of sharing. Everything true can be increased by sharing only. Sharing is not only wise; it is the denial of loneliness, the opportunity for joy and the only way of increasing our love. Judging by the physical life we have, we may not regard ourselves as holy. There is a lot of confusion and dirtiness in the world that led to senseless dramas and tragedies. All those are products of ignorance, belief in the fantasies of our introverted minds, backed-up by egotistical pride. When we chose to follow our impulses over God's advice, we raised our flag of specialness; we hastily built a trap and pretentiously called it "independence" and proudly stepped into it. One may wonder why we drifted so far away and why didn't God stop us. From God's perspective, the answer is simple:

First: He has given us the freedom of choice that we highly appreciate and highly misuse. For Him, to interfere in our decisions means to violate the freedom He granted us, which, like any decision He makes, is well thought and eternal. We may ask, knowing that we may misuse our freedom, why did He give it to us? The obvious answer is, because we cannot fully benefit from our freedom if we don't freely experience it. Physicality is a learning environment. There is a big difference between being set in a certain environment chosen by somebody else, and choosing the same environment ourselves, in complete freedom. While both ways aim to the same outcome, each one of the two identical choices has a different personal significance. The difference is that we have a limited personal attachment to the choice that is freely given (take it or leave it), while the desired and pursued choice has a personal appeal. Excited about their newly found freedom, Adam and Eve chose to replace God's truth with the "truth" they liked. Our world is the consequence of our thoughts; our creation that enjoys our full support. Unfortunately, once in our physical environment we built ourselves a cozy nest which we don't want to abandon.

Our reality is not as pretty as it could be but, it is ours. In His fairness, God doesn't want us locked in our lower condition. He offers His advice and helps our return to the ideal life He prepared for us. But again, He won't force us to adopt His way. We either decide to change, or stay with our fantasies. We are free!

Second: He took care that whatever we do on earth, we cannot cause any permanent damage to ourselves. This earth is a kind of playpen where we can run our foolish games, suffer the consequences and learn their values at our individual speeds. Whatever we do here has short term consequences and, doesn't call for His interference. Our temporary doings in our temporary life are permanently erased afterwards. We are not created as bodies and, we are not bodies. Our physical bodies are transient tools, of no value beyond physicality. Jesus' experience shows how little the body meant to him. The worst we can conceive, the death of our bodies, is of no significance. "Do not be afraid of those who kill the body but cannot kill the soul." (Matthew10:28) We are our souls! On the eternal perspective, physical bodies are useless and death doesn't exist. "I raised the dead by knowing that life is an eternal attribute of everything that the living God created," Jesus said. (157) What we call death is only a transition from one form of existence to another. Death is the elimination of all fantasies we did consider to be true and clogged our minds with them. Pain and suffering we physically experience, are consequences of our physical fantasies only. We will understand them.

Third: starting with Adam, we adopted this different value system; the one we use today. Based on the pride of judging good and evil, Adam and Eve along with their descendants created this new habit of judging, classifying, comparing, accusing and, lived with it. This individual mentality is disconnected from our Father; it is our human understanding which doesn't understand much. God never judges and compares. He never accuses. His creations are units with no parts, no alternatives and no replacements. God never judges because there is nothing to blame or judge. His creation is perfect. We cannot understand God with our ego mentality and God cannot take the aberrations of ego into consideration. We tried to incorporate the divine concept and created our prized church of ego, a product of our minds that cannot help much. The reason for its inefficiency is that we try to mend two unrelated mentalities: ego's relativism, and God's truth.

Because the two do not mix, we must choose one of them. It seems, we chose materialism while keeping spirituality as a spare hope. Physical aberrations bring us to a point of crisis! Jesus started to teach us the way to eternal joy but, before fully succeeding, his life was cut short. To develop knowledge takes time. "I have yet many things to say unto you, but you cannot bear them now." (John 16: 12) As for the future, Jesus will always be available to guide us to the truth. After his departure, religious authorities, deeply self-righteous, afraid to lose their prerogatives and unable to fully understand him, diligently combined the two contradictory concepts and created the compromise that is our religion. At the receiving end, people struggle to answer questions left unanswered and paste together different ideas in a way that makes sense to them. Their answer is not truth, but the highest understanding they could accept. Left alone, we further slid into our physical ways… . This makes our return to Heaven impossible. We don't address the real issues in a valid way. The real issue is how to atone for all our mistakes. The valid way is the understanding of truth: the return to love and holiness. The only purpose of life on earth is to learn and free ourselves from misconceptions. As mentioned, salvation is "escape from guilt" and guilt is the consequence of our misunderstood life and confused values.

A common way of avoiding responsibility is claiming predestination. Predestination is our believe that God is choosing certain people for certain duties. Interesting theory! Except, God doesn't predestine any one for any job, except for excellence. If predestined for any reason, it means that we are not free and that He doesn't honor His pledge of our freedom. It means that His love is selective, His creation is not even and we have different worth. It also means that He evaluates people the same way we do here, on earth. If God uses predestination, this means that His creation is not fairly handled and perfection doesn't exist. Predestination avoids improvement through experience, which is God's initial intention. It makes forgiveness a placebo and, promotes stagnation. If so, no one can be guilty because everyone is that which he is predestined to be, that we have unequal purposes, and, are selfishly used by God. This drastic form of control is a human way, run by ego and arbitrarily attributed to our perfect God!

Jesus, on the other hand, taught us that the quality he achieved, any one of us can achieve too. What brought Jesus to a higher understanding can bring us also. He implies that we are equally well created. Where Jesus is, anyone can be and, anyone should be. "There is nothing about me that you cannot attain." (158) This is his message to us and the purpose of his teachings. "Do as I did." "For I have given you an example that ye should do as I have done to you." (John 13: 15) Don't limit your sense of reality. You can extend it to whatever degree you allow your awareness to go. Our minds are deeper and more spacious than our bodies. Mind exists inside and outside our bodies, strongly and powerfully. This extension is what people perceive as "my space" or "my comfort zone," for lack of a better term. We don't feel comfortable in narrow spaces. The existence of our minds outside of our bodies is usually understood as intuition, understanding, telepathy, prognostication, feeling, and so forth. Our nature allows one to feel another's thoughts and emotions and, share our minds. Aim high, for there is your place!

"God created man in His image and likeness" doesn't mean identical. In this statement, 'image' should be understood as 'thought,' and 'likeness,' as of a like quality". "God did create spirit in His Own Thought and of a quality like to His Own. There is nothing else," (159) is Jesus' message. Comparisons like "as," "more" or "less" are the products of perception, a human trait that wants to quantify, organize, accept, and reject. Truth, on the other hand, simply is above any comments, thoughts, and interpretations. God gave us individuality because joy and happiness can be increased only by sharing them and, in order to share, more than one individual is needed. We should be aware that individuality doesn't mean physical bodies. Physicality only pushes individuality to its extreme and, assigns to it new, unintended meanings. For a successful share, both sides must be of equal abilities and of similar qualities. We had not been created to compete, fight, and be separated, but to love and share. What you give is what you receive because there is nothing else to receive. In the Kingdom of God there is no difference between having and being. There, you have access to everything there is. God keeps no secrets from His Sons. It is only on earth where to be, means to have and to have means to take.

God created the human spirit in His own mind and of a quality like His Own; love from love and wisdom from wisdom. We are not identical, obviously; we only share ways and means. This is how God freely shares everything with His Holy Son. His Son is, as a matter of fact, a Sonship, since all His Sons have some of God in them, (160) and live as a unit, exchanging, creating, enhancing their happiness, and enjoying their peace and love for each other and for our Creator, in total freedom. But then, one got the idea of a physical world that can make us feel special and, since then life changed for those that joined it. Obviously, Jesus is not one of them.

We believe, knowledge is facilitated by our intelligence. If so, why has most of what we achieved since the Tree of Knowledge, been used for increasingly destructive purposes? Peaceful technologies have been generally by-products from military research. Meanwhile, the important issues like the awareness of who we are and what is life or the understanding of love, stagnated and often regressed. The truth has become a matter of opinions. Intelligence is understood as whatever one may think of it. Technology, that is supposed to make our daily lives so much easier, separates one person from another more than ever before. Typing on a computer keyboard deprives us of the emotions involved in direct communication. Easy access to an abundance of information diminishes the meanings of particular findings. Speed is to the detriment of the deepness of thought. Knowledge is not wisdom. Fast and repetitive information reduces independent thinking. New expressions like "cognitive exhaustion," "suckers for irrelevancy," "wasters of attention" or "perennial plugged ins", have appeared. Critical thinking is not taught any longer in schools. Ego is on the rise! All right, but where is our intelligence?

What have we learned from the huge communist experience? Almost nothing. People are still attracted to communist slogans, are still unable to evaluate the meanings behind their claims, are still floating in a fog of make-believe and ego-pleasing falsehoods, and, are still transferring the responsibility for its failures to others. Some look for a new and useless revolution. So far, revolutions we have had, created a lot of changes, damages, changed the players, but, did not improve our awareness of truth and maintained selfishness. We generally prefer the comfort of self-rightfulness and personal opinions. Television brings you commentators with their opinions and inserts a piece of equipment between you and the facts; a physical tool to push you further away from the action (reality). The news media doesn't expose one to the truth, but to a party's opinion. You become the victim of others' agendas rather than a free thinker. There was a time when media was proud to relate facts as they are. Did we truly progress?

Those questions motivated me to introduce some quotations:

Jesus said once: "unless you are guiltless, you cannot know God." (161) Only in a state of guiltlessness we can feel our connection with Our Father. "Therefore, we must be guiltless. If you do not have the necessary qualities for knowing God, you have denied Him, while He is all around you." (161) "God is in everything I see." (162) He created everything there is, from the only source available: Himself. If we don't know Him, we miss the truth and believe that some weird ideas of some self-righteous people, may be true. "There is but one God, the Father, of whom all things are, and we in him." (1 Corinthians 8: 6) Therefore "The only knowledge there is, is the knowledge of God." "God is everywhere and in everything forever." (163) He is everlasting because He is not damaged by opinions, influence, specialness, and so forth. He and His creation are the singular expression of pure and indestructible truth.

We should always remember that God created His Holy Son, from His spirit, guiltless for eternity. (164) The perfect God could not produce a faulty son. We all are His sons, but not all are sharing His truth and wisdom. "His equal love is given equally to all alike." (165) Once Adam chose his own line of thinking apart from God's, he empowered his ego and lived according to its rules for the rest of his physical life. People forgot that Heaven is not a place, but a condition. Heaven is an awareness of perfect oneness and the knowledge that there is nothing else; nothing outside this oneness and nothing else within (166). "The Kingdom of God is within you." (Luke 17:21) God gave to His Son the knowledge of Himself since there is nothing else to give. The belief that someone can give and get something other than knowledge, cost Adam and his descendants the awareness of Heaven and the Identity God awarded him. Everything is within our minds and of our minds, Heaven included. There is nothing outside of Mind. The universe is of God's Mind and, because of that, it has no limits. We don't see it because we burdened our minds with half-baked opinions and self-satisfying illusions that prevent us to see the light of truth. Truth is love and, love is all that matters.

1.

A Reminder

Sin is not a negative thought delivered by an evil genius; it is one's own desire to pursue a selfish goal. Cain's ego made him kill his brother Abel, because Abel received a higher evaluation from God. Cain couldn't accept being second place. Sin is the thought of a man who claims to be better than he is and, deserves more than he should. Cain believed by killing the winner, he will "rightfully" be recognized as number one. His ego fulfilled its selfish duty and motivated him to kill his brother. This kind of reasoning could make sense only in the physical world where the competition for specialness thrives. Only there, superiority is considered glorious.

Sin and ego are thinking systems raised by the Original Family in response to God's uncomfortable observation of their mistakes. Instead of admitting their transgression, they argued: we did it because…. Even the glorious future King David, afraid of King Saul's hate, decided to "speedily escape into the land of the Philistines; and Saul shall despair of me,… so shall I escape out of his hand.""And David arose, and passed over with the six hundred men that were with him into A'-chish, the son of Ma'-och, king of Gath" (I Samuel 27:1, 2). And David made a raid "against south of Judah, and against the south of the Je-rah'-me-el-ites, and against the south of the Ken'-ites. And David saved neither man nor woman alive, to bring tidings to Gath, …in the country of the Philistines." "And, A'-chish believed David, saying, He hath made his people Israel utterly to abhor him; therefore, he shall be my servant forever." (I Samuel 27:10,11&12) David massacred his own Israelites to save himself from King Saul's pursuit to kill him. He found in his mind that the safest way of saving himself is to kill his own kind; thus giving to the Philistine's leader the feeling that he, David, is truly separated from his Israelite brethren and, dependent on the Philistine's for protection. In his raid, David didn't leave any survivors who possibly could tarnish his reputation. All this: for his own self-preservation (ego).

Adam and Eve couldn't accept their error either. They interpreted their disobedience as something trivial, a simple curiosity about that forbidden fruit. They turned their backs against their kind and fair Father. Their self-righteousness didn't allow them to doubt the quality of their own decisions. Going their way, they created nations and those nations, run by egos, started to plunder each other. In the short run, sin proved to be more profitable than truth. For physically independent people, each one taking care of himself, it's easier to eliminate a competitor rather than improving their own performance! From ancient times people acknowledged God's greatness through displays of personal meekness and ceremonies; but, these are no more than attempts to please God, the way humans understand pleasing, and secure His leniency for their misdeeds. Likewise, people assume God shares human-like values, (Genesis 1: 27) human-like bodies, human emotions and thoughts and that He can be flattered pretty much like humans are flattered.

Alongside the experience with polytheism, people started to return to the awareness of one God. Moses, who is still venerated today, became the most influential promoter of monotheism. For the Old Testament writers, physicality is truth: it is constantly perceived with all our senses and it constantly feels real. Consequently, people conducted their lives according to their physical needs. They went as far as to sacrifice their own sons, on occasions (see Genesis 22:2, Jeremiah 32:35, Micah 6:7), in order to prove their utmost contrition for their other sins committed and be forgiven. This physical assumption is not shared by God; He "established no sacrifice." (167) The Old Testament presents God as physical; enjoying the smell of cooked meat. During the beginning years of Christianity, some said "that Christians need not bother reading the Old Testament; that the God of the Old Testament is not the highest God nor the creator of the world." This idea had been circulated among Christians of the 2nd century and, represented the views of the Gnostics, Valentinians, Docentists, Marcion and others. The sacrifices were not meant to please or benefit God. They had been intended to alleviate their own guilt felt for their own sins. The writers of the Old Testament assumed that sacrifices would please God and, make Him be more forgiving. This was an early idea of redemption by worshipers. The price for their forgiveness had been established by the sinners themselves and, paid for with the innocent lives of others. For the people of the Old Testament, everything and everyone had a price. Consequently, people did take this pay-off into consideration and continued living as they saw fit. Nevertheless, God doesn't punish and doesn't run transactions; humans do. All He wants from us is to return to the quality He gave us. When useless sacrifices and rituals became a wide-spread gripping practice, the mold had to be broken and truth reestablished. It's time to wake-up! How can killing an innocent other atone for one's sins? To be fair, only coming back to our senses, reviewing our values and being honest, can atone.

At this critical point, Jesus entered human society to straighten it up from inside out. He came as a simple teacher who raised the issue of truth and common sense that any man could relate to; with a power only a superior being (God) could have. No evil was ever created (by God) but imagined by humans. No self-aggrandizement and no opinion can stand for truth. All we need is to search for truth and love. Can one do that on earth? It seem difficult, but it is possible. His righteousness is beyond doubt and, He became our trendsetter whose impact restarted our calendar from number one and shook our existing value-system: He is the son of God!. He pursued us to renounce our mistaken thoughts: "Salvation is escape from guilt." (168) Replace self-satisfying thinking with knowledge of truth. It makes no sense to commit a crime and then interpret it as a pay-off for the forgiveness of previous other crimes; only a inconsiderate opinion can come with such idea and present it as divine wisdom. Humans being humans, instead of completely eliminating this idea of sacrifice, they came up with the idea of a super-sacrifice that would take care of all sins, forever: the sacrifice of the holiest man on earth, Jesus Christ. Jesus pointed the way to God. He gave us the tool for achieving something the physical world forgot: the return to truth, also known as Heaven. This tool was not the old bargain of sacrificing for acquittal. This tool introduced by Jesus is the change of mind's interest from opinions to truth. Renounce the assumption of an outside evil and clean-up your own mind of selfish assumptions. By adopting love, which is truth, sin is not only forgiven but eliminated.

What Jesus meant, stands against our physical culture and seems hard to accept. Our minds are set to follow the way of ego. Jesus follows the way of truth. For us, matter is real while for Jesus and for God, it is not. "God is a Spirit: and they that worship Him must worship Him in spirit and in truth." (John 4: 24) While people value what they see, Jesus values the truth He knows. What's more real than something we can touch, see and smell? You may be surprised but, in Heaven, we can also touch, see and smell. The materiality we experience is our understanding of life. But, "The world we observe is not the ultimate reality. It is the manifestation of a reality that lies beyond the plan of our observation." We interpret our world as a solid mass while, as a matter of fact it's a space filled with waves of energy. God is not a physical person, and neither are we. Sometimes we have visions that cannot be explained and, sometimes, we don't see the physical objects around us. We are the creations of His Mind yet, prefer the creations of our minds instead. Many believe that once physically dead, we still exist in an immaterial form, which is our indestructible reality that lies beyond our physical appearance. After we physically die, we are not dead; we are released from our physical illusions. Three days after being crucified, Jesus came back to greet his supporters and prove that He is not dead; that there's no death. Even before his crucifixion, Jesus brought Lazarus back to life three days after his physical demise. He knew that death is fiction so, He claimed the truth of Lazarus's existence and Lazarus manifested himself. Jesus also reportedly brought back to life a man in the city of Naim (Luke 7:11-14) and the daughter of Jairus (Luke 8:41 and Mark 5:21-30). People believed that these miracles could happen only because Jesus is special: the only Son of God and part of Trinity. Meanwhile, Jesus never claimed to be the only Son of God. On the contrary, He called us his brothers. The Christian Church did declare His divinity, based on the assumption that He was fathered by the Holy Spirit and not by physical man, as we are. Meanwhile, Jesus called himself the "Son of Man". He repeatedly claimed that we, the common people, are His brothers who, once restored to our original condition, could do everything He did "and more". Regardless of who our physical fathers are, our true primordial Father is God. Our physical parents give us our physical qualities and, take charge of our upbringing. "For whosoever shall do the will of my Father which is in Heaven, the same is my brother, my sister, my mother." (Matthew

12: 50) "I said, ye are Gods." (John 10: 34 and Psalm 82:6) "To us there is but one God, the Father of whom are all things, and we in Him." (1 Corinthians 8: 6) "The rich and poor meet together: the Lord is the maker of them all." (Proverbs 22: 2) "One is your Master, even Crist; and all ye are brethren. And call no man your father upon the earth: for one is your Father, which is in heaven." (Matthew 23: 8, 9) God doesn't create different sons in different ways, some more special or better loved than others. We all are equally well equipped and equally loved. We are as created, healthy and living forever. Jesus based his miracles on his knowledge that death and illness do not exist except in our beliefs. For Him, miracles are the removal of the illusions we burden our nature with. He refused to believe the human fiction of sickness and death and relied on his Father's reality. He told those he restored to health: "your faith has healed you," meaning, faith in the perfect Creation. That, is our reality. No doubt, the faith of the one who was healed had been endorsed by the unwavering faith of Jesus and, the truth of health manifested itself.

His gift of miracles and his new spin on scriptures, stated with confidence, induced those who knew Jesus to perceive him as Messiah: the one who would come to save the Jewish nation (again, an intervention from outside, not an inner raised awareness). He truly is the savior of all people from their ignorance. He came as teacher of truth so, "He that believeth in me, the works that I do shall he also do; and greater works than these shall he do." (John 14:12) This statement shows that he saw himself as a work in progress: more, than what he did, can be achieved. It is possible that, as mentioned before, his passage through physicality, contaminated to some extent his mind. He was not changed but, he understood people's thinking. Nevertheless, Jesus knew that his as well as our minds can be and will be clean of any contamination. He was a man who could perform miracles through his faith and knew that any other man can, if he shares the truth. Miracles are not gifts that can be given to someone but, the removal of the misconceptions that overwhelmed someone's mind. In other words, miracles are not favors. They are a return to normal. "There is no situation to which miracles do not apply, and by applying them to all situations you will gain the real world." (142) "Every child of God is one in Christ, for his being is in Christ as Christ is in God." (169) With our physical mentality, we cannot claim miracles because we confuse knowledge of truth with opinions about it. Our contamination with physical concepts, is perfect.

The apostles quoted Jesus as saying during their last supper, while raising the cup of wine: "this is my blood of the New Testament, which is shed for many for the remission of sins." (Matthew 26: 28) These words made the experts believe to be a fore-ordained atoning sacrifice for the salvation of "many." According to the Jewish tradition, "almost all things are by the law purged with blood; and without shedding blood is no remission." (Hebrews 9:22) The Jewish religious establishment couldn't consider salvation as being the result of adopting higher values. They thought that they already have the right values and, those values must be guarded by their stern physical laws. Those laws are their claim of valor. Jesus, because he upheld different values, had been accused of transgression and, executed. He stated that salvation means rising to the mentality that endorses love for all, not the mercantile mentality of specialness and subjection to external, conventional laws. For humans, external, physical laws, overrun the divine internal laws of love and wisdom, in their attempt to fix the human belief system. If touched, the perfection of divine meaning is altered and, it is not perfect any longer: "Christ also suffered for us, leaving us an example, that we should follow his steps." (1 Peter 2: 21) Follow His steps means to share His values, not the values of the world. There is one fundamental law, the law of love, that sustains life and, this is not even a law as we understand law. This law of love is our given nature that we should respect. The prevalent opinion among religious scholars is that the remission of sins could be achieved only through the merciful killing of God's Son, as an atoning sacrifice "by which we are sanctified" ... "once and for all." (Hebrews 10: 10) Could God have His son killed to pay for His other sons' misjudgments?! This is the conclusion of a mercantile mind: everything has a price. The atoning sacrifice of an innocent other was considered a fair price for buying back a sin. (Psalm 111: 9) This could be eventually accepted if the victim would consent but, the victim is not consulted and not even aware of the coming ordeal. Even more surprising, the price for the sinner's "atonement" is set by the sinner himself and considered the will of God. Not to mention that the sinner doesn't even pay with his personal assets; he does, with the life of the innocent other.

The apostles were simple people who didn't have enough time to absorb Jesus' totally new metaphysical vision of life. At his premature death, the apostles were still confused and not wholly ready to follow him. The three years spent together were not enough for those uneducated, most of them illiterate, followers to understand it all. Many of our students today, after twelve years of general education and four years or more of college and universities don't fully comprehend their new professions until they spend more years building their own experience in the field. Could the apostles grasp Jesus' metaphysics in three years? If not, we should ask why did Jesus come to them and not to the more educated others? The answer can be found in the mentality of the learned of that time. They worked to formulate high concepts and opinions, polished them up and considered them "truth". Proud of their understanding, they closed their minds. Job done! "from what you want, God does not save you." (170) Nevertheless, "If any man thinks that he knows anything, he knoweth nothing yet as he ought to know." (1 Corinthians 8:2) From this perspective, it comes as no surprise that the learned of that time decided to have Jesus killed rather than review their own well-established, self-righteous, publicly accepted opinions. Accepting Jesus' understanding of life, would nullify their qualification as spiritual leaders. This was too much to bear in our physical culture. Jesus was not interested in opinions. He is concerned with truth: "Seek first the kingdom of God." (Luke 12:31) Everything we value in our short journey on earth is obsolete in eternity. People look for God's mercy to save them instead of evaluating their own mental quality. They valued physical achievements through outside interventions: miraculous healings, generating food, winning wars, lucky situations, supremacy over others, wealth and so forth. They all had been excited to see miracles produced for them and never considered to produce those miracles themselves. The way they had been, they could not perform any miracle and they didn't even dream of being any different. When Jesus' physical demonstrations stopped, they abandoned Him. There was nobody who could inspire them any longer and they reverted to their old egos. Many projected their insufficiencies on Jesus:... 'if He is the Messiah, why didn't He free them from the Roman occupation...?'... 'Why didn't He free himself from being nailed on the cross...?' Judas himself, after spending time with Jesus, listening to his speeches and witnessing his miracles, abandoned Him in disappointment and anger when he realized that Jesus is not interested in physically bringing them the prophesied glory. He was angry because Jesus didn't do what he expected him to do. Judas didn't see the Roman Empire as a means for disseminating Jesus' teachings worldwide. He trusted instead his and others' myopic opinions of physical, special glory, versus the glory of the highest civilization of the time and, lost sight of Jesus' spiritual objective. Judas didn't want to give to Cesar what belongs to Cesar and neither give to God what belongs to God. He gave credence to his own opinion: if Jesus is the Messiah, then he's supposed to do what ancient scrolls said the Messiah would do: free Israel! He valued the promises of the Old Testament writers more than he valued Jesus' words. When he finally realized his mistake, Judas couldn't live with himself and committed suicide.

Our return to the Kingdom of Heaven, known as salvation, is all we need. It seems confusing that salvation doesn't happen as we had been told it would. Now, the Bible assumes that at His second coming, Jesus will make a glorious entrance: "behold a white horse; and he that sat upon him was called Faithful and True, and in righteousness he doth judge and make war. His eyes were as flames of fire, and on his head were many crowns; and he had a name written, that no man knew, but he himself. And he was clothed with a vesture dipped in blood: and his name is called The World of God. And the armies which were in heaven followed him upon white horses, clothed in fine linen, white and clean. And out of his mouth goeth a sharp sword, that with it he should smite the nations: and he shall rule them with a rod of iron: and treadeth the winepress of the fierceness and wrath of Almighty God. And he hath on his vesture and on his thigh a name written, KING OF KINGS, AND LORD OF LORDS." (Revelation 19: 11-16) Compare this glorious scenario with a straight, nonceremonial release from ignorance through love and wisdom! "He that doesn't love does not know God; for God is love." (1 John 4: 8) Besides, we had been told that for God "salvation is of the mind," where learning takes place and where our values are.

Salvation is not a flashy and theatrical appearance but freedom from confusion; the unrecognized goal that supersedes all other goals, and not a physical show. Salvation is, as a matter of fact, escape from guilt, (168) a rise above misjudgment. For as long as we believe that guilt is justified, whatever the reason, we will not be able to look within ourselves. There the guilt lays, there the atonement must take place. Between guilt and atonement cannot be any compromise. "The undoing of guilt is the essential part of the holy Spirit's teaching." (171) We can choose only one of the two: guilt or atonement. Organize your house and sieve what you need from what you don't! Return to wisdom. Do you prefer to be resurrected as son of God, or redeemed as a human being on another earth? Redeeming is a pay back, the equivalent of paying a ransom, a release from blame or debt, so one can have his credentials restored. It is a physical process. Resurrection instead, means the revival, the raising back to the life we are intended in its spiritual, unaltered form.

If we believe that guilt is real, the reconciliation with God (the atonement) is impossible. The only choice we have is the choice between the two opposite beliefs: guilt and innocence, which is the same as the choice between illusion and truth. There is no other way. Because sin and guilt are interconnected, if sin is forever, so is the guilt that follows. Fortunately, sin is an option, an opinion that, like any opinion, can be either dismissed or accepted. Atonement cannot atone as presented in the Bible because it only pardons the sin but doesn't deny it out-right (it is an ego safe procedure). True atonement is turning away from sin. It is the dismissal of sin and guilt. Sin is your creation and your responsibility. It is within your ability to deal with.

For as long as you believe that we are bodies, you will believe in sin. (278) The Son of God was created innocent (172) and, remains innocent because this is his given nature. He did many mistakes, but those don't damage the quality of one's creation; one is eternally innocent and, does necessarily return to his innocence. Sin is a learning experience. Denial of sin is not achieved through prayer or ceremonies but by understanding its meanings as well as all the meanings of life. Laws or ceremonies do not change a sinful mind. Understanding, enlightenment, does. If you continue to harm, you remain bound to earth until you will finally get the meaning of life.

While the church of ego interprets the Kingdom of Heaven as something outside of you, God created it as you. You have the Kingdom of Heaven in the pristine mind and soul you have been gifted with. You hold the key to your happiness. Sin is not a fixture, but a misjudgment.

"Whosoever is born of God doth not commit sin,"..."because he is born of God" (1 John 3: 9) "For in Him we live and move and have our beings,"... "For we are also His offspring." (Acts 17: 28) You cannot change your reality as Son of God unless in a dream of an alternative life. "Thought cannot be made into flesh, except by belief." Jesus said (173). Therefore, believe the truth! Accept the awareness of who you are. Separation can be possible only in the physical state. The body is ego's home because we can have ego only if we see ourselves as separated bodies. Only then can we compare, promote, compete and enrich ourselves to the detriment of others. Physicality is a trap.

"This world is not the Will of God, and so it is not real." "But every mind that looks upon the world and judges it as certain, solid, trustworthy and true, may believe in two creators; or in one, himself alone. But never in one God." (174) We have not lost the knowledge of who we are, we only forgot it. (175)

God is lonely when the minds He created do not fully communicate with Him" (88). He cannot share His joy with you until you know joy with your whole mind. Every mind that is changed back to its original quality, ads joy throughout the Kingdom.

God did not create evil, and does not hold "evil" deeds. The idea of Him punishing you is not His and has no value. The punishment, will never happen. To burn forever in tar or to be tortured in any way for "sin", is not justice but a frightening revenge fostered by human minds. God knows you are the way you have been created: holy forever. No mistake is forgiven by Him because none is real and therefore none is regarded. God does not believe in retribution (176) and in all that bargaining with pay-offs and punishment, which our existence on earth is so concerned with.

The best way to describe the idea that God sacrificed His Son is: "an anti-religious concept." (177) "I am incapable of receiving sacrifices." (178) "The power of love is in His gentleness. Therefore, He cannot crucify nor suffer crucifixion." (179) "Vengeance is Mine, sayeth the Lord" is a misconception by which one assigns his own "evilness" to God, Jesus said (180).

"This world is not the will of God." (181) This world happened because Adam decided to see the Garden of Eden as his territory, run his way. In the same way, we recently decided to see communism as a panacea and, as known, this concept collapsed under its own ignorance. Likewise, we try to glorify socialism today by introducing a form of radical democracy, based on a form of self-righteousness, glorified as "progressive". Poverty is of the ego, never of the truth. (182) All opinions feel justified to accuse others and claim to be truth. By the way, God is not a killer and doesn't ask anybody to kill.

2.

JESUS

Jesus introduced a new era to history. Multiple gods had been abandoned to mythology, live sacrifices had been considered obsolete and life on earth acquired a new purpose: return to love and to the quality we had been awarded at our creation. Who would have thought that our high aspirations would stumble from its first steps into the most hideous crime of the most distinguished son of God that came to help us: Jesus Christ.

Religious beliefs had just been established among the most influential churches of the more prosperous countries on earth. Those gods had been given the most exciting stories that filled mythology books. It seems it was the opportune time to reintroduce the knowledge of the only true God and of His expectations of us. True, but those people most concerned with a true God, had their own mythology in place and reacted in a strong way to a real divine presence, the Son of God, that had a different message than local mythology did. The authorities of the Jerusalem temple had been so upset over Jesus' message (God's son) that they requested his crucifixion. The Roman governor of Israel, in order to satisfy the local leaders and avoid a rebellion, didn't find any reason for Jesus' execution but, in order to keep the peace, granted to have Jesus executed. It is difficult to fight a strong ego. During his short life on earth, Jesus made a strong impression. For once, the way to salvation from our harsh, restrictive living, had been revealed: know the truth. It still remains to know the truth and adopt it. This proved difficult because we have a long history of living a physical but wrong life. At the end of it, we still don't know if we are physical beings or spiritual ones. It is important to know who we are because each kind of existence comes with its own important consequences. Because we have had a physical life for thousands of years, we are surprised to find out that we may be spiritual beings after all. Some believe they already know the truth and, few are interested to know more than what they already believe. Then, there are those who want to organize the whole political-economical system in ways they consider fair. I lived through the well advertised and poorly applied materialism in communism: a simple mentality that may be socially comfortable but, it is hardly a compliment and, seldom successful. Brilliant Socrates was sentenced to death for thinking differently than the majority in democratic Greece. Stalin sent to the gulag most of his independent thinkers. Jesus was killed because of his higher mindedness. So, the forced message: think average! In the US, schools are focused on group activities to the detriment of knowledge, critical thinking and learning; creativity gets stifled.

Faithlessness, that is mental sickness (183), had been considered enlightenment in our physical, popular mode. Ego (selfishness) is more practical than the more sophisticated love.

Still, the singular voice of Jesus dusted our faint memories of God like a breath of fresh air, and Christianity spread. Jesus' physical similarity to regular people, his ability to directly relate to our challenges and his familiar way of verbal communication made him so real that people felt they have a chance to reach amazing heights if they follow him. Jesus' purpose was to raise people's awareness to the ability of having an ideal life, and join Heaven. The obstacle to this awareness is that people could not accept to renounce their egos. So religion ..., got Jesus killed. Ego versus truth! His disciples suddenly leaderless, frightened and confused, interpreted his crucifixion in their traditional Jewish way as a form of atonement. They did not understand that:

- Jesus is not a body and neither are we. We are the minds and souls using those bodies.
- Love and truth are not something we can rationalize. They simply are.
- Life is an indestructible perfection. Physical death is only the collapse of our physical opinion about the nonphysical.
- By traveling back and forth from body to spirit in front of our eyes, Jesus proved immortality.
- The purpose of life is to learn from our mistakes, renounce them and return to our God given perfect values.

- Our happiness is complete when we achieve the completion of love.
- Jesus taught us how to achieve the same quality as His: using truth and love as the foundations of life.

In the beginning God was the only existence in the universe and He created everything that is. The difference between physical and metaphysical is the difference between what we believe and what God knows. To the laws of physics any action has a cause. If so, what is the cause (what makes it happen) to make matter organized into life and run by precise laws? We should notice that matter is inert, it doesn't think or create. The only creative force is the abstract mind, which makes sense of everything happening in the universe. God, being above anything physical, is not subjected to anything physical. He works as He thinks and, His creations are dependent on his mind.

If we start to dissect the truth, we destroy it. Truth, like anything given by God, comes as a unit. No individual part or organ of ours is separately functioning. Only the complete, functioning collection of organs is the human. The same is true for the Creation of the universe. So far, we attempt to disintegrate its wholeness by paying attention to its units. We built on earth a way of living based on physical selfishness (the assumption that we are individual and independent beings); a system that affects the Creation's wholeness. If we believe we know what we need to know, we don't know what knowledge is. The church we've created encourages us to expect God to step in and change our lives for us: "For by grace are we saved, through faith; and that not of yourselves: it is the gift of God: not of works, lest any man should boast." (Ephesians 2: 8, 9) Salvation is presented by the Church as a personal gift from God, while it is our responsibility to trace back our steps and reconnect to the way we had been created. God already gave us everything we need to accomplish this job. Now, we have to show our willingness to get saved from the limitations of physicality; follow Jesus' advice!

Ego's Church borrows ego's interest in physical matters. Its most outrageous idea is the substitutional atonement: an atonement through the physical sacrifice of an innocent other. The "sinner" is a spectator to the drama of his "assumed" reconciliation by the sacrificing of someone else to his behalf. This so called "atonement" is a crime. Equally nonsensical is the idea of being admitted into Heaven due to the Church's mediation and, the assumption of God's mercy. Access to Heaven requires a heavenly quality; "the knowledge of truth." Heaven cannot be accessed by another's (God's) mercy. (No exceptionalism!) So we either upgrade our standards or can continue to be as it is now and, we will stay in the environment that fits our values. We have the given ability but, we usually miss the commitment to improve. We believe we belong where we presently are. We tell ourselves what we want to hear:… 'we had been created as physical beings and, we should stay that way until God decides to save us. …' That means to be saved from our own creation of ourselves?! No one is special in the eyes of God; we are all equally created. We may not seem equal because we adopt a wide variety of choices that bring us to the most unusual conditions but, we are equally gifted.

Does improved mentality come through the grace of God, (an outside intervention), or through personal effort? We have been created ably to clean our house and all its hidden corners. It seems logical to allow people to correct their misjudgments and discover their given nature on their own and by their free will. We should reclaim our original quality. This is dignity. We prefer instead to rely on the comfortable and backward mentality of ego. Ego tells us we are special and fine just the way we see ourselves. This is the continuing "age of ignorance".

Ego is the belief that soothes our failures. It picks pieces of truth and rearranges them to our liking. We did it for so long that we don't know God any longer. "Knowledge cannot dawn on a mind full of illusions, because truth and illusions are irreconcilable" (355). Jesus guided us to abandon the illusions of our rules-laden faith so we would be able to rediscover God. This is the return to the perfection that allows us access to eternal life.

The established religion's initial reaction to Jesus' teaching had been to squash his new movement. Jesus was executed for being found guilty of truth and his small following became hunted down. Nevertheless, the new religion struck a chord, touched inner needs and gradually spread. Not clear about the details of the new faith, people displayed strong and diverse doctrinal opinions as they tried to harmonize Jesus' teaching with their understanding of life. Each group upheld its "rightful" idea of divinity. Particularly debated was the nature of Jesus, as both human and divine.

After centuries of fierce conflicts, leaders slowly settled around a compromise that satisfied the majority. Tired of struggle, many in North Africa adopted the newer and more concise Muslim religion of their conquerors. The Muslims believe that we have only one physical life in which we do our best to cleanly live the kind of faith we have. At the end of it, God decides if we "deserve" to be kept alive or not. This is a harsh concept upheld by harsh people. The Jewish religion is somewhat similar,: one either lives by a set of laws or, ... nothing good would come from it. By Christian beliefs, we misjudge, make mistakes, and once corrected we become aware again of our renewed selves with a clearer understanding. For us, on earth, Jesus' teachings came as a breath of fresh air: all our mistakes can be corrected by correcting the thoughts that produced them. We can then enjoy such unbelievable possibilities that we would not conceivably return to the petty mentality and simple practices we had used before. Our imperfect past would be abandoned, along with our bodies and their opinions. Only our divine essence will live forever. The difference between what we have on earth and what we can have in Heaven is so dramatic that, once aware of it, we cannot possibly prefer to stay physical.

More than two thousand years after Jesus' crucifixion, we still had not found our answers. The undisputed truth is too different from our current understanding. The fact that Jesus was submissive and allowed the temple authorities to apprehend him, knowing well the outcome, was interpreted by the early Christians as fulfilling God's will. God is, after-all, aware of everything. Sacrificing one's son was still considered very special at the time. Imagine sacrificing the "Only Son" of God with his Father's approval! Such a high and holy sacrifice must be, they thought, due to the most holy purpose of all: a pay-off for the sins of all humanity, forever. Very dramatic but, does anybody see that Jesus was not sacrificed but executed for political reasons? Can anyone figure out that Our Father didn't send him to be sacrificed (God doesn't recommend killings) but that Jesus himself, aware of his freedom of choice and of his immortality, decided to go through this experience as a demonstration of what life's reality is? Jesus knew that through his execution he will prove the truthfulness of everything he taught, so that we can have a valid credibility. No doubt the crucifixion is a traumatic experience but his commitment to stand behind his teaching is the best test of His truthfulness. No doubts possible.

At the time, substitutional atonement was a traditional practice well known and accepted by local culture. Nevertheless, can the Creator of life allow the killing of his "Only Son"? "God established no sacrifice," (184) "God weeps at the sacrifice of His children who believe they are lost to Him." (185) Nevertheless, Jesus' sacrifice was Jesus' choice for the reason of proving the truthfulness of his statements. His followers, fearful and embarrassed, gave him their highest honor they could imagine:… 'He atoned for all our sins….'. They even interpreted his murder as the expression of God's love!?

Jesus said: "Teach only love, for that is what you are. If you interpret the crucifixion in any other way, you are using it as a weapon for assault rather than as a call for peace for which it was intended. The apostles often misunderstood it for the same reason everyone misunderstood. Their own imperfect love made them vulnerable to opinions and, out of their own fear they spoke of the 'wrath of God' as His retaliatory weapon.'" "If the apostles had not felt guilty, they never could have quoted me as saying, 'I come not to bring peace but a sword.' This is clearly the opposite of everything I taught. Nor could they have described my reactions to Judas as they did, if they had really understood me. I could not have said, 'Betrayest thou the son of man with a kiss?' unless I believed in betrayal." "Judas was my brother and a Son of God, as much part of the Sonship as myself,". (186) Judas was only confused by his contradictory thoughts and emotions: if Jesus is the Messiah, why doesn't he fulfill his promise to free Israel from Roman occupation? (see the Gospel of Judas). Because atonement, as presented by the apostles, is not meant to deny sin, the future was open for sin's further use. This explains why the Church requires continual prayers for protection against sins.

Freedom of choice is God's will and, Jesus chose to stay with his teaching of truth and love. If he would avoid the crucifixion, his life's work would allow doubt and interpretations much beyond what we doubt today. So, in order to uphold the relevance of his teaching, Jesus chose to back-up his words with his own life. He could avoid the ordeal of crucifixion, but this would undermine his credibility and this He couldn't allow. By subjecting to execution, He demonstrated his love, the truth of his teaching and the permanence of life. He did it in the open for everyone to see and under the most adverse conditions. Love and faith are either eternal or they are mere fiction. Jesus didn't hesitate to prove them to be an eternal truth.

If any doubt of Jesus' understanding of sacrifice, He said: "Sacrifice, in any way, is a violation of my injunction that you should be merciful even as your Father in Heaven is merciful." (187) God doesn't want anyone to suffer or to sacrifice but to live a happy life. "God does not believe in retribution." "Sacrifice is a notion totally unknown to God." (188) Jesus said: "I am as incapable of receiving sacrifice as God is, and every sacrifice you ask of yourself you ask of me. Learn now that sacrifice of any kind is nothing but a limitation imposed on giving." (189) Sacrifice takes lives away. It takes victims away from their experiencing the physical world. It takes away victims' freedom of choice. For God, happiness is the free exchange of love that has the quality to return amplified to the one sharing it. This system works to everyone's benefit. We can never say enough: God is a God of life, not of death. Aware of the human misunderstanding of their own nature, Jesus came to teach us the way we should live in order to harmonize with the meaning of life. He didn't come to atone. He came to teach atonement. Atonement has a limited value because it refers to the sin committed in the past. But God didn't create past. Because the past is gone, the atonement which is also in the past, has no value. The bible writers assume that Jesus' sacrifice atones for any future sins, too. This means that we may sin again, possibly indefinitely, and, the Scripture writers assume that through His sacrifice, we may be forever forgiven. Again, as presented, sins are forgiven but, their presence and importance are endorsed by the act of sacrifice itself. This is not sin's dismissal! Even if so, how forgiven are we if we still have to continually pray for forgiveness? Shouldn't we renounce our sinful thoughts once and for all? Wouldn't this correction be the true atonement? It should, if it is true. Understand atonement as a mental upgrading and then "those who accept the Atonement, are invulnerable." (191) "The gift of union is the only gift that I was born to give." Jesus said. (190) This means that substitutional atonement, is a placebo, a feel good moment, an ego tactic. Atonement is a highly personal process, not one size fits all. If properly understood, atonement is the result of personal enlightenment, of personal commitment to love and not simply a gift dropped from outside. If gifted, the atonement would circumvent introspection and free choice. If given, it is not personally chosen and personally executed. In order to atone,

one must prove his commitment to love by loving. God wanted Jesus to teach and enlighten people; not to be killed by the alarmed self-righteous leaders of the day. His death was the decision of the established church, crystallized in its self-righteous system of laws and rituals. "The crucifixion did not establish the Atonement." (192) "Its only message is that you can overcome the cross." (193) Truth belongs to God. Jesus' decision to submit to local religious authorities was due to His understanding that, in spite of the expected cruelty, He finally had to confront the system He wanted to be replaced. Not facing his detractors would mean a failure on his part, a desertion He couldn't accept. He realized he had to make his closing statement, to live what He taught and demonstrate the truth behind His words: "Fear not them which kill the body, but are not able to kill the soul." (Matthew 10: 28)

The apostles, taken by surprise by the unexpected and fast unfolding tragic events, felt frightened and confused. Overwhelmed by the cruelty of Jesus' drama and fearful for their own lives, they missed the meaning of the momentous occurrence. They didn't understand why did God let this cruelty unfold. They lost sight that God gave us freedom of choosing our actions and that He couldn't retrieve what He once gave. The apostles missed the truth that life cannot be killed. They couldn't accept what they never thought was possible. Jesus' subjection to crucifixion was Jesus' own choice and not an atoning sacrifice ordained by God the Father. Atoning sacrifices had been common occurrences in the Jewish culture: "without shedding of blood is no remission of sin." (Hebrews 9: 22) Sins can be washed by blood alone! They never thought that "The crucifixion is the symbol of human ego." When confronted with the truth of guiltlessness of God's Son, ego pursued to kill him. Ego's reason is the claim of guiltlessness is blasphemous to God. "If we say that we have no sin, we deceive ourselves, and the truth is not in us." (1John, 1:8) Ego assumes the position of God's defender, when it fits its purpose. It interpreted Jesus' claim of guiltlessness as the final guilt that fully justifies murder. When Jesus acknowledged that He was the Christ, the Son of God, "the high priest rent his clothes, and said, What need we may further need? And they all condemned him to be guilty of death." (Mark 14: 63 and 64)

Jesus said: "I was created like you in the first, and I have called you to join me in the second." (194). His faith, made him unique and also an example that can be followed. God "has called you to join me," Jesus said (195). What happened afterwards was the best demonstration of what faith and love can do; a demonstration nobody else could perform. It was the only such demonstration humans could witness and the only one that could change history. Jesus' submission to crucifixion showed His faith in the reality that nobody else could see: the evilness of ego and the permanence of life. It also showed His love for us and the purity of Creation. Truly, His crucifixion and resurrection that followed are the most powerful pages of Jesus' teaching and the most misunderstood ones. This crucifixion is not in any way an atonement for bystanders' sins, but, a mind changer. His crucifixion showed that no matter what cross one may face, he can overcome it. Life cannot be destroyed. The crucifixion is what ego does. When it was confronted with the real guiltlessness of God's Son, ego tried to kill him; and attempt to put the whole thing away. Ego itself claimed the status of God and interpreted human guiltlessness as the final guilt that fully justifies murder. (196) (Also see 1John 1: 8) "Crucifixion is always ego's aim. It sees everyone as guilty and, by its condemnation, it would kill. Whom you perceive as guilty, you crucify. The Holy Spirit sees only guiltlessness, and in His gentleness, God would release us from fear and re-establish the reign of love. The power of love is in His gentleness. Therefore God cannot crucify nor suffer crucifixion." (197)

If God wanted Jesus crucified as a ransom for our salvation, to whom was this ransom paid? To Himself?! He had already forgiven us. (God is "good and ready to forgive; and plenteous in mercy" - Psalm 86: 5 and " thou hast delivered my soul from the lowest hell" 13: 13) "To the lord our God belong mercies and forgiveness's, though we rebelled against him": (Daniel 9: 9), "The Lord is longsuffering and of great mercy, forgiving iniquity and transgression" (Numbers 14:18.) Atonement is a personal change of mind from sinful to sinless, not the torture of another to one's benefit! God showed the lack of value of the physical body, and of all physicality for that matter. He showed the nature of death beyond any assumption. He never made amends, never favored some over others, never mentioned atoning by killing and never accused anyone of sins. "Whosoever is born of God doth not commit sin." (1John 3: 9) Sin is a creation of those who forgot their Father and built their own unreal "reality". It cannot entail death because death doesn't exist. Bodies are not us and we never die. If no consequence, there can be no cause. More than that, the apostle Paul said, "God has shown me that I should not call any man impure or unclean." (Acts, 10: 28) If Jesus didn't die, will we, his brothers die? Again, what dies is the physical image we adopted and all its related values, while the divine reality of us lasts forever. We should remember that Jesus never changed the dynamics of this world and never showed any interest in doing so. His interest was the disclosure of truth. If we understand the truth of ourselves, we understand God and, all issues that occupy our minds get resolved.

Reading the Bible, we can see that Jesus never claimed paying for our sins with his sacrifice, or in any other way. In one of the earliest letters of the Bible, written in the 50's of the first century, the 1 Corinthians 11: 24, apostle Paul quoted Jesus: "This cup is the new covenant in my blood. Do this as often as you drink, to remember me." I Corinthians was written many years before the Last Super. During the Last Super this covenant was mentioned slightly different by Luke: "This cup is the new testament in my blood, which is shed for you." Jesus didn't mention earlier, to Paul, of his blood being shed for us. He only asked Paul to remember him, meaning, to remember his teachings. Only after the crucifixion, the apostles attribute the new significance to the event: A cup of wine is not to remember Jesus, but to remind the readers that He died for us. It seems obvious that Jesus never connected his crucifixion with atonement. Nevertheless, the clergy makes this connection the central piece of the scriptures, ever since.

For Jesus, His crucifixion was just another attack with a full range of intensity and violence. He considered his body as of no value: "To sacrifice the body is to sacrifice nothing," (198) and, consequently cannot pay for anything. As mentioned before, the body is only a tool while the mind, which is responsible for our bodies' actions, cannot be sacrificed. So, why sacrifice his body? His "sacrifice" was meant to silence Him. The lesson of his crucifixion is that the destruction of the body is not the destruction of life; anything that is destructible cannot be real and is therefore inconsequential. One's bodily destruction cannot justify anger (199). If you respond with anger, you must be equating yourself with the destructible, and you are therefore regarding yourself insanely. "I have made it perfectly clear that I am like you and you are like me, but our fundamental equality can be demonstrated only through joint decision. You are free to perceive yourself as persecuted if you choose. When you chose to react that way, however, you might remember that I was persecuted as the world judges, and did not share this evaluation for myself. And because I did not share it, I did not strengthen it. I therefore offered a different interpretation of attack, and one which I want to share with you." (200) "As I have said before, 'As you teach so shall you learn.' If you react as if you are persecuted, you are teaching persecution. This is not a lesson a Son of God should want to teach if he is to realize his own salvation. Rather teach your own perfect immunity, which is the truth in you, and realize that it cannot be assailed. Do not try to protect yourself, or you are believing that truth is assailable." (201) "I elected, for your sake and mine, to demonstrate that the most outrageous assault, as judged by the ego, does not matter .... That is the only way in which I can be perceived as the way, the truth, and the life .... You are not persecuted, nor was I." (202). "Forgiveness is the answer to attack of any kind." "The message of the crucifixion is perfectly clear: teach only love for this is what you are. If you interpret the crucifixion in any other way, you are using it as a weapon for assault rather than as a call for peace for which it was intended. The apostles often misunderstood it, for the same reason that anyone else does. Their imperfect love made them vulnerable to projection [versus knowledge] and out of their own fear they spoke of the 'wrath of God' as His retaliatory weapon. Nor could they speak of the crucifixion entirely without anger, because their sense of guilt had made them angry. These are some of the examples of upside-down thinking in the New Testament, although its gospel is really only the message of love. If the Apostles had not felt guilty, they never could have quoted me as saying,'I come not to bring peace but a sword.'This is clearly the opposite of everything I taught. Nor could they have described my reaction to Judas as they did. I could not have said,'Betrayest thou the Son of Man with a kiss?'" (203) "Judas was my brother and a son of God, as much part of the Sonship as myself." (204) We may conclude that crucifixion was the result of opposing thought systems coming to a head. In other words, it was nothing but a clash of cultures, a conflict between two ways of thinking: ego and the Holy Spirit. The crucifixion is a crime with no other significance than an expression of human misjudgment. Crucifixion is ego's choice; its customary response to a challenge. The interpretation of crucifixion as an atoning sacrifice was meant to protect the established opinion at the time, despite the fact that God never asked for sacrifice or crucifixion for any reason. It is the resurrection that symbolizes the release of guilt through guiltlessness. The apostles who ran into hiding after Jesus' capture, fearful and still unable to completely understand their master's teaching, got the shock of their life when days after his execution, Jesus came to their hiding place behind "shut" doors. The disciples "were assembled for fear of the Jews, when Jesus came and stood in the midst, and said to them, Peace be with you." (John 20: 19) Their bewilderedness went beyond reason and they concluded that Jesus' resurrection could happen only to Him because he is special. The thought of specialness had been highly accepted in Jewish culture: Jesus is the only son of God and, therefore special. Regardless of what anybody thought, Jesus never claimed He paid for anything with his execution. For Him, sacrifice gets nothing. "I want mercy not sacrifice," Jesus is quoted (Matthew 12:7). "No one can die for anyone, and death does not atone for sin." (205) Sacrifice is an idea solely born from people's imagination, an attempt to show their love for the one to whom they dedicate the sacrifice, while in and of itself, sacrifice is nothing but murder and thus a departure from love and a promoter of guilt. "To sacrifice the body is to sacrifice nothing." (206) Those who believe that sacrifice is born out of love, must learn that sacrifice is separation from love. It is amazing how truth can be interpreted in order to suit someone's stout opinion. Fortunately, truth is unassailable and the truth is that "sacrifice is a notion totally unknown to God. It arises solely from fear, and frightened people can be vicious. Sacrifices in any way are a violation of my injunction that you should be merciful even as your Father in Heaven is merciful." (209)

Resurrection demonstrates that because death doesn't exist, its cause, the sin, doesn't exist either. Some people come up with a temporary idea of sin that will disappear when the person believing so, dies. Truth and love instead, last forever as people live forever. They are indestructible because they are built flawless. Everyone will awaken in due time, through the dawning in their minds of what is already there: truth, love, knowledge. This awakening is accomplished by the union of one's will with the Father's. Once released from the grip of materialism, everybody will understand the nobility of their inborn nature. Resurrection is a coming home; oneness reestablished. The choice of Heaven is too obvious to miss. God helps us at every step because the reawakening of every Son of God is necessary to enable the Sonship to know its wholeness. We all have been formed from the One and the One is not whole if any one of its parts is missing. It is only a matter of time before we all will figure out the truth.

Resurrection in its original, spiritual understanding is the complete triumph of Christ over ego, truth over perception, achieved by transcendence. Each day, each hour and minute, even each second, you are deciding between the crucifixion and resurrection; between the ego and the Holy Spirit. Ego is requested by guilt; the Holy Spirit is defined by guiltlessness. The decision is yours.

Jesus said: "I am your resurrection and your life. You live in me because I live in God. And everyone lives in you, as you live in everyone. We all are created by God from Himself. Can you then perceive unworthiness in your brother and not perceive it in yourself? Can you perceive it in yourself and not perceive it in God? ['We and the Father are one'] Resurrection is the will of God" (208). "The God of Resurrection demands nothing because He does not require obedience, for obedience implies submission. He would only have you learn your will and follow it in the spirit of gladness of freedom, not in the spirit of sacrifice and submission." (207) Regardless of everything you may think, the Resurrection is salvation achieved through atonement and, atonement is your will. You cannot atone until you want it. There is nothing more that you can have, in addition to what God offers you. What else could be in your best interest other than an eternity of everything?

The Second Coming of Christ is described by Jesus as "merely the correction of mistakes, and the return of sanity. It is a part of the condition that restores what was never lost, and re-establishes what is forever true. It is the invitation to God's World, the willingness to let forgiveness rest upon all things without exception and without reserve." It "is Christ restored as one Identity, in which the Sons of God acknowledge that they all are one." (194/425) The restoration of mind is done through one's personal decision.

There are people that will say, "A bird in the hand is worth more than two on the fence." This is the power of ignorance, ego at its best. The bird in your hand is your surety of the physical possession. The birds on the fence are life and freedom. The bird in your hand will die in captivity; the birds on the fence will perpetuate in freedom. All the inconsistencies, inaccuracies, tribalism and exaggerations of the scriptures are due to people's inability to distance themselves from their physical condition. We tend to believe we are created as bodies but, bodies are narrow limitations; God wouldn't confine us in such small quarters. If aware that God is a Mind and we are extensions of Him, then the truth will appear totally different. We are minds also and create as He does, communicate as He, and can think as high as He. If God is a mind, His apparent indifference to our physical suffering would be His lack of recognition of our physical fantasy where nothing fits as it should. Jesus willed to come to us in a body in order to relate with people on even grounds.

An important lesson of Jesus' later experience comes from His refusal to blame anyone for His crucifixion. "When he was accused by the chief priests and elders, he answered noting. Then said Pilate unto him, Hearest thou not how many things they witness against thee? And Jesus answered him to never a word; insomuch that the governor marveled greatly." (Matthew27: 12-14) Why didn't He? If you believe that you had been attacked and your attack in return is justified, then should you not defend yourself? This way, your brother deserves a returned attack rather than love. An eye for an eye and a tooth for a tooth, seems to be a fair assessment. The only objection is that attacking a body is attacking something that is not you, nor him, and consequently is insignificant. If your body is meaningless, your returned attack has no justification. If you respond with attack, you downgrade yourself for being angry for so little. Your anger is more damaging to you than any damage is to your body. You cannot claim to answer to anything coming from outside of you, because your answer is only to your inner thoughts. Anger is your answer to the false perception of yourself. The attack makes you angry and you react to your own anger. Again, your thoughts of pride and anger are the products of your ego. Anger is a form of attack and one cannot attack the created without attacking the Creator. This explains why Jesus was never angry and never recommended anger to others. "And the servant of the Lord must not strive; but be gentle unto all men," (2 Tim. 2:24.) "Put in [your] mind to speak evil of no man, to be no brawlers, but gentle, showing all meekness unto all men." (Titus 3:1, 2) "The meek shall inherit the earth" means that the defense that cannot attack is the best defense. "They [the meek] will literally take it over because of their strength." (211) "They shall inherit the earth because their egos are humble, and this gives them a truer perception." Anger always involves the projection of separation that perceives humans as unrelated and alone, competing and arguing. Little do they notice that the projection of separation is contrary to the unity provided by God and, must be accepted as one's own responsibility. As you give, you shall receive. If you forgive others, you will be forgiven. (Mathew 6: 14) "O man, whosoever thou art that judged: for wherein thou judge another, thou condemn thyself; for thou judgment does the same things." (Romans. 2: 1) This connection between what one does to another and to himself is not strictly physical.

People had restrained their thinking in the totalitarian countries because they considered it prudent not to contradict or even be of concern to the political power. Dreaming and creating, require freedom to unfold. Creating is being. Once you stop thinking you start dying. For this reason, totalitarian countries (communism in particular) did not produce any creative advancements. The feeling of mental stagnation and, of spiritual incarceration, made me renounce all my physical possessions I eagerly accumulated in communist Romania. I initially thought that the possessions I desired, would offer me freedom from communist dependency. Once achieving that degree of independence, I realized that independence is much more than physicality can offer. I became a dissident and started to rebuild my life from zero. Those who admired my success in Romania, had been puzzled. They thought I wanted more possessions. For my own self-preservation, I couldn't tell them that what I wanted was the freedom to know and do, in a country where both knowledge and achieving are not limited by government rules. The totalitarian government's big mistake is its self-praising idea that it is the only reliable defender of public fairness and safety. The communist government is the biggest jailor ego could build. Free communication makes that government afraid of the spread of feared politically "incorrect" opinions so, it tries to control it. In my birth country, knowing the truth was considered not only politically incorrect, but a threat to communist's own nature and purpose. I felt suffocated. Truth is undeniable. Life is free knowledge and I wanted to know more than the government allowed me to know. The physical redistribution of assets is not the key to success; nonphysical awareness is the key. Success is not physical but spiritual. Fairness is love and wisdom. Jesus understood the importance of the Father's values and chose to share them. He understood love and love prompted him to come and try to save men from their own illusions. Thus, he became a Christ, no longer a man, but a guide for us to do the same. "A guide does not control; he directs, leaving it up to you to follow." (212) Control is against God's given freedom and an insult to the abilities we had been gifted with at our creation. God knows that one has no need for help to enter Heaven. He has never left it. One only needs to liberate himself from the false beliefs that keep him away. As one washes the sweat and dust from his body, so he can renounce the misguiding thoughts and be pure. This is the symbolism of baptism. No unclean thing shall enter the Kingdom of Heaven.

"No man cometh to the Father but by me does not mean that I am in any way separate or different from you except in time, and time does not really exist. The statement is more meaningful in terms of a vertical rather than horizontal axis. You stand below me and I stand below God. I am higher because without me the distance between God and man would be too great to encompass." (213) Jesus presented to us what we, in our condition, cannot see or understand with our means. It seems, there is nothing to understand. All we need is awareness of truth.

Jesus' first coming on earth had the purpose of teaching us the way to holiness. He taught us the basic concept of love and added: "I have many things to say unto you, but you cannot bear them now." (John 16: 12) In order to say all that He wanted to say, He chose to dictate his message printed on more than 1200 pages to Helen Schucman, a psychologist at the Columbia Presbyterian Medical Center in New York City. Jesus identified himself to Mrs. Schucman and convinced her, who initially was a resistant atheist, to take the job. The book, "A Course in Miracles", was finished in the fall of 1972. It is the main source of inspiration for this book. Since Jesus' purpose was to teach, this comprehensive course can be considered the fulfillment of his promise. In an abstract way, this may be considered his Second Coming. By peacefully dictating this book, He could say more than He could, by talking to people. To no surprise, like on His First Coming, his message was met once more with resistance. The Church of ego gave Him no recognition. We just ironed out our acceptance of what He said during his First Coming and feel we don't need another shakeup, no matter how divine it may be.

How does love save you? If you love, you forgive, deny ego, sin and guilt, and return to the Self you had been created. Since God and His

Creation are perfect, we all are eternal. Perfection perpetuates and constantly amplifies itself by loving. We reach the gates of Heaven together with those we love; something one cannot do alone. If alone, your love is less than perfect. The measure of your love lies in how you see your brothers. Your completion is found in the complete dismissal of your sin and guilt. Seeing your brothers as holy is the recognition of your own holiness and the purity of our Creator.

3.

ATONEMENT

In the Garden of Eden, "A deep sleep fell upon Adam, and he slept." (Genesis 2:21) Nowhere is it mentioned that he woke up, because he didn't. In his dream, he created his own world different than the one he came from. As his Father loves His creation, so Adam loved his own except he did it in his state of dream. Adam's world, being imaginary, is inherently temporary, imperfect and not true. As God created Adam from His own perfection, Adam conceived his own creation from his own imperfection. He had to figure out how his world will work, weight his choices and decide the values he had to live by. Unlike other Sons of God, Adam let his emotions get the best of him and, built his own world accordingly. It is his world! No one should come to tell him what to do and how. His descendants learned the ropes, built values and ways to match their environment and, with each passing generation become even more human. Since ancient times, observant people noticed our steady decline and predicted a cataclysmic conclusion. We will reach a time when we will be so far away from God that we won't be able to reconnect. This is when "the Day of the Lord" will come; the day when we will have no hope and He will come and save his overwhelmed human experiment. That will be our last chance to wake-up. He will show us what we are unable to see now, and change course. Again, God will not change our way for us. He will help us understand where we got off the road, we will understand what we missed and agree to change back to normal… or not.

In order to evaluate and judge the others, Adam had to see humans as separate beings inhabiting separate bodies. People believe it is reasonable for God to share their opinions they are so proud of, rather than they to share God's. God considers every person worthy because He created everyone worthy and, they are worthy under their load of mistakes and illusions. Jesus stated that the Final Judgment contains no condemnation because God sees no flaw in His creation; only the confusions of us, who are those who decided to live the physical life. Physicality is imagined, therefore not real and forgiven. In our human state of opinionated self-righteousness, we judge our neighbors in terms of right and wrong according to Adam's evaluation. For God, "All things are lawful"…"but not all things are expedient." (I Corinthians 10: 23) Things that are lawful, but not "expedient", are not punishable. We are "punished" enough by our own wrong choices. We are allowed to live this kind of life because it is useful to understand our mistakes and, would show us what is useful and desirable to have, instead. The plan went wrong when the humans, instead to returning to the group, started to adjust to their new physical condition. Human opinions are closer to our heart than advices coming from the invisible God. Their independence is mesmerizing and their free access to the infinite world of ideas pulled them away from the idea of perfection. All ideas are attractive but, only one is true; only one is eternal. Sure, we are free to think whatever we want but, we are inclined to favor what fits our physical environment. Our creations are precious to us. God respected our freedom. He expected us to learn from our failures but, we fell into a state of self-righteousness supported by mental tactics that drew us deeper in our delusions. "The natural man receiveth not the things of the spirit of God for they are foolishness unto him." (1 Corinthians. 2:14)

Confused between what we see and what we are, people tried to combined the two faces of "reality" even if no bridge is possible between them. Still, we try to put them side by side and believe that it can work. Our Bible is a good example of this attempt. We are not aware that "The world of bodies is the world of sin." (214) Physicality welcomes the soothing presence of ego, while spirituality relies on truth provided by the spirit of God. Do we want to grow and know how everything is, or to stay put and enjoy what we have? Physicality tries to either appease or condemn; spirituality enlightens. We are hesitant in choosing between our human arrangement and God's perfect plan. Our creation is our baby, heaven is His. What God created is certainly better, but it doesn't feel like our idea.

Try to compare love and jealousy. Both are the consequence of loving someone, but one of those two feelings is the opposite of the other. Jealousy implies possession while love implies giving. Jealousy, revenge, and discrimination are what ego wants, for the reason of "protecting" your condition. Jealousy is a lack of quality that doesn't make you right, but it makes you feel in control. Its formal association with love, forgiveness and fairness, gives jealousy a façade needed to make us feel clean without being holy. This self-satisfying mixture makes the separation between truth and illusion, difficult. We consider the two sides of understanding, acceptable: one as a fact of life, the other as a moral demand. Both being the expression of who we are.

Jesus and the Holy Spirit teach us that we are God's Children: "You are part of God," (215) Being created by God, from Himself (there is nothing else to be created from), means that God, who is perfect, built us according to His perfection, as part of the Holy Trinity (216). The fact that we created for ourselves this kind of life we have on earth and believe it is true, doesn't mean that this opinion is correct. There is so much more beyond our physical awareness than is within it! Truth cannot be influenced by opinions as light cannot be affected by darkness. Nevertheless, we usually dismiss what is not our idea and doesn't look that attractive. We hesitate to investigate the truth; we prefer to interpret the truth in a way that fits our opinions.

Truth is, undoubtedly, the only way that leads to Salvation but, one cannot know truth if he doesn't know what is not true. The chance to evaluate alternatives is the reason of having the Tree of Knowledge of Good and Evil. For one to be right, the other must be wrong and wrong doesn't exist beyond an example. Evil is an illusion. God didn't create anything wrong or anything evil. Still, we like those games of right and wrong, love and jealousy, up and down. In ego's understanding, sin entails death. ("the wage of sin is death" / Romans 6: 23) Consequently, ego comes with the idea of atonement achieved through sacrifice. According to scriptures: someone must die in order to pay for the damage (sin) that one did to another. The surprise is that the perpetuators are left untouched: they do not pay for the atonement, do not pay a compensation, do not apologize, do not change their attitude and, are not even mentioned. The one who is sacrificed for atoning purpose, as mentioned, is not the perpetrator of sin, may not even understand what happens and why and, consequently, cannot atone. Nevertheless, being practiced for a long time, the idea became traditionally accepted without checking its value. This time, faced with the unexpected crucifixion of Jesus, people paid their respect to him by assuming that he paid for the sins of all those who believed in him, forever. This was again, an emotional decision because, it is not possible to pay for one's misjudgment by doing another injustice (a crime of killing an innocent other). Sin is not a merchandise and, cannot be physically evaluated. Also, if Jesus, knowing how little the body meant for him, ("Body is meaningless." 217) would he offer his meaningless body to us, the ones he loves? (218) Could he teach us that physical bodies can unify us mentally? "The body is the symbol of what you think you are." (219) So far, we see us as separate individuals, while we are a part of a holy unit. Jesus' body was not of any greater value than ours (our bodies can be equally revitalized) and certainly not a source of salvation. His value is his mind: "Salvation is of the Mind,"…"This is the only thing that can be saved." (220) Jesus never claimed of saving his believers from sin through his own death. This is nonsense! This claim was made by his confused and guilt feeling apostles. "No one can die for anyone else, and death does not atone for sin," Jesus said (221). This kind of "atoning sacrifice" is a useless crime. Sin is annulled by its own abstract nature. It is a fantasy and a mistake; consequently it is unreal. Killing a body for the sin committed by one's weird thought, is absurd. Why kill the body for a mistaken thought? It would be reasonable to kill the thought that created the sin.

As for the pain Jesus suffered at the crucifixion, keep in mind that He could control bodies. He healed the sick, removed infirmities and brought people back from death. Couldn't He control his own pain? We are told that He didn't complain and didn't make a noise while crucified. Also, He died within hours, much faster than usual. The nails didn't create lethal wounds. Crucified people had been left to die slowly, in public view, some times in a day or two. By subjecting to the cruelty of crucifixion, Jesus certified what he taught: reality is not physical and life doesn't require a body. Life is of the mind. How can we expect to know the truth, while living a physical fiction? How can we pretend that forces that supposedly exist outside of us (Satan) are responsible for how our minds work? We choose our explanations that can cover for our mistakes and allow us to feel reasonably innocent. We are not misled by forces outside of us. We invite those improper ideas for personal reasons. We prefer to pass our mistakes to someone else like Satan and, claim innocence. Jesus came to us as a teacher: "for I have given you an example that you should do as I have done to you." (John 13: 15) He is an honest, well-intended and competent adviser, not a pusher. We decide what to accept from others and what to resist.

A physical sacrifice cannot atone for mistaken thinking and, death doesn't atone for sin. Jesus understood us as He understood himself. The only difference between He and us is the difference in the level of understanding life. In other words, it is the knowledge of truth. God amplifies His happiness by sharing messages with us, for the benefit of All. He is All. For this reason, selfishness and specialness cannot fit in God's perfection. Selfishness and special abilities only apply to our physical understanding of life as separate individuals living independent lives and comparing one with the other. Only the human writers of the scriptures could claim that Jesus is special because He is the only son of God, "begotten not made". Jesus knows that we are all built the same as he is and differ only in our level of awareness. We can read in the Bible that "We are gods; and all of you are children of the Most High." (Psalm 82: 6) Jesus never claimed to be the only son of God: "I ascended unto my father, and your Father; and to my God and your God." (John 20: 17) More than that, He asked people to follow his example and raise to the awareness that allows us to do everything he, Jesus, did and more (John 13: 15). This performance is not possible if one is any less than He is. Therefore, the difference between Jesus and us can be found only in our level of awareness. Jesus' death, like any death, doesn't atone for sin. No two persons perceive the same situation the same way in all its details and come to the same conclusions. One's mind's intricacies are best known by its owner. This means that only the owner of that mind is able to clean it all and only if he is committed to do so. "No one can die for anyone, and death does not atone for sin." The personal significance of sin makes the atonement a strictly personal affair. It is impossible for someone to atone for somebody else's sin. One's life is strictly that person's duty to handle.

We are not punished for choosing wrong; we suffer the painful consequence of it. The importance of life on earth consists in our opportunity to meet challenges head on. In other words, life on earth is school that one should take seriously, for his own good. One may flunk but, why does he? "It takes great effort and great willingness to learn." (222) It is much easier to stay ignorant.

Unfortunately, instead of updating our minds, we complain, justify our will, cultivate self-righteousness, and do new mistakes in an attempt to compensate for the previous ones. We are more aware of other people's mistakes than of our own. The others have to improve, not us! We dig in our heels and continue to believe we are justified to believe in what we do. So many times we believed the solution to our problems is around the corner: populism, communism, technology, escape into drugs, religion, emigration, etc. The life we've created is our mental baby, the only life we know and, we hold it as precious. Those who believe in socialism consider themselves advanced thinkers. Is the accusation of others, advanced thinking? It most likely is an emotion enhanced by catchy slogans. All mistakes are correctable. Communism is Karl Marx' mental creation and he is considered by his supporters to be a major philosopher. We had been bold to claim that he found the end of social evolution by prescribing a formula for finally ending social inequality but, he based his philosophical system on mistaken premises. He had been mistaken to demand the forceful removal of the social disparity without addressing the cause of that disparity. The cause of financial disparity is not the disparity of income, as Marx claims, but the disparity of interests, education and commitment. If one doesn't remove the cause, he cannot avoid the repetition of its effect. And, Marx didn't. Because of that, communism world-wide collapsed. People's desire to have goods, freely think and plan their own lives, brought down communism. No one can be free while dependent on government hand-outs. No one can grow if forced to comply to only one mentality and one way of living, set for all. More recently we have a follow-up group of "progressives", who focus mainly on motivating the indifferent or deviant pupils at the expense of neglecting the mentally alert ones who can bring society forward.

Unfairness is caused by selfishness, which is something beyond Marx's thinking range. He chose his physical understanding to the disregard of the nonphysical. Marx committed the major mistake of demanding people to think like himself. He thought that because he has the "answer" to the problem of social injustice, he is not only right but that he could demand everyone to think the same as he does. Freedom of thinking, dreaming and planning are prerequisites for life. To stop thinking freely, means to start dying. Freedom was the reason for the American emergence and, lack of freedom was the reason for communism's collapse. Some people appear to have more than others because people have diverse ideas, goals and motivations or commitments but, Karl Marx didn't even touch these issues of personal interests. He had been only interested in coercing people to adopt his simplistic formulas. Preventing people from being diverse and from following their dreams is not, by any stretch of the imagination, a social "heaven." As evidenced, communism didn't produce any meaningful creations or discoveries. It exceeded instead in stealing intellectual properties and economic ideas from the capitalist realm, while blaming it at the same time. Marx's philosophical world is ego's desire for control and self-preservation supported by popular conditions. Can this be an intelligent answer to social problems? His "popularity" excited the imagination of those who are unaware. The imperfect physical world we have, is our choice. "God did not choose this sorry path for you." (223)

If God would prevent us from experiencing the consequences of our poor decisions, we would never search for solutions. If we want to remain in the status-quo of this world, which is as close to hell as it gets, we will. Nevertheless, in the end we will all come back to what is our metaphysical home where a fulfilled, joyous life is waiting for us. It is only a matter of time before we realize where we are. The choice is too obvious to miss. Jesus came to make it easier for us to understand and believe that this process is doable.

All the laws that we accept now are of no value in the Kingdom of God. They belong to our fictitious world only. All the miracles that we refuse to believe possible on earth are natural in the Kingdom because there, perfection is reality. Miracles are not divine gifts for special people. Miracles just restore life to its original quality that is offered equally to all.

Jesus did believe in the truth existing in spiritual values when He was a man like us and, He became the one we revere today. "I was a man who remembered spirit and its knowledge," (224) he said. He gave credence to the value of his higher thoughts and, his thoughts proved to be true. "The Kingdom of God is within you." (Luke 17:21) This means, it is in your mind and soul. We are created as part of the Kingdom of God. As God created the world in His mind, (the only existing reality) likewise, we created our world in our minds. Because we believed in the validity of our world, we made it our reality. "Thought cannot be made into flesh except by belief." (225) When we believed in the truthfulness of our thoughts, we seamlessly drifted into the world of our beliefs. Adam believed in the physical world and drifted smoothly into it. Our physicality requires words that express only what we want to express and, for this purpose we use our voice. Jesus didn't go along with popular demands, as politicians do, but with what he knows is true. This is what the Holy Spirit softly advised him, and Jesus listened. He chose that which is obvious to the mind over what's obvious to our physical interests. There is nothing about him that any one of us cannot also attain. "For I have given you an example, that ye should do as I have done to you." (John, 13:15) "They [His disciples, past and present] are not of the world, even as I am not of the world," (John 17:16). The apostle Paul agreed: "I am in this world but not of this world."

All humans are divine. We are created by Him from Himself, through His will. "You shall know that I am in my father, and you in me, and I in you." (John 14: 20) God is all that is. There is nothing else to create from. Consequently, "you are the holy Son of God Himself." (226) Returned to Heaven, Jesus maintains his commitment of helping us to come back. "I am with you always, even to the end of the age." (Matthew 28:20) All that I wrote here is Jesus' recent message to us; presented the best I can.

The world is incomplete when the prodigal son (any one of us) is running astray, not fulfilling the purpose of his creation. God is missing you as you are missing Him. God offers us the opportunity to atone whenever we want to renounce our physical life. Taking this opportunity is the atonement; the abandonment of our mistaken ways. We are not the helpless opportunists waiting for Jesus to do the work of atonement for us. "I cannot unite your will with God's for you, but I can ease all misperceptions from your mind if you will bring them under my guidance. Only your misperceptions stand in your way," (227) Jesus said. "You are the Kingdom of Heaven, but you have placed this belief in darkness so, you need a new light. The Holy Spirit is the radiance that helps you banish the idea of darkness. This is the glory before which dissociation falls away, and the Kingdom of Heaven breaks through into its own." (228) We are in possession of the needed abilities. We can access the awareness that would make us follow Jesus' teaching and his example. "Be ye therefore perfect even as your Father which is in heaven is perfect." (Matt 5: 48) Jesus was a human as we are and he ascended, as we will. We must forgive our past mistakes because, once forgiven, they are gone. Each of us is who he/she wants to be.

God created everything that is, in His Mind. His creation is straight and as pure as His meanings: no alternatives, no variations, no confusions, no contradictions, no dualities. Humans instead, found a delight in imagining complications, hidden meanings, interpretations and so forth. God created us and I believe I am as created. The Christian theologians believe there are at least five types of creation. The first type is called "begotten". It applies to Jesus alone and means God incarnated. The Old Testament "mistakenly" called the first generations of humans, begotten. The second type of creation is the "creation" of Adam. He was "formed from the dust of the ground, and breathed into his nostrils the breath of life; and man became a living soul" (Genesis 2: 7) These different kinds of births allow religion's "experts" to justify their opinion that we can never be like Jesus. The third type of creation was the creation of Eve, from Adam's rib. (Genesis 2: 21, 22). No man has a missing rib due to this kind of creation for a woman. This probably means that this procedure took place once only, for Eve. The fourth type of creation is each of us, the ones "born" from women, as known today. And, the fifth type is that applied to the creation of the "Son of Man". The masters of the Christian Church believe that this change happened through God's grace; from human to the holy son of God. The Bible said succinctly that " God created man in His own image," (Genesis 1: 27) This is how far theology goes in splitting hairs and claiming deepness of thought. God has one creation applied to us all. We are all of Him, through His will, to fulfill His meaning. Besides, who was there to witness those "different" kinds of creations? Creation is one process used for one purpose, period. It takes the one and only straight thinking to know the way leading to Heaven and, adopt it.

Due to his holiness Jesus is qualified to, "Leave the 'sins' of the ego to me." No blood has to be shed. Left up to Him, our sins will be dismissed. One doesn't have to worry and be concerned about HOW is Jesus going to dismiss our sins! "That is what Atonement is for. But until you change your mind about those whom your ego has hurt, the Atonement cannot release you. While you feel guilty, your ego is in command, because only ego can experience guilt." (229) "The Holy Spirit knows that all salvation is escape from guilt." (230) God never considered us to be sinners so, there is no sin to be washed. As for our sinful thoughts and mistaken opinions, they can be dismissed by the humans themselves. God "gives the Son of God the power to forgive himself of sin." (231) Our mistaken decisions can be easily discarded into the pit of endless choices. Sins are mistakes that cause a deeper emotional reaction. Jesus calls sin "a mistake you keep hidden; a call for help that you would keep unheard and thus unanswered." (232) Because we are sons of God, we are qualified to eliminate our sins if we want to. "The wages of sin is death," explains our limited life span. The Bible talks about the death of our sinful thoughts, but, not about the sinful person. The sinful thought can be dismissed, but not the person who created that thought. The person simply has to live with his creation until he decides to discard it into the past. As perfect creations of God, we have a permanent life. All mistakes we do on earth are the product of our temporarily self-deluded minds and, are not permanent. Because sins ruin one's self-image, we customarily defer our sins to someone else; usually to Satan. If deferral makes one feel better, it suggests that we can also defer our atonement as well and feel an even deeper relief. But, this process of deferral is imagined and cannot eliminate one's sinful feeling. The real meaning of Atonement can be described as the healing of the perception of sin and, its replacement with a knowledge of peace. Atonement undoes all errors (233) without punishment, and replaces them with truth. It unites all creations with their Creator. Thus, "Atonement is the way to peace." Only ego can believe that atonement can be accomplished through an attack (sacrifice) against another.

In our pre-separation condition, known as the Garden of Eden, we had a state of mind in which nothing was needed. Now, in our physical condition we have many needs that make us compromise our purity; and life has become never the same since. The acceptance of the real atonement means the clear consciousness that enables someone to realize that his/ her errors never really occurred. There is nothing, other than nightmares, in Adam's deep sleep from which one can easily escape by waking up. We are not whom we thought we are and, we cannot be punished for whom we are not.

We generally interpret God in a way acceptable to our egos. But setting ego in charge, hides the truth and leads us astray. Because we don't follow our Creator's advice, we are still here where Jesus found us, two thousand years ago. People do not want their comfort disturbed and, settle for stagnation in the material world where we built comfortable justifications and appeasing pay-offs. The concept of time that exists in our minds only, among other advantages it offers the past as a place where we can discard all our embarrassments. We can leave there all past memories, if we want, and start a new and clean day. The past is dead. Life can be compared with a hypothetical eternal present where we are able to find new and interesting information, new projects and create. In the Kingdom where pure thoughts and meanings are the way, "things you are not proud of", no matter how well hidden, cannot enter. Remove them first from your mind. Once aware of their selfish stupidity, you will be unable to consider them again. Life was created in God's mind and is extended in ours. Atonement doesn't require someone else's physical sacrifice. It requires only to shake off the mistaken opinions that clog our minds and burdened your life.

Separation as physical bodies allows comparison, the feeling of specialness and the misunderstanding of love. "The world of bodies is the world of sin." (234) While fascinated by specialness, we miss the fact that separation from your brothers is separation from God and, a decision against the atonement. Atonement enables you to realize that your errors never really occurred (235). You produced errors while unaware, in a state of confusion, which disqualify those error's validity. Atonement is the act of uniting all creation with their Creator for the purpose of restoring everything to the original intention. No atonement can pay for an abstract mistake with physical means.

Remember that where your heart is, there is your treasure. So, the real question is, what do you treasure and how much do you treasure it? Atonement corrects the thoughts that caused your past errors (236). You did what you did, but it is all inconsequential in the world of Truth (reality). Renounce the past doings and, live your higher quality in the present.

Our long-term goal cannot be any other than to undo the separation and restore the wholeness of mind. "When God created you, He made you part of Him." (237) God and His creation are completely dependent on each other. Until we return to this perfect trust, we burden our minds with useless attempts to justify our physicality. Creation is a unit. Separated, its parts are of no value. The parts of a car are not the car. God's creation is incomplete without you and you are incomplete without Him. Again, your brother/sister is your way to salvation. The other's creation is similar to yours; if you don't see him/her worthy, you are not worthy. In this realm of ego, as we take from others, so it is taken from us. Sow respect and love and you will receive respect and love.

The only purpose of this world, as seen by the Holy Spirit, is the healing of God's Son. Until you see the healing of the Son as all you wish to be accomplished by the world, you will not know the Father nor will you know yourself. (238) To love yourself is to heal yourself of all your damaging thoughts.

We shall look on our brothers and see in their freedom, ours, for such it is. Do not see sin in him/her, or you both shall be kept in this hell. His/her perfect sinlessness releases you both. Never forget, your brother is your key to salvation because you see yourself in him. You and he/she are created equal. The differences are the different choices we make. God put part of Himself forever in you and your brother's holiness that you might see in your brother the truth about yourself (239). Because you are of God, you are part of His Trinity and the Creation is not complete without you. We are as we see our brothers. When you see the other as a beautiful and perfect creation of God, you feel the same exalting purity in you and in all others. Your right perception is necessary before God can communicate directly to you (240). The function of love is one for all: seeing love in everyone, is seeing love in God.

4.

TRUTH AND PERCEPTION

It is hard to believe that the physical universe is the product of a Mind. Can a thought create things? We prefer to believe that matter was ever existent and, it organized itself to the extent that it could create life, humanity included. Is this more believable than the idea that God created everything in His mind and of His mind? It's preferable to accept Mind over matter: in the beginning He, Mind, was the only creator and the only source of everything. From our life's experience, all that we need to exist is physical. We are physical creatures living in a physical environment for a relatively long time. We became dependent on material items! Nevertheless, there is nothing to work with or to come from other than a Mind we call God. Certainly, we are created by our parents but then, who created the first parents? Just think, isn't it a miracle that two united microscopic cells can produce a human being? Isn't it curious that after creating, growing and ejecting a baby, the mother is left with no scars? We have parents because we need to be nourished, guarded, educated and lovingly instructed by two people who believe their creation (child) is an extension of their identity into the future; their contribution to life itself. To them, their child is their most precious creation. Once we mature, we may start asking questions we never asked before and, explore the edge of our knowledge. Can physical matter organize itself in such a way that made the biological reproduction possible or, is it a superior Mind that made the whole process possible? "God is everywhere." (241) "Every blade of grass is a sign of God's perfection". As we know, physical matter doesn't think or create; it is inert. As for our brains, they are physical and serve the physical purpose to coordinate our bodily functions, but cannot create them. Brains are physical parts of our physical bodies. Nevertheless, Jesus stated that by believing, thought can be made into flesh (242). If so, the whole world can be created by firm beliefs.

The quantum world is a world of possibilities, after all! If we believe in physicality, physicality becomes our reality. If we believe in our thoughts, we can accept that we can create our own realities. We don't lose sleep trying to understand how this process took place. We use what we have and call it life. Still, what is life?

Since life itself is well organized, it means that it is set by an organizing Mind. We call this creative mind, God. He must have had created everything that is, we included. Since the mind cannot be created, we can accept that we have fragments of the divine mind God had given to us at the time of our creation. This is the connection that justifies our cooperation among ourselves within the creation. We are conceived as creators too. We've created our physical world by firmly believing that this is what we want without a shadow of a doubt. We may not have even noticed when this transition from spiritual belief to physical perception happened. It was a smooth and willing change from what we had been to how we are. We look the same as before our spiritual switch and have the thoughts that made this change comfortable. Afterall, our thinking desired this new world. "One believes what he made" in his mind. "Belief produces the acceptance of existence." (243) "God did not create bodies" so, our bodies are the way we always knew them. Because our world is created by us, in our minds, "This world is not the will of God, and is not real." It is the manifestation of our thoughts. The imperfections of our physical world attest to our human imperfection. To God, we may not be seen as sharply separated as our individual bodies are, but seen as a spiritual unit. This is the proof that we are one creation of one God. It is significant that in some cases, people who just suffered a clinical death can clearly see, hear and think from outside of their bodies, before the medical doctors can revitalize them. We call these phenomena, Near Death Experiences. More importantly, those individual experiences have many striking similarities. It is interesting that having our bodily functions stopped and eyes closed, our minds can see and think in a clearer way than when we are alert under the control of our brains. It seems that physical restraints create a blur rather than help to our awareness in those situations. If these Near Death Experiences are samples of eternity, they suggest that we can live rather comfortably during our spiritual life. It is surprising that Jesus said: "Your kingdom is not from this world because it was given to you from beyond this world." (244)

"Every mind that looks upon the world and judges it as certain, solid, trustworthy and true, believes in two creators, or in one: himself alone, but never in one true God." (245) I do remember only one personal message that I received from God: it was during one of my first days as a U.S. immigrant. At that time, I depended on welfare assistance. I didn't have money nor an American dental license and I barely spoke English. I did some simple work where, surprisingly I was treated with more respect than I expected. Unfortunately, those jobs didn't give me enough time to study for the Dental Board. So, I decided to do janitorial work. The jobs were either in the evening or nocturnal, thus leaving me the best part of the day to study for the American Dental License (I never took English classes. I knew my medical terms and I could translate the connecting words with a dictionary). I could afford a couple of hours break to look around for new jobs. One night after cleaning a movie theatre I grabbed my two large black plastic bags full of debris and, after a deep breath I walked toward the trash bin at the end of the parking lot. For a moment, I felt concerned over my sticky and dirty hands and the physically demanding work. I asked myself if I will ever be able to use these hands for delicate dental work? At that moment, I heard a clear and soft voice saying to me: "This is the chance you have now. Use it." And, I did. That work allowed me to buy a car, a house and to qualify for the lease of a dental office days after I received my California Dental License. I would like to hear God again but, He never spoke a word to me since. Nevertheless, God became a new and firm belief that I could not have had in communist Romania. I discovered that "The fundamental conflict in this world is between creation and miscreation. Fear is implicitly a miscreation; therefore, the conflicts of this world are between love and fear." (246) Love is truth and divine perfection. Fear is an opinion, a human arbitrary feeling, and an expression of insecurity. Love is creative and uniting; fear is destructive and separating. We designed our living environment! Our world doesn't work as God's does, obviously. Therefore, the two worlds, God's and man's, cannot be grafted. "What you find difficult to accept is the fact that, like your Father, you are an idea (a thought). And, like Him, you can give yourself completely, wholly without loss and only with gain. Herein lies peace, for here there is no conflict." (248) In God's world there is no strife for survival. God's Creation is the enjoyable way of living. The world created by humans "is the belief that love is impossible" (249); that life is organized by opinions that don't include neither truth nor love. If our world is imperfect, it is "the world of scarcity, [where] love has no meaning and peace is impossible." (234 /320) Fortunately, the two years I needed to Pass the National Board and the California State Board, had been as peaceful and successful as they could be.

At any time, nothing exists but God. "I am the first, and I am the last; and beside me there is no God." (Isaiah 44: 6) "I am the Lord that maketh all things; that stretcheth forth the heavens alone; that spreadeth abroad the earth by myself;" (Isaiah 44: 24) Since nothing can be produced from nothing, God must be the source of everything and be the energy that keeps everything moving. "God depends on no one for His existence and everything depends on Him for its existence." "God is all in all in a very literal sense." (250) God being a mind, invites the question: how does it happen that the universe is ever-expending? Where does the universe get all its materials for its continuous expansion? What is the source of energy necessary for its parts' continuous movement? Because we cannot answer this and other questions, we had better not ask and accept everything as it is. We still believe that this process of creating matter from thoughts is not possible. Still, all that ever exists is God's Mind and Soul; therefore, He must be the only source of the universe. Our "rational" thinking concluded that life is the result of physical evolution from substances we assumed were forever available. Our knowledge is rather sketchy about such a distant past as forever but, coming closer to our time, after the solar system came to be, we feel we have more data to support the commonly accepted theory of evolution. Once the solar system came into existence, we can argue that the earth had been built from a certain amount of solar matter, already around, and that matter is able to support our physical understanding of life. But, still, how did the solar system come to be? It evolved from what?

The permanent existence of matter that can sustain life is dependent on a constant supply of energy that cannot be created by the matter itself. Life is energy, constant movement; while matter is inert and dependent on that energy. The only life is the universal mind and, therefore, the only source of everything. It is therefore possible that imagining something can make that something manifest to our senses. Therefore, that matter is created by His Mind. Einstein came with the well-known $E = MC^2$ which relates energy to matter. Scientists even managed to produce some elementary particles from a lot of sheer energy; but can anyone produce a sandwich, not to mention the whole universe from sheer energy?! I believe it can if matter is imagined by a firm thought. To continue, matter is seen as a micro cosmos, due to its similarity with the planetary macro cosmos. As we see the sun with its planets gravitating around it, so we can see small electrons gravitating around the atomic nucleus. In this arrangement, we have large empty spaces that separate the tiny electrons from each other and from their nucleus. The planets are similarly separated from each other and from their suns. Still, when I look on my desk, I don't see the large spaces between its elementary particles. I only see the mass of particles themselves.   Scientists also found that the deeper we go into the structure of matter, the "mushier" those small elements are. They seem to be vibrations or energy waves. Can this make sense? Is it possible that we see only what we want to see? To add to this puzzle, the atoms that are assembled in molecules are also widely spaced among themselves and, the molecules are themselves generously spread from each other too. We are entitled to ask if the space between particles is a void, or if it contains something we don't know yet. … possible waves of energy. The atoms' nuclei are made of subatomic particles that are also separated by huge spaces for their size. If we go even further, those subatomic particles are made of even smaller ones that may not even be particles, but jolts of energy. Physicists found that matter's elementary particles do not resemble small balls, but, small strings, like spaghetti, that are in a state of continuous movement, in specific ways. These strings seem to be hybrids between physical particles and energy waves. My desk and for that matter any physical object in sight is about 99.99% empty space which we don't see. We only see the 0.01% of constant moving particles that may not even be solid, but we see them that way, assembled as objects.

The fact that those particles are in constant vibration, may make them appear bigger than they are. Still, they are only 0.01% of any object. It seems, the particles' movement is more important than their physical existence. With no movement they may not be significant, or not be at all. Life is movement. The moment the movement of subatomic parts stops, the particles collapse together, the empty spaces between them disappear and mighty solar systems type of arrangement that once made them look like objects, disappear into what we call black holes. When our physical bodies die, they shrink and disappear too in their own black holes. Then, our physical elemental particles come back to the nonphysical intention that created them. Due to their flexibility and constantly vibrating particles, we may consider that physical objects are alive! If so, their lives originate in the energy provided by God. Therefore matter exists due to the constant vibration (energy) provided by God. Every movement requires energy. The whole universe must consume a huge amount of energy that doesn't seem to ever diminish. Where does all this energy come from? It certainly doesn't come from anything physical. Physicality is the beneficiary of movement, not its cause. Evolution of any kind means energy, not dead weight.

A good observation is the condition of the substance we call water. Molecules of hydrogen and oxygen had been created from pure energy. They connect as molecules of water, that under proper conditions become either frozen hard like a rock or, liquid water. Even the Rock of Gibraltar went through the same phases of pure energy, independent particles, fog, liquid lava and solid rock. The existence celebrated by materialists is, as a matter of fact, an uneven energy field seen in a certain stage of manifestation. What makes it change? It is not only the environment that changes, our minds do too and, we see things differently at different times. We invent things: we see something we want to see and, we didn't see it before. We may see the same person as having various attitudes at different times. Jesus healed people because he believed they are created healthy and are consequently healthy, so, He claimed their true, healthy condition and, their health manifested itself. We believe they changed. People who love themselves are healthier than those who don't. All that is physical changes due to non-physical conditions. The process of healing requires more than a wish. It requires a definite, intimate belief. Healing takes place at a level where our minds can influence our energy field.

Physicality is our creation. Truly, we should be able to see through objects and be able to travel through them. Neutrinos are known to travel through any planet, in a straight line, undisturbed. From this perspective, I wonder why do we see through glass but not through sheet metal? It would be perfectly rational to be able to, unless, we decided that this is impossible and therefore is impossible. As a matter of fact, it's a miracle that we see those solid objects as we do. We decide how to see what we see and, we share those decisions. Then, we all agree to see everything as such, build an experience and a consensus and thus, we have our world. Our sight has only one way to perceive things that, objectively, are quite different than the way we observed them.

I remember a story shared with me by one of my respectable, older patients. When she was a young girl, one day she was playing in their yard and her mother was on her chair nearby mending some garments. At one time, the girl raised her eyes and saw a pleasant man standing not far from her with a kind smile on his face.

"Mom, there is a man in our yard," she said with a calm voice.

"Go and shake hands," the mother smiled, undisturbed.

My young patient got up and advanced towards him but, as she advanced, he stepped backwards, or so it seemed. Once he touched the wall of the house behind him, he gradually sunk into it effortlessly, his garments and all. The girl ran into the room on the other side of that wall to see him but, he was nowhere to be seen. I asked that lady permission to give her name in my book but, she hesitated to agree. She didn't want to get any public attention.

When Adam disregarded God's advice, he started to understand good and evil. He disobeyed but he couldn't accept he was the only disobedient person around. The same thoughts had been certainly shared by others around him. He supposedly was curious to know what's wrong with that forbidden fruit, the only forbidden fruit in the whole Garden. He was the only one we know that had the curiosity to check-out that fruit. There's no reason to feel guilty. On the contrary, he should be proud for having that courage to find out what is the problem here. Adam was not mature enough to evaluate the multitudes of interesting possibilities offered by the world and, he became trapped by the fantasies he discovered. God gave us the freedom to choose ways and values in order to understand what is good for us, what is not, and why. Then, we have Adam who thought that those fantasies are real life and, offer really good choices to consider. He didn't only observe those options, he defiantly stepped with both feet right into the middle of them. It's possible others also felt the dangerous attraction of the fantasy world and, kept their distance. It seemed obvious that if doing something which is right, doing the opposite can be wrong and eventually evil. To understand the difference between truth and opinion requires evaluation. Evaluation implies awareness. Awareness, in its turn, requires hard work. Are you willing to do it? It is much easier to enjoy what you have. Self-righteousness is satisfying, unchallenging and unproductive. Adam assumed if he is right, the others who have different opinions must be wrong and, many times, he perceived the wrong in the others. The forbidden fruit experience made Adam more confident: he experienced the courage it took to check out that mystery fruit. After this courageous experience, he started to explore other avenues he didn't consider before. Building a shelter, working the land and hunting gave him a sense of independence and control he never had before. The forbidden fruit incident became an increasingly distant event, soon forgotten. His new condition required a new environment run by new rules and values that fit his new role as the builder of a new life. He saw himself being independent of others and, his independence was expressed by his physical uniqueness. Only physicality could offer him the new kind of independence and authority he enjoyed. His specialness allowed him to judge and therefore project his shortcomings to others who had not been any different or better than he. He felt like a leader, an overseer of others. The whole world became physically apparent and, it worked by different laws in different ways than before. The spiritual world didn't offer the uniqueness and the pride he discovered in his new world. Tilling the land, building a house, providing for his family had been stimulating; and, being able to discern good from evil made him feel like a leader... this is life! The world of ego offered him the kind of pride the world of God didn't. In time, the past became forgotten and the material world started to appear as the only reality that is. He acquired a new understanding of life and a new philosophy based on his new value system. This was the start of the new age that I call "The Age of Ignorance." This is the world of criticism, separation, taking advantage of people; a world of incomplete knowledge, the glory of selfishness and breaking the unity of creation. In the middle of all this excitement Adam probably lost sight of this: that the alternative to truth must not be truth but, a source of mistakes. So, in our proud isolation we built this "world where the belief that love is impossible," (249) while this is not true. The way we see love on earth is so incomplete, practical and temporary, that it cannot be an integral part of the eternal life set by God. In people's minds, the meaning of life got confused with personal interests. Our physical interests are so much simpler and practical, easy to understand and handle. Because we forgot our true nature and drifted more and more into the physical issues, it became important to that someone who knows us intimately, should come to earth and remind us of our nature, abilities, and higher knowledge. Because of that, "As God sent me to you, so I will send you to others." (251) Jesus said.

Alright so, what is truth? Scientists discovered that "cosmos expanded from the size of a tiny subatomic particle … to 100 trillion trillions times its original size, at a rate faster than the speed of light." What they haven't discovered yet is "what triggered [that expansion] in the first place." What is that mysterious expanding force, that defeats the physical attraction and, it is faster than light? If the universe is the creation of God's mind, its expansion must also be related to His Mind. (252) As a matter of fact, Mind is the only thing that is, the only source of everything and, the only creator of everything that exists. Thought can manifest as matter, by believing it (253). At creation, God gave to His sons pieces of His mind to use. Those pieces of divine mind have the same quality as their source and, could be equally creative. As for "faster than the speed of light", that could be only the speed of thoughts. Mind's thoughts can travel from one end of the universe to the other, instantaneously. Einstein called this phenomenon "spooky action at a distance," where cause and effect happens at the same time across large distances, like there is no space between them; it fulfills His purpose.

For mind, space doesn't exist. Mind is not subjected to the rules of space and time because mind is their creator and master. Speed of light is the fastest speed a material object can achieve but the mind is not material; it is its creator, thus, independent of it. Nothing is outside of God. Mind is not only the master of the universe, but the universe itself. The Universe expands as minds are expanding and their creativity diversifies. The creative power of mind builds new worlds. This may explain why "scientists don't understand how the matter of the universe exists at all." Their understanding still revolves around the politically correct, general understanding of physicality. Meanwhile, physicality exists because a mind decided to conceive it (253). The desk I am writing on, was made from a tree that supposedly comes from a long line of evolution starting from simple elements assembled in a way that allowed them to grow and reproduce. In its state now, this inert and fashioned piece of wood mixed with glue and veneered shiny, exists because of the moving elementary particles that comprise it. The energy needed for their constant movement is provided by God, obviously; it fulfills His purpose. We need tables, we got them! God created us in his mind, of a quality like His own, so our communication is of an even quality and of absolute fairness. This was until we decided to monitor what we say and created our controlled verbal communication. With this, absolute fairness is gone. Everything has a meaning that upholds a purpose. If so, who formulates that purpose? It must be a Mind that makes sure that its implementation is a well-coordinated process. Eternity must be justified by truth.

Things are the way we visualize their purpose in our minds. Adam saw his world differently than the world is seen by God, and his world became different. As mentioned, God didn't expel him from the Garden of Eden. Adam expelled himself by seeing his own life differently than God did. He transgressed and his world became a way to justify his transgression. "The world we observe is not the ultimate reality. It is the manifestation of a reality that lies beyond the plane of our observation." "For Plato, the world we experience with our senses is a secondary world, a world we mistake for reality." This opinion was shared by Pythagoras, the Indian mystics and others. Adam didn't share this opinion. For him, the world we see is ultimate reality.

In the fall of 2012, a new state of matter was discovered, called FQH (Fractional Quantum Hall). This discovery suggests that the particles that compose matter, are excitations of an underlying non-material matrix. The excitations appear as waves as well as particles as previously hinted by Maxwell. For Plato, "The world we experience with our senses is a secondary world, a world we mistake for reality." "All things are created first in the world of spirit, and then, their counterparts are brought into physical existence." "Physical birth is not a beginning; it is a continuing. Everything that continues has already been born." (254) Mind seems to be terribly downrated on earth, while in the Kingdom of God it is everything. "Thought is the most powerful thing one can possess. It is pure energy that belongs to the energy of the whole creation". Here, on earth, we consider the brain to be the creator of the mind, while, the reverse is true. Mind created the body and the body needs a brain to coordinate its functions and to transmit the consciousness to it. If we understand brain as a biologic computer, then mind is its programmer, the giver of meanings that brain can then process, memorize, and use. (255) Brain is an efficient executor, not a creator. Creator is the Mind. When God gave us minds, our thinking acquired a divided ownership: our minds belong partly to its creator and partly to the created. (256) Our brains can temporarily influence it, but can never change it. "Would I not rather join the thinking of the universe, than to obscure all that is really mine with my pitiful and meaningless 'private' thoughts"[as used on earth]? (257) Jesus asked. We pollute the universe with our verbiage.

Looking at identical (monozygotic) same sex twins, who are coming from the same egg, and generally live their formative years under the same conditions, we would expect them to think the same. But those twins, despite many similarities, are never identical. They have God-given personal minds, independent of their striking physical resemblance. This invites again the question, is the mind a product of the brain, or is it of a different origin, and independent of anything physical?

God created his Kingdom that works in a perfect way, as He is perfect. God is, as expected, a supreme Mind that gave parts of His own to His creation, so we can all be connected. Therefore, we can easily share ideas and feelings among ourselves and with God. This is why we can be "as perfect as our Father in Heaven." This is why the Father knows us better than we know ourselves. We all think with His Mind, can understand His thoughts and share His values, united by love. We are one. His oneness is perfection, truth, holiness and wisdom. Adam, who departed from his Father's way, chose his own understanding of life centered on separation. This separation is manifested through criticism, judgement of good and evil, exploitation, abuse etc. Meanwhile, evil is non-existent because "what is opposed to God does not exist." (258) God did not create dichotomies or versions to His meanings. "In the Kingdom there is no teaching or learning, because there is no belief. There is only certainty" (259). Our world, being based on relativism, sees everything as subjected to interpretations, while reality is singular. "Spirit is immortal and, immortality is a constant state."... "It is not a continuum, nor is it understood by being compared to an opposite. Knowledge never involves comparisons." (260) What is not of God, is not true. In our materialist way of thinking, life allows us to claim as true and valuable a variety of opinions that are not real, even if, many consider them true. "Truth implies no change at all." It is continuous and, "never involves comparisons." What is not true, leads to failure. God would never accept the practice of judging another because His goal is harmonizing, not analyzing. People are diverse, and their diversity brings them, to different angles of seeing the one single truth. There is nothing that can be judged regarding the one who is created perfect. Judgment precludes love and therefore precludes truth. Truth is the proverbial narrow path; the only path among so many others that leads to our best interest: eternal fulfillment.

We are His creation from Himself, for the purpose of communication. Communication is the only way God's perfection could be further improved. "Only beings of like order can truly communicate". (261) We can communicate with God only if we can relate to Him, meaning, if we are as perfect as created. Our "existence rests on communication." "Communication is the will of God. Communication and creation are synonymous," Jesus said. "God created beings that have everything individually, but who want to share to increase their joy. Nothing real can be increased except by sharing. That is why God created you." (262) Once the original couple's minds gave more attention to guilt (run by ego), the Age of Ignorance had begun. Our history began when a new mentality started to be used and it changed the dynamics of the world. This is when humanity changed from the original, divine, spiritual ways to Adam's physical choices of existence; a turn for the worse that became our world. Once he did what his Father asked him not to do, Adam felt guilty, naked and insecure. How could he overcome it? As we already know, he had two alternatives: one was to admit his misjudgment and atone, which would have resolved the crisis once and for all. The second, was to deny the wrongdoing, internalize it, build excuses, feel guilty and attribute that guilt to someone else. He discovered an abstract helper, the ego, which spread into a world-wide excuse for one's mistakes enacted in our physical life. Guided by his ego, Adam tried to explain why he disobeyed. This attempt was ineffective; "sin" stays with the "sinner" until he atones. If internalized, the idea of sin erodes one's mind for as long as it is retained. Since denial is not effective, and its acceptance could not be considered, ego tried to motivate our mistakes (generators of guilt) and defer one's guilt to somebody else. Ideally, people deferred it to the undefeatable Satan or to God Himself. This choice remained the standard solution to personal mistakes, used by his descendants, for the duration of history. Our standard assumption is that guilt belongs to the other person, who should be punished for having it. This attempt at transferring sin is a feel better tactic that doesn't address the cause and, doesn't eliminate the guilt. Guilt stays where it is produced, regardless of the opinions and reasons used to separate Adam from his misjudgment. Guilt chipped away people's confidence, stopped or slowed down personal growth, eroded one's identity, separated people and motivated them to fight and conquer so they could feel special. Once they lost the connection with God, people started to rely on alternative support systems, crafted by their own ego. "The carnal mind is enmity against God." (Romans 8: 7) The carnal mind (ego) projected its sin away and, people became suspicious. These questionable thoughts (opinions, accusations) people created certainly crossed through other people's minds too, they being mostly common excuses or expressions, so, even having no proof people can be predictably accused of the others' sins. People thus damaged their mutual love and trust. So, we cannot know the truth any longer. In addition, we created the materialistic church that is neutral in regard to killings and conquering. The physical understanding of life, being constantly told and routinely practiced, appears acceptable, it dulls people's awareness and, made impossible for those using it to return to what they had been meant to be. We created an alternative reality that we trust and, seemingly prefer. So, by being angry, guilty and disappointed, Adam projected his frustrations to those around him. Those projections had been accepted by his mind, seemed real, and had been also accepted as real by the world. Misunderstandings separated those who were supposed to happily cooperate. Separation opened the door to selfishness, self-righteousness, rating each other, specialness and a whole array of harmful behavior that led to ignorance, deviousness, abuse, resentment and so forth.

Being blessed with creative abilities people built their own fortress, also known as the Tower of Babel, standing for the protection of their besieged self-righteousness and, for safety. Guarded by guilt, anger and vengeance with ego in command, this tower became our world. Somebody else could be held wrong and punishable, but not those who sought safety in their physical achievements. The Bible claims that people's towers fell apart when the tongues of the construction workers had been confused and they couldn't communicate effectively any longer. Once the idea of sin and guilt were incorporated, people separated from each other, started growing in different directions, became suspicious, built personal opinions and started to compare, judge and accuse. A range of worthiness had been created. A variety of different, unexpected ideas and attempts to manipulate others had been introduced. Yes, we don't communicate any longer. We talk instead. The cohesion among people in this physical world is provided by our physical needs, services, procurement of goods and accumulation of means, deferred guilt and of suspicions…, not by love. Selfishness and projection of guilt, brought conflicts and the human unity deteriorated. It became a world of divergent selfish ideas, motivated dominance, a world of have and have-nots that experience a whole array of unhappiness. It is a world created by us, where we are responsible for the way it works. It is poorly conceived, no doubt and, fortunately, doesn't last. After all, this world is Adam's aberrant dream shared by his descendants.

This world is everything we know, something we don't have anything to compare with. The Bible tries to present God to us but, as shown, the Bible is not that tight. Even Jesus is not always presented correctly. But, yes, we do believe what the Bible says. We need to believe in something as solid as truth and, the Bible is the closest available to that goal. If anything written in the Scriptures appears to be out of line, we find believable explanations that confuse our observations and, stops our search for answers. Some do not take those inconsistencies into consideration and, keep walking along the old lines; others dismiss religion with its apparently useless rules and ceremonies and become materialists. For lack of choices, many started to be dependent on the scriptures as they are, accept their explanations and eventually add plausible interpretations of their own that support their church. Others stand by, waiting for new facts and thoughts to correct those inconsistencies to their satisfaction. If there is a God out there, He will help those who are confused, and honest. Well, He does help those interested but cannot do much for those who wait for others to do the job of enlightenment for them. Jesus already tried to enlighten us but, did anyone try to replace his own beliefs with Jesus' teaching without adjusting or bending it with palatable explanations here and there? We have access to truth. We can figure out what makes sense and what doesn't. We can answer the contradictions using our wisdom and common sense. Connect to God, ask Jesus for help and He will. Build a pristine church in your mind and hold it high. It is a terrible thing to be lost in this weird, physical world. It is legitimate to know our Father, to grasp the truth and remember our birthrights. The problem we face with this attempt is the delusion of our own minds. Our minds have been trained since birth to think ego's way. We learned this early on by observing those around us. We seem to be trapped in our physical experiences. We are not motivated to go beyond the conventional wisdom and find the truth about life. We are encouraged to wait for an outside divine intervention to save us from our own, collective ignorance. The problem is that by waiting, one wastes his life. Nothing comes from doing nothing. It is our prerogative to return to holiness. God helps us, the moment we start moving forward. But, as mentioned, one cannot find his answer for as long as he believes that he already knows it, … that he is right. You don't grow if you don't move out of your thinking box. Be who you honestly feel you should be.

The immaterial, while invisible to those using sight, is obvious to those employing vision. On earth, we take in order to have and speak in order to promote our interests, while in God's kingdom we have by giving, and, communicate to exchange pristine thoughts and affection. On earth we judge, compare and separate one person from another, while in His kingdom we accept everyone as a perfect creation in his own right, love their originality, accept them as they are, and enjoy their company. It doesn't take a super intellect to figure out which place is better. We only need to want to upgrade our mentality to higher standards. Do not wait for the others to do what you are supposed to do yourself. The difficulty of taking action rests in the fear to abandon the kind of comfort our egos set for us. If we believe we are right, or that we are satisfied with what we have, why should we change? Many fear the unknown that lays beyond our physical existence. Salvation is a private desire that cannot be transferred. "The kingdom of heaven is within you." Find it! Honor it! To this there is nothing to add or subtract. Heaven is an exclusive neighborhood where you cannot pay, cannot talk your way into it or short-cut your admission. You cannot be admitted there out of pity, favor or mercy. You must have the quality that fits. For now, you have the quality that fits you to the place where you are, on earth. All you need is to return to being the Son you had been created and take the place that had been reserved for you from the beginning. You chose to move away, now you have to want to come back. You cannot return the fruit of the Knowledge of Good and Evil, but you can stop judging your brothers, abusing and categorizing them. Eliminate any motivation you have, but love and honesty.

Realize that God is in charge and is fully competent. Not being the least, keep in mind that if you blame your brother, you are, as a matter of fact, blaming yourself. You don't react to your brother's behavior; you react to your opinion about him. You blame yourself for your interpretation of your brother's words and deeds. Somebody's inner workings are intimately known to him but, to no others. For this reason, no one else can clean your inner flaws. In addition, your ignorance creates separation which comes with a lot of unwanted and uncalled-for consequences. Be aware of your divine creation. Forgive your brothers because you love them as you forgive and love yourself. Look at the others to see you. If you see them holy, you are holy. It is your job to clean up your own mind and find the treasure buried there. Of course, God can clean up your mind for you but, if so, you accept that you are incapable to do it and downgrade your own quality.

The most profound influence in human history belongs to Jesus Christ. He came to present God to us in ways we couldn't otherwise know Him. "My mission was simply to unite the will of Sonship with the Will of the Father by being aware of the Father's Will myself. This is the awareness I came to give you, and your problem in accepting it is the problem of the world." (263) God is not a distant superpower, independent of us. He is Us and everything around Us. He loves us because He loves Himself. It is probably incorrect to call Him Father, because a father is, in our experience, a different person, cast in a separate body, outside ourselves. Also, if we have a father, we assume, we must have a mother too. God created every one of us from Himself, the only existing "Person" at the time. God is in everything that is, us included. He is also most difficult to follow in our condition, due to the seemingly insurmountable differences between where He is and where we fell. Nevertheless, we should never abandon our willingness to join Him. He wills us back and, provides us with the answers and the help needed to succeed. What we need to succeed is the determination to do so.

Love is the full appreciation of God and His creation. It is also impossible to describe. Love is so trivialized in our physical world that it become improper to attribute it to Heaven. We are more concerned about sins than about love while, it is no such thing as sin. Sin is a human thought, an illusion, while love is truth created by God. Sin is the result of our mistaken thinking. If we understand our brothers, we know their perfect creation. If you understand them, you forgive them as you forgave yourself for the mistaken thoughts you once had, and probably still do. Only then can you love your brother/sister. The way to recognize your brother is to recognize the Holy Spirit in him. "Love one another as I loved you." (John 13:34) "Because we are Sons, God hath sent forth the Spirit of His Son into your hearts." (Galatians 4:6) As already mentioned, our brother's mind is part of yours and, also part of God's (264). Honor it!

As you love your brother, you love yourself and you love the Creator. Your brother is your passport to Heaven. Without love for him, you cannot access it. If your love for your brothers is not complete, you are not complete and, you are not ready for Heaven.

God never considered forgiveness because He doesn't consider that someone needs it. We are all perfectly created. Our many aberrations are exclusively ours. Dismiss them! One can join God only if he finds nothing to forgive in his brothers. By seeing your brother whole, you are whole because, we are all created equally well. Once our minds are returned to the awareness of our Father's mind, we are connected to the only reality there is. "Knowledge cannot dawn on a mind full of illusions, because truth and illusions are irreconcilable." (265)

INDEX

A Course in Miracles, Text, Chapter 2, Page 23, 3: 1

27. Ibid. Text, Chapter 22, Page 467, 1: 4
28. Ibid, Chapter 21, Page 453, 9:2
29. C. Leonard Woollley "The Sumerians" Page 32
30. Ibid. Page 32,33
31. A Course in Miracles, Chapter 1, Page 12, 3: 3
32. Scott Alan Roberts and John Richard Ward "The Exodus Reality" Page 210
33. A Course in Miracles, Text, Chapter 7, Page 119, 7: 4
34. Ibid. Text, Chapter 20, Page 437, 5: 1
35. Elaine Pagles, "Revelations", Page 163
36. Bart D. Ehrman, The Orthodox Corruption of Scripture, Page27 Ibid. A Course in Miracles. Text, p. 41, 42, and 25
37. Bart D Ehrmam, "Misquoting Jesus", Page 65
38. Elaine Pagels, "Revelations", Page 163
39. Elaine Pagles, "Revelations", Page 162
40. A Course in Miracles, Text, Chapter 4, Page 61, 6: 1
41. Ibid. Text, Chapter 4, Page 62, 9: 2
42. Ibid. Text, Chapter 6, Page 105, 2: 1. Also, Manual for Teachers Page 56, 5:5
43. Ibid. Text, Chapter 31, Page 651, 1: 5
44. Ibid. Workbook for Students, Page 32, 3:2
45. Ibid. Text, Chapter 2, Page 23, 3:1
46. Ibid. Text, Chapter 2, Page 23, 3: 1
47. Ibid. Text, Chapter 6, Page 105, 3: 2
48. Ibid. Text, Chapter 6, Page 104, 1:3
49. Ibid. Text, Chapter 2, Page 23, 3:1
50. Ibid. Workbook for Students, Page 315, 2: 2
51. Ibid. Text, Chapter 2, Page 23, 3:1
52. Ibid. Text, Chapter 8, Page 144, 3:7
53. Ibid. Text, Chapter 7, Page 134, 2: 5
54. Ibid. Clarification of Terms, Page 85, 5: 5
55. Ibid. Text, Chapter 7, Page 134, 2:5
56. Ibid. Workbook for Students, Page 85, 5: 6
57. Ibid. Text, Chapter 8, Page 147, 2: 8
58. Ibid. Text, Chapter 7, Page 120, 4: 5
59. Ibid. Workbook for Students, Page 378, 8:6

60. Ibid. Manual for Teachers, Page 56, and Text, Page 105, 2: 1
61. Ibid. Workbook for Students, Page 54, 7: 5
62. Ibid. Text, Chapter 5, Page 78, 1: 4; and Workbook, Page 85, 5: 6
63. Ibid. Text, Chapter 9, Page 179, 9: 8
64. Ibid. Text, Chapter 18, Page 390, 2: 5
65. Ibid. Workbook for Students, Page 362, 9: 4
66. Ibid. Text, Chapter 13, Page 261, 6: 2
67. Ibid. Text, Chapter 24, Page 502, 3: 1
68. Ibid. Text, Chapter 1, Page 11, 3: 1
69. Ibid. Text, Chapter 31, Page 652, 3: 1
70. Ibid, Clarification of Terms, Page 85, 3: 8
71. Ibid. Text, Chapter 19, Page 402 4: 1
72. Ibid. Workbook for Students, Page 217, 6: 3
73. Ibid. Manual for Teachers, Page 12, 1: 2
74. Ibid. Text, Chapter 31, Page 652, 5: 4
75. Ibid. Text, Chapter 7, Page 11, 7: 4
76. Ibid. Text, Chapter 7, Page 118, 2: 2
77. Amit Goswami, PHD "The Everything Answer Book", Page XI
78. Ibid (The Everything Answer Book), Page XII
79. A Course in Miracles, Text, Chapter 14, Page 277, 13: 4
80. Ibid. Text, Chapter 31, Page 651, 1: 5
81. Ibid. Text, Chapter 4, Page 70, 1: 4
82. Ibid. Text, Chapter 16, Page 344, 12: 7
83. Ibid. Text, Chapter 16, Page 349, 9: 4
84. Ibid. Text, Chapter 24, Page 514, 12: 5
85. Ibid. Text, Chapter 31, Page 664, 10: 6
86. Ibid. Text, Chapter 18, Page 373, 6: 6
87. Ibid. Text, Chapter 7, Page 134, 2:5
88. Ibid. Text, Chapter 13, Page 239, 9: 1
89. Ibid. Workbook for Students, Page 262, 11: 3
90. Ibid. Text, Chapter 13, Page 237, 1: 5
91. Ibid. Text, Chapter 31, Page 662, 7: 1
92. Ibid, Workbook for Students, Page 217, 6: 4
93. Ibid, Text, Chapter 18, Page 386, 7: 4

94.   Ibid, Text, Chapter 12, Page 221, 5: 1
95.   Ibid, Text, Chapter 7, Page 119, 7: 4
96.   Ibid, Workbook for Students, Page 262, 11: 3
97.   Ibid, Text, Chapter 5, Page 84, 4: 1
98.   Ibid, Text, Chapter 4, Page 66, 4: 1
99.   Ibid. Text, Chapter 6, Page, 100, 1:6; and 2: 3
100.   Ibid. Text Chapter 8, Page 144, 3; 4,5
101.   Ibid. Text, Chapter 3, Page 50, 3: 2
102.   Ibid. Text, Chapter 3, Page 42, 2: 3
103.   Ibid. Text, Chapter 4, Page 58, 8: 4
104.   Ibid. Text, Chapter 4, Page 65, 1: 6
105.   Ibid. Text, Chapter 8, Page 155, 1: 5
106.   Ibid. Text, Chapter 12, Page 221, 5: 1
107.   Ibid. Text, Chapter 6, Page 105, 3: 2
108.   Ibid. Text, Chapter 4, Page 70, 3: 3-6
109.   Ibid, Workbook for Students, Page 214, 6: 3
110.   Ibid. Text, Chapter 9, Page 161, 5: 1
111.   Ibid. Text, Chapter 4, Page 69, 8: 3,4
112.   Ibid. Text, Chapter 24, Page 514, 12: 5
113.   Ibid. Text, Chapter 13, Page 237, 3: 2
114.   Ibid. Text, Chapter 12, Page 235, 8: 8
115.   Ibid. Text, Chapter 2. Page 21, 2: 2
116.   Ibid. Text, Chapter 16, Page 349, 9: 4
117.   Ibid. Text. Chapter 20 Page 441, 7: 7
118.   Ibid. Text, Chapter 4, Page 59, 1O: 3
119.   Ibid. Text, Chapter 15, Page 319, 10: 4
120.   Ibid. Text, Chapter 6, Page 91, 1: 3
121.   Ibid. Text ,Chapter 15, Page 319, 10: 3
122.   Ibid. Workbook for Students, Page 305, 9: 5
123.   Ibid. Text, Chapter 30, Page 631, 3: 7
124.   Ibid. Text, Chapter 10, Page 187, 2: 5, 6
125.   Ibid. Text, Chapter 28, Page 604, 2: 2
126.   Ibid. Text, Chapter 28, Page 604, 2: 5-7
127.   Ibid. Text, Chapter 28, Page 589, 1: 1, 2
128.   Ibid. Text, Chapter 19, Page 404, 4: 9
129.   Ibid. Text, Chapter 10, Page 191, 9: 9

130. Ibid. Text, Chapter 6, Page 100, 2: 3
131. Ibid. Text, Chapter 6, Page 100, 1:6
132. Ibid. Text, Chapter 6, Page 100, 2: 5
133. Ibid. Text, Chapter 25, Page 536, 9: 11
134. Ibid. Text, Chapter 16, Page 344, 15: 3
135. Ibid. Text, Chapter 19, Page 403, 6: 5
136. Ibid. Text, Chapter 11, Page 210, 1: 1
137. Ibid. Text, Chapter 11, Page 211, 4: 9
138. Ibid. Text, Chapter 4, Page 69, 8: 2
139. Ibid. Text, Chapter 22, Page 471, 11: 9
140. Ibid. Workbook for Students, Page 230, 4: 4
141. Ibid. Text, Chapter 12, Page 229, 1: 4
142. Ibid. Text, Chapter 19, Page 402, 3: 1 And, Page 525, 9: 1
143. Ibid. Text, Chapter 19, Page 402, 4: 1
144. Ibid. Text, Chapter 19, Page 402, 5: 1-3
145. Ibid. Text, Chapter 16, Page 336, 5: i0
146. Ibid. Text, Chapter 18, Page 390, 2: 5, 6
147. Ibid. Text, Workbook for Students, Page 224, 12: 2
148. Ibid. Text, Chapter 1, Page 12, 3: 2, 3
149. Ibid. Text, Chapter 16, Page 341, 3:1
150. Ibid. Text, Clarification of Terms, Page 85, 5: 9
151. Ibid. Text, Chapter 16, Page 345, 1:1
152. Ibid. Text, Chapter 17, Page 353, 5: 1
153. Ibid. Text, Chapter 14, Page 278, 17: 1
154. Ibid. Text, Chapter 19, Page 412, 17: 8
155. Ibid. Text. Workbook for Students, Page 85, 5: 6
156. Ibid. Text, Chapter 4, Page 65, 11: 7
157. Ibid. Text, Chapter1, Page 7, 3: 10
158. Ibid. Text, Chapter 3, Page 45, 7: 1, 2
159. Ibid. Text, Chapter 6, Page 100, 2: 1-5
160. Ibid. Text, Chapter 14, Page 280, 7: 1
161. Ibid. Workbook for Students, Page 93, 4: 5
162. Ibid. Text, Chapter 14, Page 274, 8: 7
163. Ibid. Text, Chapter 13, Page 265, 12: 6
164. Ibid. Text, Chapter 14, Page 278, 17: 1
165. Ibid. Text, Chapter 18, Page 384, 1: 1 & 6

166. Ibid. Text, Chapter 24, Page 514, 12: 5
167. Ibid. Text, Chapter 14, Page 277, 13: 4
168. Ibid. Text, Chapter 12, Page 229, 6: 1
169. Ibid. Text, Chapter 12, Page 233, 14: 6.
170. Ibid. Text, Chapter 12, Page 233, 14:
171. Ibid. Text, Chapter 10, Page 19, 9: 9
172. Ibid. Text, Chapter 8, Page 152, 7: 4, 5
173. Ibid. Workbook for Students, Page 315, 2:4, 5
174. Ibid, Workbook for Students, Page 93, 5: 3
175. Ibid. Workbook for Students, Page 73, 1: 1
176. Ibid. A Course in Miracles, Text, Chapter 3, Page 36, 2: 7
177. Ibid. Text, Chapter 15, Page 324, 2: 5
178. Ibid. Text, Chapter 14, Page 284, 10: 9
179. Ibid. Text, Chapter 3, Page 36, 3: 1
180. Ibid. Workbook for Students, Page 315, 2: 2
181. Ibid. Text, Chapter 12, Page 221, 4: 7
182. Ibid. Text, Chapter 28, Page 605, 5: 6
183. Ibid. Text, Chapter 24, Page 514, 12: 5
184. Ibid. Text, Chapter 5, Page 89, 4: 5
185. Ibid. Text, Chapter 6, Page 95, 15: 8
186. Ibid. Text, Chapter 3, Page 37, 4: 3
187. Ibid. Text, Chapter 3, Page 37, 4:1
188. Ibid. Text, Chapter15, Page 324, 2: 5
189. Ibid. Text, Chapter 15, Page 324, 3: 4
190. Ibid. Text, Chapter 14, Page 276, 10: 1
191. Ibid. Text, Chapter 3, Page 36, 1: 2
192. Ibid. Text, Chapter 4, Page 52, 3: 8
193. Ibid. Text, Chapter 4, Page 64, 10: 3
194. Ibid. Text, Chapter 4, Page 64, 10:3
195. Ibid. Text, Chapter 19, Page 403, 6: 5-8,
196. Ibid. Text, Chapter 14, Page 284, 10: 6
197. Ibid. Text, Chapter 15, Page 328, 7: 3
198. Ibid. Text, Chapter 6, Page 92, 4: 2-4
199. Ibid. Text, Chapter 6, Page 92, 5;1
200. Ibid. Text, Chapter 16, Page 336, 6: 8
201. Ibid. Text, Chapter 6, page 92, 5: 3,4

202. Ibid. Text, Chapter 6, Page 94, 13: 2 and 95, 15: 5
203. Ibid. Text, Chapter 6, Page 95, 15: 8
204. Ibid. Text, Chapter19, Page 412, 17: 8
205. Ibid. Text, Chapter 15, Page 328, 7: 3
206. Ibid. Text, Chapter 11, Page 208, 5: 6, 7
207. Ibid. Text, Chapter 11, Page 208, 4: 1-8
208. Ibid. Text, Chapter 3, Page 37, 4: 1-3
209. Ibid. Workbook for Students, Page 449, 9: 1
210. Ibid. Text, Chapter 2, Page 20, 7: 3-5
211. Ibid. Text, Chapter 1, Page 9, 4: 6
212. Robert B. Stinnett, Days of Deceit, the truth about FDR and Pearl Harbor, 2000
213. The Course in Miracles, Text, page 240, paragraph 6: 1-3
214. Ibid, page 284, paragraph 10: 1-9
215. Ibid, Page 95, paragraph 15: 8
216. Ibid, Page 69, paragraph 8: 4
217. Ibid, Page105, A, paragraph 5: 3
218. Ibid, Page 104, A, paragraph 1: 3
219. Ibid, Page 41, paragraph 5: 11
220. Ibid, Text, Chapter 19, Page 412, 17: 8
221. Ibid. Text, Chapter 5, Page 75, 3: 10
222. The song of Prayer,(A course in Miracles' extension) Page 14, 4: 2
223. A Course in Miracles, Text, Chapter 3, Page 43, 7: 3
224. Ibid, Text, Chapter 8, Page 512, 7: 4
225. Ibid, Workbook for Students, Page 364, 11: 6
226. Ibid, Text, Chapter 3, Page 43, 7: 7
227. Ibid. Text, Chapter 5, Page 76, 4: 1
228. Ibid. Text, Chapter 4, Page 63, 5: 3, 4
229. Ibid. Text, Chapter 14, Page 277, 13: 4
230. Ibid. Text, Chapter 25, Page 536, 9: 11
231. Ibid. Text, Chapter 19, Page 404, 4: 8, 9
232. Ibid. Text, Chapter 1, Page 10, 5: 7
233. Ibid. Clarification of Terms, Page 85, 5: 5
234. Ibid. Text, Chapter 2, Page 18, 4: 4
235. Ibid. Text, Chapter 2, Page 19, 1: 13, 14

236. Ibid. Text, Chapter 6, Page 100, 2: 1
237. Ibid. Text, Chapter 24, Page 512, 4: 3
238. Ibid. Text, Chapter 24, Page 512, 7: 6
239. Ibid. Text, Chapter 3, Page 41, 6: 1
240. Ibid. Text, Chapter 14, Page 274, 8: 7
241. Ibid, Text, Chapter 8, Page 152, 7: 4
242. Ibid. Text, Chapter 1, Page 14, 4:4
243. Ibid. Text, Chapter 3, Page 51, 6: 9
244. Ibid. Workbook for Students, Page 315, 2: 4
245. Ibid. Text, Chapter 2, Page 32, 3: 13
246. Ibid. Text, Chapter 8, Page 144, 3: 7
247. Ibid. Text, Chapter15, Page 315, 4: 5, 6, 7
248. Ibid. Text, Chapter 8, Page 144, 3: 7
249. Ibid. Text, Chapter 7, Page 119, 7: 4
250. Ibid. Text, Chapter 8, Page 144, 3: 10
251. Ibid, Text, Chapter 7, Page 132, 4: 1
252. Ibid, Text, Chapter 8, Page 152, 7: 4, 5, 6
253. Ibid, Text, Chapter 5, Page 81, 2: 4, 5
254. Amit Goswami, PHD, The Everything Answer Book, Page 108
255. Ibid, Text, Chapter 5, Page 78, 1: 4,
256. Ibid, Workbook for Students, Page 85, 5: 7
257. Ibid, Workbook for Students, Page 262, 11: 3
258. Ibid, Text, Chapter7, Page 114, 3: 4, 5
259. Ibid, Text, Chapter 4, Page 60, 11: 12
260. Ibid. Text, Chapter 4, Page 70, 3: 8, 9
261. Ibid. Text, Chapter 4, Page 70, 5: 1, 3
262. Ibid. Text, Chapter 8, Page 144, 3: 4
263. Ibid. Workbook for Students, Page 55, 1:7
264. Ibid, Text, Chapter 10, Page 187, 2: 5
265. Ibid, Text, Chapter 10, Page 192, 14: 8

www.ingramcontent.com/pod-product-compliance
Lightning Source LLC
Jackson TN
JSHW022107220225
79392JS00021B/12